Katja Levy (Ed.

Commemorating the 30th
of the PRC Constitution

Berliner China-Hefte

Chinese History and Society

Edited by
Mechthild Leutner

Ostasiatisches Seminar
der Freien Universität Berlin

Vol. 45

LIT

Commemorating the 30th Anniversary of the PRC Constitution

Edited by

Katja Levy

LIT

Bibliographic information published by the Deutsche Nationalbibliothek
The Deutsche Nationalbibliothek lists this publication in the Deutsche
Nationalbibliografie; detailed bibliographic data are available in the Internet at
http://dnb.d-nb.de.

ISBN 978-3-643-90633-5

A catalogue record for this book is available from the British Library

© LIT VERLAG GmbH & Co. KG Wien,
Zweigniederlassung Zürich 2015
Klosbachstr. 107
CH-8032 Zürich
Tel. +41 (0) 44-251 75 05   Fax +41 (0) 44-251 75 06
E-Mail: zuerich@lit-verlag.ch   http://www.lit-verlag.ch
Distribution:
In the UK: Global Book Marketing, e-mail: mo@centralbooks.com
In North America: International Specialized Book Services, e-mail: orders@isbs.com
In Germany: LIT Verlag Fresnostr. 2, D-48159 Münster
Tel. +49 (0) 2 51-620 32 22, Fax +49 (0) 2 51-922 60 99, E-mail: vertrieb@lit-verlag.de

In Austria: Medienlogistik Pichler-ÖBZ, e-mail: mlo@medien-logistik.at
e-books are available at www.litwebshop.de

Contents

Commemorating the 30th Anniversary of the PRC Constitution

Calligraphy: Chen Ning
Orders: Lit-Verlag Münster-Hamburg-London, Grevener Str. 179, D-48159 Münster, Germany, lit@lit-verlag.de.
Submission of Manuscripts (Articles, Reports, and Reviews):
Chinese History and Society/Berliner China-Hefte, Freie Universität Berlin,
Prof. Dr. Dr. h. c. Mechthild Leutner, Goßlerstr. 2-4, 14195 Berlin.
Manuscripts should conform to the style of Chinese History and Society/Berliner China-Hefte: <http://www.chinesehistoryandsociety.de>

Introduction

The constitution of a country stipulates the core elements of a country's legal, political and societal structures. Since the foundation of the People's Republic of China (PRC) in October 1949, four different Constitutions have been promulgated. While the first (1954) was heavily influenced by the Soviet model, the following two (1973 and 1975), long after the Sino-Soviet break, were shaped by the political developments of their time, particularly by the "Great Proletarian Revolution", and should therefore be seen as political-historical documents rather than as the basis of a functioning legal system.

The fourth Constitution of the PRC, the 1982 Constitution, which is still in force today, was drafted after the reform and opening policy had already been launched. Although modelled after some hundred international model constitutions, parts of the 1982 Constitution show some particular "Chinese characteristics", for example, the references to Chinese revolutionary history in its preamble and to the special overall "leadership" status of the Communist Party. The current Constitution has lasted longer than any of the others and has been amended four times (1988, 1993, 1999 and 2004). All the Amendments were first approved by Party Resolutions of Party Congresses, usually in the autumn of the preceding year; the Constitution was then amended in the following annual session of the National People's Congress in spring. The earlier changes mainly aimed at adapting the political and constitutional system of the PRC to the new conditions resulting from Deng Xiaoping's economic reforms after 1979, most importantly, the change from a planned economy to a market economy. The existence and development of the private sector in the PRC was acknowledged as supplementing the state economy, and the 1988 Amendment, for the first time, allowed for the transfer of land use rights. In 1993, the second Amendment replaced certain terms in the Constitution, for example, the term "state-run enterprise" (*guoying qiye* 国营企业) was replaced with "state-owned enterprise" (*guoyou qiye* 国有企业) and "planned economy" (*jihua jingji* 计划经济) with "socialist market economy" (*shehui zhuyi shichang jingji* 社会主义市场经济). At the political level, the most important change was introduced with the 1999 Amendment: a new paragraph was added to Article 5 of the Constitution, reading "The People's Republic of China governs the country according to law, establishes a socialist rule of law state" (*zhonghua renmin gongheguo shixing yi fa zhi guo, jianshe shehui zhuyi fazhi guojia* 中华人民共和国实行依法治国, 建设社会主义法治国家). This reform is generally referred to as the introduction of the rule of law to China, although the term *fazhi guojia* 法治国家 in the Chinese sense does not refer to the same complex of ideas as the Anglo-American "rule of law" or the German "Rechtsstaat". The 2004 Amendment to the Constitution marked another milestone in Chinese politics, with the adding of two provisions related to human rights: the protection of human rights by the state in Art. 33 and the protection of private property in Art. 13. However, since 2004 no further amendments have been added and several constitutional law cases have shown that the implementation of the rights and provisions of the PRC Constitution is far from complete. Many issues still seem to have remained unchanged and many problems unresolved. Does this Constitution from 1982, which came into force only six years after the end of the Cultural Revolution, still match the needs of today's society in China? Where is Chinese constitutionalism heading? Are there any plans for improving the implementation of the Constitution? How do Chinese legal experts view the future of their Constitution?

In the summer of 2012, 30 years after the 1982 Constitution came into force in the PRC, we had these and other questions in mind when the China Studies Department of FU Berlin, with the generous support of the Deutsche Forschungsgemeinschaft (DFG) and the Heinrich-Böll-Stiftung, organized an international conference on "Social Change and the Constitution – a Conference on the Occasion of the 30th Anniversary of the Constitution of the PRC of 1982". The aim of the conference was to bring together researchers from China, Europe and the United States to discuss current trends of constitutionalism in the PRC.

We were thrilled at the enthusiastic response from the invited speakers and enjoyed two full conference days of stimulating discussions based on the excellent papers presented by the participants.

Now, we are pleased to publish some of the papers from this conference in the current issue of *Chinese History and Society / Berliner China-Hefte*, i.e. the articles by Benjamin Liebman, Gao Quanxi, Huang Hui and Chen Hsien-wu/Lin Po-wen.

Benjamin Liebman analyses Art. 41 of the 1982 PRC Constitution which is supposed to protect the rights of Chinese citizens with regard to the various ways in which they are allowed to voice their criticism of the government. The rights referred to in Art. 41 allow Chinese citizens, for example, to complain about decisions made by the state or by the courts. Liebman's astonishing research result is that these rights "appear to be designed to provide a mechanism for redress even where a law has explicitly rejected formal adjudication or administrative review". In other words, while Art. 41 is not – as one might expect at first sight – a provision that creates an independent or autonomous authority or institution to deal with complaints against state authority, it tends to deprive any court decision of its finality, because there is no limit to the complaints that can be submitted according to Art. 41.

Gao Quanxi, as a proponent of the so-called political constitutionalist school, provides the readers of this issue with a rare insight into the debate among different schools of constitutionalism in the PRC, showing how each of these schools employs different methods to give meaning to the Constitution within a political and legal system that, on the one hand, is trying to introduce elements of the rule of law and on the other, remains "under the leadership of the Communist Party".

Huang Hui describes herself as a proponent of one of the other constitutional schools, that is, the normative constitutional study school. In her article, she proposes a new methodological approach for Chinese constitutional scholars to tackle the problems related to the implementation of constitutional provisions. While she acknowledges that the Chinese legal system already provides for some, albeit not perfect, approaches for the reviewing of constitutional cases, she suggests a form of case by case comparative constitutional study that, in her opinion, could improve constitutional practice in the PRC.

The two scholars from Taiwan, Chen Hsien-wu and Lin Po-wen, look at Taiwan's constitutional system and show how, in some ways, the Western idea of the rule of law has already become part of constitutional practice in Taiwan, although the term "rule of law" is not mentioned in Taiwan's Constitution.

4

Zhu Yi, another speaker at the conference, makes a short critical comment[1] on the Amendment to the Criminal Procedure Law of the PRC, which took effect in March 2012. Articles on more subjects follow this short *Forum* section: The editor of this issue of *Chinese History and Society / Berliner China-Hefte* analyses the academic debate on the abolition of the Re-education through Labour System with particular regard to the stability maintenance concept in this debate. Mechthild Leutner and Martin Leutner present the findings of their research on the impact of National Socialism on China Studies in Germany. And finally, Emmelie Korell gives an insightful analysis of the construction of a Chinese county's identity during its transformation into a tourist site.

We hope that our readers will find the contributions presented in this issue stimulating and that the results of the research made available here will provide many new insights into the current state of the Chinese Constitution and beyond.

Berlin, February 2015
Katja Levy

---

[1]   As a contribution to the *Forum* section this essay was not peer-reviewed.

Benjamin L. Liebman

Article 41 and the Right to Appeal[*]

Extensive discussion of the Chinese Constitution focuses on the ways in which the Constitution is under-enforced or not implemented.[1] Many leading Chinese academics used the occasion of the thirtieth anniversary of the enactment of the 1982 Constitution to discuss ways in which enforcement of the Constitution could be strengthened.[2] Similarly, much of the discussion at this conference concerned possible ways to make the Constitution enforceable. This essay takes a different approach, examining one clause in the Chinese Constitution that is arguably at times over-enforced, providing constitutional authorization for challenging legal determinations outside the legal system.

This essay's focus is Article 41 of the 1982 Constitution. Article 41 protects the rights of citizens to criticize (*piping* 批评) and make suggestions (*jianyi* 建议) to state actors and to file complaints (*shensu* 申诉), charges (*konggao* 控告), or exposures (*jianju* 检举) against illegal conduct of state actors. Article 41 also requires state actors to deal with such complaints.[3] My central interest is in the meaning of the right to file complaints.[4] My goal in this essay is to examine the ways in which the concept of *shensu* is used to provide a basis for challenges to state action both within and outside the formal legal system. My central argument is that Article 41 provides insight into structural tensions inherent in China's constitutional framework.

My interest in Article 41 stems from an ongoing empirical project that examines the impact of petitioning on two Chinese courts.[5] That project aims to show how and why

---

[*] This essay is adapted from comments delivered at the conference, "Social Change and the Constitution – a Conference on the Occasion of the 30th Anniversary of the Constitution of the PR China of 1982", held at the Free University in Berlin, June 15-17, 2012.

[1] Some recent scholarship has moved beyond this traditional framework of analysis, most notably Keith Hand's important work (Hand 2011: 60).

[2] For examples of recent discussions, see the work of prominent scholars Zhang Qianfan, He Weifang, and Tong Zhiwei (Zhang 2012a; He 2012; Tong 2012). For an excellent summary of recent writing on the Chinese constitution see Yan 2013: 2 f.

[3] The full text of Article 41 states: "Citizens of the People's Republic of China have the right to criticize and make suggestions regarding any state organ or functionary. Citizens have the right to make to relevant state organs complaints or charges against, or exposures of any state organ or functionary for violation of the law or dereliction of duty; but fabrication or distortion of facts for purposes of libel or false incrimination is prohibited. The state organ concerned must deal with complaints, charges or exposures made by citizens in a responsible manner after ascertaining the facts. No one may suppress such complaints, charges and exposures or retaliate against the citizens making them. Citizens who have suffered losses as a result of infringement of their civic rights by any state organ or functionary have the right to compensation in accordance with the law" (1982 Constitution, Art. 41).

[4] At times *shensu* is translated either as "filing a complaint" or as "filing an appeal". Yet "appeal" in the context of *shensu* is distinct from an appeal in litigation, because few procedures govern the filing of *shensu* and *shensu* are usually brought after court appeals have been exhausted or are not connected to court proceedings. To avoid confusion I use the Chinese term *shensu* throughout this essay.

[5] I have also discussed the impact of petitioning on China's courts more generally in prior work (Liebman 2011).

petitioning, even by individuals, is an effective mechanism for influencing the courts. Court records reveal that petitioning is often an effective tool for individuals and groups seeking to change already final court decisions or seeking direct compensation from the state. Assessing the merits of such petitions is of course difficult. Some such cases almost certainly involve wrongly or unfairly decided cases. Yet others involve grievances brought by individuals facing hardship where courts likely have done nothing wrong, in particular in cases where decisions are unenforced because defendants cannot be located or lack resources to pay judgments. My interest in petitioning has led me to take a greater interest in the concept of *shensu* – filing a complaint or appeal, a term that appears not only in the Constitution but also in a number of specific laws. The concept of *shensu* is not limited to complaints filed to the courts, but it is of particular importance in the courts, when *shensu* are often handled alongside petitions and where the ability to *shensu* provides recourse for litigants even after appeals have been exhausted and the time for filing a formal rehearing petition has expired.

What does Article 41's reference to the right to file a *shensu* mean? The provision has received little scholarly attention. Scholarly discussion of Article 41, in China and the west, largely consists of general references to the concept of a right to complain or notes the relationship between Article 41 and the petitioning system. Sometimes the media cite Article 41 as supporting the media's right to "supervise" the state (Liu 2013; Feng 2013). Few scholars discuss the specific meaning of Article 41, in particular the right to *shensu*, or how it is enforced.[6]

The right to file a *shensu* includes a broad range of mechanisms for challenging state action: petitioning through the letters and visits system, filing an administrative appeal, administrative litigation, and filing a formal application for rehearing in a court case (Zhang and Gu 2011: 33-35). There is debate within China on whether to understand Article 41 as providing a procedural right to challenge state action or a broader political right to speak out and contest state action.[7] Yet it is clear that the right to *shensu* includes both the right to use formal procedures to contest state action and also to seek redress outside of such formal procedures when such procedures either are not available or are not effective. *Shensu* includes the right to challenge final court decisions through the legal system and to challenge state action outside the legal system when legal procedures have

---

[6] For example, see Chen (2009), arguing that the right to *shensu* means the right to file a complaint or charge against state organs. One exception to this trend is the detailed study of Zhang and Gu (2011), discussed further below, which analyzes the right to *shensu* and related statutory provisions in detail from the perspective of administrative law. Zhang and Gu also provide an overview of existing literature on Article 41.

[7] Those who argue that the right to *shensu* is a procedural right focus on the ways that the concept is implemented through formal law. Those who view Article 41 as providing a political right tend to define *shensu* more broadly to include a range of action inside and outside the legal system. Zhang and Gu (2011: 33-34) provide a good summary of existing debates on the meaning of Article 41. They argue that legal provisions governing *shensu* can be broken down into four separate meanings: a basic right under the constitution, a mechanism for seeking redress under administrative law, a means of initiating rehearing procedures in the courts, and a mechanism for initiating the renewal of formal administrative proceedings (Zhang and Gu 2011).

been exhausted and when legal remedies do not exist. Article 41 thus includes the right to challenge final decisions in the courts, but it is not specifically targeted at the courts. *Shensu* petitions can be filed with a range of state actors.

In addition to the Chinese Constitution, 31 Chinese laws mention the right to petition (Zhang and Gu 2011: 32).[8] These provisions largely fall into two categories: those that provide a formal procedure for challenging decisions and those that provide a general right to relief outside of formal legal procedures (Zhang and Gu 2011: 33). Yet the boundaries between formal and informal and between *shensu* and other mechanisms for challenging state action are often unclear.

The role of *shensu* in procedural laws

Examination of the concept of *shensu* in China's three primary procedural laws[9] provides insight into how Article 41 has been translated into practice in the courts and also into some of the ambiguity that continues to exist. All three laws provide a legal basis for challenging already final court judgments, although the particular terms and procedures used to describe such challenges vary. Scholars cite these provisions as a mechanism by which the constitutional right to file a *shensu* is made effective.

The concept of *shensu* is most clearly articulated in the Criminal Procedure Law. The Criminal Procedure Law states that parties to a criminal case, their legal representatives, or close relatives may challenge already decided cases by filing *shensu* petitions (2012 Criminal Procedure Law, Art. 241). The recently revised criminal procedure law states that courts should retry cases in response to a *shensu* petition where there is new evidence proving there was an error, where there was insufficient evidence or evidence should have been excluded, where the original judgment included a misapplication of law, where there was violation of procedure that might have affected the fairness of the outcome, or when a judge handling the cases was involved in corruption or other illegal conduct (2012 Criminal Procedure Law, Art. 242).[10] There is no time limit on when *shensu* may be filed. The Supreme People's Court has also specified requirements for *shensu* filings in criminal cases (Criminal Procedure Law Interpretation, Art. 372) and has instructed courts to respond within three months, which may be extended to six months (ibid., Art 375). If the court determines that a *shensu* has merit the court then initiates (or orders a lower court to initiate) a retrial. The 2012 Criminal Procedure Law added significant detail regarding the specific requirements for filing a *shensu* compared to the 1996 Criminal Procedure Law.[11] The new law thus provides a quasi-formal mechanism for challenging final criminal judgments at any time through the filing of a *shensu* petition.

---

[8] The Basic Laws of Hong Kong and Macao also use the term, but are not relevant to the discussion here and thus are not included in the 31 laws listed.

[9] China has not yet adopted an Administrative Procedure Act, only the narrower Administrative Litigation Law. Scholars in China generally refer to the Criminal Procedure Law, Civil Procedure Law, and Administrative Ligitation Law as China's three primary procedural laws.

[10] The SPC's interpretation in the Criminal Procedure Law also makes clear that a non-party to a case may file a *shensu* petition if he or she believes that an incorrect final judgment has adversely affected his or her legal rights (Criminal Procedure Law Interpretation, Art. 371).

[11] For a discussion of the changes, see Zhang and Jiang 2012: 353-358.

In contrast to the Criminal Procedure Law's extensive reference to *shensu*, the Civil Procedure Law largely speaks of litigants having the right to file a formal application for a retrial, or *zaishen*, to challenge an already final court judgment.[12] The filing of a *zaishen* application is time-limited: prior to 2013 litigants had two years from the issuance of a final judgment to request a retrial. As of January 1, 2013, the time for filing a *zaishen* application is six months (2012 Civil Procedure Law, Art. 205). The 2007 Civil Procedure Law had appeared to provide for a broader right to challenge final decisions: the 2007 law also stated that challenges to already final cases should be handed as *shensu* (2007 Civil Procedure Law, Art. 111), thus suggesting a right to *shensu* in addition to a right to file for retrial through *zaishen* proceedings. The 2012 revisions changed this provision to state that litigants seeking to challenge already final court decisions should be instructed to file for a *zaishen*, or rehearing (2012 Civil Procedure Law, Art. 124); there is no longer reference to a right to file a *shensu*. The change appears designed to limit the use of *shensu* outside the formal retrial process. Yet even after the six month time period for filing an application for retrial has expired a court or procuratorate may initiate a retrial on its own initiative at any time. In practice this means that after the formal time period for filing a request for a retrial has expired, litigants may nevertheless seek to convince courts or procuratorates to initiate retrials.

In a recent book on civil rehearing procedures in the courts authors from the Supreme People's Court (SPC) attempted to address confusion about the difference between *shensu* and formal retrial (*zaishen*) applications in civil cases. According to the authors, the difference between *shensu* and *zaishen* is that *zaishen* petitions follow specific legal requirements, while there are no constraints on or rules governing when and how a litigant (or non-litigant) may file an application for a *shensu* (Su 2010: 1). The right to file a *zaishen* is a procedural right; the right to seek redress through *shensu* is a constitutional right. There are no time or jurisdictional limits on filing a *shensu*, and no limits as to who may file such a petition. The authors thus explicitly state that in some cases a litigant may use *shensu* procedures even when the challenge does not meet the legal requirements for a *zaishen* (ibid.: 2). The SPC book further noted that the legal standard for courts deciding whether to reopen a case is different depending on whether a litigant challenges a decision through a *shensu* or a formal application for *zaishen*: in a *shensu* case a court must determine there was an actual error before reopening the case. In a *zaishen* proceeding, in contrast, the court determines that the procedural requirements set forth in the Civil Procedure Law and relevant SPC interpretations have been met. The court then proceeds to examine whether an error has in fact occurred. Thus in theory a court should not reopen a case in response to a *shensu* unless the court determines there has been an error; in the

---

[12] Prior to recent revisions to both the Civil Procedure Law and Criminal Procedure Law the concept of *zaishen*, or retrial, was also used in the criminal context. The revised Criminal Procedure Law appears to try to separate out the concept of *shensu* in criminal cases from the more formal *zaishen*, or retrial, proceedings in civil cases (Zhang and Jiang 2012: 353). Nevertheless, the terms continue to be used interchangeably, even in official publications, because a successful criminal *shensu* leads to a formal retrial. The Criminal Procedure Law continues to use the term *zaishen* to refer to retrials undertaken by the courts, but does not use the term *zaishen* in the context of requests by individuals to reconsider final judgments.

more formal context of rehearing courts only need to find that a party filing for a rehearing has shown that an error has likely occurred.

One notable aspect of the SPC's explanation of the scope of *shensu* is that the provision of the Civil Procedure Law that the SPC authors suggest is relevant to filing a *shensu* does not actually mention the term. Article 177 of the 2007 Civil Procedure Law, incorporated as Article 198 in the 2012 Civil Procedure Law, states that when a court president believes that an error has occurred and that a case should be retried the court president shall refer the matter for discussion and decision to the court adjudication committee. Clearly one of the mechanisms for court leaders to become aware of such errors are *shensu* or petitions or protests in cases that fail to meet legal requirements for retrials.

China's Civil Procedure Law thus implements Article 41 of the Constitution both through formal *zaishen* retrial procedures and through creating a catch-all mechanism for courts to reopen cases at any time when errors are discovered. This is particularly likely in response to *shensu* complaints from litigants who fail to meet the procedural requirements for applying for a retrial. Article 41 thus provides a base both for formal legal procedures and for litigants to seek redress even when they do not meet the requirements of such procedures.

China's Administrative Litigation Law and Court Organization Law also mention the right to *shensu*. The Administrative Litigation Law states that a party to a case may challenge a final court decision via a *shensu* (Administrative Litigation Law, Art. 62).[13] The Court Organization Law likewise states that courts shall diligently handle any *shensu* petitions concerning final court decisions (Court Organization Law, Art. 13). Neither provides detail regarding how courts should handle such complaints.

Although the terms *zaishen* and *shensu* are often mixed, it is clear that the right to file a *shensu* challenging a final court decision is broader than the right to file a rehearing request. *Shensu* may be brought at any time, and outside the criminal law context there do not appear to be limitations on who may file a *shensu*. In practice, however, within the courts *shensu* petitions may be converted into rehearings. One recent study found that most formal rehearing cases begin as *shensu* (Zhang and Gu 2011: 34). This is particularly likely when litigants are challenging court decisions after the two year limit (now six months) on filing a retrial application in civil cases has expired.

The role of *shensu* in administrative law

China's three procedural laws provide the most important examples of how the right to *shensu* is incorporated in statutory law. Yet the impact of Article 41 is not limited to litigation. Examining the roles Article 41 and the right to *shensu* play in administrative law in China shows a range of ways in which the right to *shensu* has influenced legal development. Many of the 31 laws that make specific reference to *shensu* are substantive administrative laws. Three aspects of the impact of the concept of *shensu* on administrative law are of particular note.

---

[13] Although the Administrative Litigation Law uses the term *shensu* and makes no mention of *zaishen* initiated by plaintiffs, subsequent judicial interpretations from the Supreme People's Court referred to the use of *zaishen* in administrative cases and imposed a two-year limit for litigants to apply for review via *zaishen* procedures. As in the civil and criminal contexts, no time limitation applies to *shensu*.

First, Article 41 provided an important argument in support of the enactment of the Administrative Litigation Law and the right of individuals to sue the government in the 1980s (Yan 2013: 9 f.). Arguments were made during debates in the National People's Congress that a key goal of the Administrative Litigation Law was to ensure compliance with Article 41. Article 41 was also cited in arguments in support of similar rights to sue the state in administrative laws governing specific substantive areas, such as the right to sue the Marine Transportation Department under the 1983 Marine Safety Law (ibid.). Thus Article 41 can be understood as providing important support for the right of individuals to sue the state.

Second, Article 41 has provided a mechanism for challenging final decisions in administrative litigation and administrative reconsideration. Put differently, in administrative cases the right to *shensu* provides a mechanism for protesting or challenging outcomes in formal procedures, both in the courts and through administrative review.

Third, Article 41 also provides a mechanism for seeking redress where substantive laws have not provided formal mechanisms for seeking redress. A number of administrative laws provide for a right to *shensu* even though they do not provide a right to bring an administrative lawsuit or file for administrative reconsideration. Even in cases where a right to sue or file for reconsideration does exist, the right to *shensu* may provide relief where the subject of administrative action has failed to challenge administrative action within the required timeframe. Thus, for example, the Civil Servants Law provides that civil servants and others hired by state actors may bring *shensu* to challenge administrative sanctions, even though such decisions are not reviewable in court or through administrative reconsideration (Civil Servants Law, Arts. 13, 90, 91, 92, 94; Zhang and Gu 2011: 34). Other laws, including the Teachers Law and the Judges Law, have similar provisions. The Administrative Penalty Act, while providing a right to bring formal challenges to the impose penalties, also provides for the right of citizens, legal persons, and other organizations to bring *shensu* challenging administrative sanctions and imposes an obligation on administrative actors to investigate such *shensu* (Administrative Penalty Law, Art. 54).

In administrative law Article 41 has provided a basis for formal legal challenges to state action (the Administrative Litigation Law), a means of challenging the outcomes in such formal challenges (through administrative review and *zaishen* rehearings), and a mechanism for raising challenges even when laws provide no avenue of redress. Article 41 thus underpins both the right to use the legal system to challenge state action and the right of individuals to perform an end-run around the legal system when dissatisfied with an outcome or where formal law does not authorize their claims.

Substantive laws also make clear that petitions may go to a range of state actors – not just the courts or administrative agencies. For example, the 2004 Organization Law of Local People's Congresses and Governments states that local people's congress deputies have the power to receive *shensu* and the "views of the masses" toward government (Organization Law of Local People's Congresses and Governments, Art. 44). Article 41 says nothing about the involvement of the courts in enforcing or protecting the rights set forth in Article 41 (Yan 2013: 9). Instead, one of the key uses of Article 41 in practice has been to provide a remedy against perceived injustices in the courts.

Article 41 and the petitioning system

Perhaps the most significant and debated manifestation of Article 41 outside of statutory law has been the petitioning system. Most scholarly debate surrounding Article 41 in China focuses not on the meaning of *shensu* in statutory law but on whether the right to petition (*xinfangquan* 信访权) is protected by the Constitution. Some scholars argue that the petitioning system is a mechanism for enforcing the rights set forth in Article 41 (Shao 2010). Many scholars view petitioning as a political right providing for redress to citizens for infringements of individual rights. Others contend that the petitioning system is a mechanism for protecting other rights and that the petitioning system is needed because the courts are unable to provide a sufficient remedy to individuals (Zhang 2010b). Still other scholars disagree, arguing that petitioning remains wholly outside the legal system, and thus that Article 41 should be understood only as providing a legal basis for specific statutory provisions regarding *shensu,* not a constitutional right to petition. Scholarly debate pays little attention to another possibility: that Article 41 provides a legal basis not just for the existence of the petitioning system (and the right to *shensu* more generally), but for the practice of petitions and *shensu* undermining court authority by providing mechanisms for challenging final court decisions.[14]

The idea of an extra-judicial route to challenge state action is not new, in practice or in the Constitution. All four of the PRC's Constitutions have protected some form of the right to file a complaint. The 1954 and 1975 constitutions spoke of the right to file charges (*konggao* 控告) against illegal state action.[15] The 1978 constitution added the right to *shensu* alongside *konggao*.[16] Scholars have argued that the 1954 Constitution imposed on the state the obligation to create dedicated entities for receiving and responding to complaints, as opposed to protecting the rights of citizens to air those complaints, something already protected in theory by the constitution's guarantee of free speech (Tu 2012). This was done through the creation of the petitioning system.

My empirical research on the influence of petitioning on the courts suggests that petitioning to the courts undermines court authority and reinforces Party-state oversight of

---

[14] Scholars inside China and in the west have argued that the petitioning system undermines the courts, but have not generally noted that tension between petitioning and the authority of courts has a constitutional basis in Article 41.

[15] "Citizens of the People's Republic of China have the right to make written or oral charges to organs of state at any level against any person working in an organ of state for transgression of law or neglect of duty. People suffering loss by reason of infringement of their rights as citizens by persons working in organs of state have the right to compensation" (1954 Constitution, Art. 97).
"Citizens have the right to lodge to organs of state at any level written or oral charges of transgression of law or neglect of duty on the part of any person working in an organ of state. No one shall attempt to hinder or obstruct the making of such complaints or retaliate" (1975 Constitution, Art. 27).

[16] "Citizens have the right to lodge to organs of state at any level charges of transgression of law or neglect of duty on the part of any person working in an organ of state. Citizens have the right to complain to state organs when they have suffered losses as a result of infringement of their civic rights by any state organ or functionary. No one shall attempt to hinder or obstruct the making of such charges or retaliate" (1978 Constitution, Art. 55).

the courts.[17] My claim is <u>not</u> that the impact of petitioning on the courts stems from the fact that the right to file complaints is set forth in the Chinese constitution. The right to petition may be more robust than other provisions in the Constitution, but this is not because of the Constitution. Likewise, the lack of finality in the legal system is not due to Article 41, although Article 41 gives litigants the right to continue to appeal or file complaints even after cases are final. Instead, the impact of petitioning on the courts reflects the same historical tradition and political structure as does the Constitution. The Constitution mirrors actual practice, whereby courts are not independent and decisions are not final, and where substantive outcomes are more important than legal procedures. Although Article 41 may have been designed to protect the right to expose and contest official wrongdoing, it is operationalized in a way that undermines judicial authority

I am also not claiming that all of the rights in Article 41 are protected. That is clearly not the case. But I am suggesting that in practice the right to *shensu* is at times more robust than provisions in the Constitution that protect the independence of the courts. [18] Independence of the courts thus may be difficult or impossible to attain in China not just due to political intervention; independence may also be impossible because of a system in which mechanisms exist to challenge final decisions both inside and outside the courts. Article 41 is one provision that mirrors actual practice, which is often not the case when it comes to the provisions of the Chinese constitution.

The practice of allowing *shensu* petitions (and the constitutional recognition of the practice) draws on China's imperial tradition and on mass line ideology. It would be a mistake to understand Article 41 as simply endorsing the practice of Party officials intervening in court decisions; Article 41 draws on a deeper historical tradition of the state providing direct redress to aggrieved individuals. There are, of course, precedents for a constitutional right to petition the state elsewhere. For example, in the First Amendment to the U.S. Constitution (although in the U.S. context the right to petition generally means the right to petition the legislature, and is in practice part of the right to free speech). What is different in China is that the right to seek redress of grievances covers the right to protest already final court decisions and implies an obligation on the courts to reopen cases when errors are discovered.

The impact of Article 41 on Constitutional reform in China

It is also important to note what Article 41 does not do. Article 41 is not a fundamental requirement of transparency or informational disclosure by the state. Some in China have drawn parallels to constitutional ombudsperson systems in other countries. This comparison seems strained. Rather than creating an independent or autonomous oversight institution, Article 41 represents a tradition in China of non-differentiation, both among between legal institutions and non-legal institutions and among various Party-state departments or entities. Article 41 reflects a system in which often overlapping

---

[17] As I have explained elsewhere (Liebman 2011), petitions regarding the courts may be filed both with the courts and with other Party-state organizations outside the courts. Within the courts there appears to be little difference between petitions and *shensu*.

[18] "The people's courts shall, in accordance with the law, exercise judicial power independently and are not subject to interference by administrative organs, public organizations or individuals" (1982 Constitution, Art. 126).

institutions resolve disputes and provide redress, not the creation of an external oversight institution. Indeed one of the curious aspects of legal provisions concerning *shensu* is that they appear to be designed to provide a mechanism for redress even where a law has explicitly rejected formal adjudication or administrative review.

What does this mean for the questions at the heart of this conference and volume, and for the future trajectory of Constitutional reform in China? Would reforming Article 41 or the petitioning system make a significant change to the constitutional structure, or facilitate better enforcement of other constitutional provisions? This essay's brief examination of Article 41 suggests three responses.

First, significant reforms to the petitioning system alone are unlikely to lead to broader change. It is possible that they might pave the way for greater acceptance of the finality of court opinions. But such changes are unlikely to make a large difference. Petitioning itself is reflective of the problem of weak court authority; petitioning is not itself the source of the problem. Likewise recent efforts to tighten requirements for the filing of retrial applications in civil cases are unlikely significantly to reduce the pressure courts face from petitioners. Article 41 suggests deeper structural issues that must also be addressed if finality and court independence are to become characteristics of the Chinese legal system.

Second, can reform take place while the current system of allowing *shensu* and petitions continues? Can constitutional rights be enforced in a system in which court decisions can be reopened in response to petitions and protests at any time? One insight obtained from analyzing Article 41 is that constitutional reform is not merely a question of allowing the courts to handle constitutional claims. Any attempt to enforce the rights set forth in the Chinese constitution needs also to confront the question of how to achieve a balance between a system that is hyper-responsive to individual grievances and a system that operates according to rules and procedures. The petitioning system sometimes helps aggrieved individuals win redress. One reason that *shensu* and petitioning continue to be important is that other avenues for seeking redress are often lacking or ineffective; formal procedures often provide inadequate remedies for addressing grievances. The fact that many *shensu* relate to administrative action – and to administrative litigation – suggests that courts are not yet in a position to address such problems (Yan 2013: 9 f.). But the continued importance of both *shensu* and petitioning also reinforces a message that legal institutions lack a privileged position for adjudicating rights.

Third, this essay also raises a theoretical question: can finality be obtained in a system that continues to have a never-ending right to appeal? If not, does the enforcement of constitutional rights require either courts to play leading roles or court decisions to be final? Most other systems that have undergone constitutional transitions have opted for finality as a core value of rule of law. China has thus far taken a different path, maintaining a system that focuses on the substantive correctness of decisions. Such an approach reflects historical tradition and concern about the legitimacy of the state.

Many in China and the west have argued that this practice is not sustainable in the context of a modern legal system. Yet this perhaps may be yet another area where Chinese legal reform has the potential to challenge conventional wisdom. In a society undergoing rapid and radical change, providing a general mechanism for challenging state action even where law does not formally provide for such challenges may be important not only for preserving state legitimacy but also for addressing injustice. Examination of Article 41 suggests that there may be theoretical justification for the continuation of the system, in particular if courts continue to lack significant power to review state action. Article 41 has largely remained in the background in discussions about the constitution and about institutional reform in China. Yet addressing the tension inherent in Article 41 may be central to efforts to enforce the constitution and to deepen institutional reforms.

References
1954 Constitution, Constitution of the People's Republic of China (1954).
1975 Constitution, Constitution of the People's Republic of China (1975).
1978 Constitution, Constitution of the People's Republic of China (1978).
1982 Constitution, Constitution of the People's Republic of China (1982).
Administrative Litigation Law, Administrative Litigation Law of the People's Republic of China (1989).
Administrative Penalty Law, Administrative Penalty Law of the People's Republic of China (1996).
Chen Dang 陈党 (2009) "Jiandu quan, qingqiu quan jiqi xianghu guanxi – 'xianfa: di 41 tiao' jiedu" 监督权,请求权及其相互关系—"宪法"第 41 条解读 [The rights to supervise and complain and their interrelationship - a reading of Article 41 of the constitution], <http://lawyer.fabao365.com/4243/article_33370>, accessed 1 March 2013
Civil Servants law, Civil Servants Law of the People's Republic of China (2005).
Civil Procedure Law 2007, Civil Procedure Law of the People's Republic of China (2007).
Civil Procedure Law 2012, Civil Procedure Law of the People's Republic of China (2012).
Court Organization Law, Organic Law of the People's Courts of the People's Republic of China (2006).
Criminal Procedure Law 2012, Criminal Procedure of the People's Republic of China (2012).
Feng Jiaowen 冯娇雯 (2013) "Chongtu yu tiaohe: Meiti jiandu yu sifa gongzheng zhijian" 冲突与调和: 媒体监督与司法公正之间 [Conflicts and Mediation: Between media supervision and judicial fairness], <http://www.chinalawedu.com/new/201302/wangying20130203115570627642290.shtml>, accessed 1 March 2013.
Hand, Keith (2011) "Resolving Constitutional Disputes in Contemporary China", in *University of Pennsylvania East Asia Law Review* 7:1, pp. 51-159.
He Weifang 贺卫方 (2012) "Sifa gaige de nandian he tupokou zai nali" 司法改革的难点和突破口在哪里 [What are the difficulties in and solutions to judicial reform], <http://news.ifeng.com/opinion/special/sifagaige/detail_2012_10/10/18149310_0.shtml>, accessed 1 March 2012.
Liebman, Benjamin L. (2011) "A Populist Threat to China's Courts", in Woo, Margaret Y. K. and Mary E. Gallagher (eds.) *Chinese Justice: Civil Dispute Resolution in Contemporary China*, Cambridge: Cambridge University Press, pp. 269-313.
Liu Jianguo 刘建国 (2012) "Wangluo fan fubai tixian gongmin xingshi ziyouquan, jiandu quan" 网络反腐体现公民行使自由权,监督权 [Anti-corruption efforts on the internet are a reflection of citizens exercising their right to freedom and their right to supervise], <http://news.sohu.com/20130219/n366391833.shtml>, accessed 1 March 2012.
Organization Law of Local People's Congresses and Governments, Organization Law of Local People's Congresses and Governments of the People's Republic of China (2004).
Shao Jian 邵建 (2010) "Xinfang quanli: xianfa baohu, hezui zhiyou" 信访权利: 宪法保护何罪之有 [The right to petition: protected by the constitution, what is the crime

there], <http://news.ifeng.com/opinion/politics/201003/0313_6438_1574323.shtml>, accessed 1 March 2013.

Su Zelin 苏泽林 (2010) *Minshi anjian shenqing zaishen zhinan* 民事案件申请再审指南 [Guide to applications for rehearings in civil litigation], Beijing: China Legal Publishing House.

Supreme People's Court, Interpretation Regarding the Use of "The Criminal Procedure Law of the People's Republic of China", Nov. 5, 2012.

Tong Zhiwei 童之伟 (2012) "'Yixian xingzheng' jiuyao quanmian luoshi xianfa" "依宪执政" 就要全面落实宪法 [Full implementation of the constitution is necessary for governance according to the constitution], in *Shidai zhoubao* 时代周报 [Time weekly], <http://time-weekly.com/story/2012-12-13/128260.html>, accessed 1 March 2013.

Tu Siyi 涂四益 (2012) "Wusi xianfa zhi gongmin quanli yiwu guifan de tedian" 五四宪法之公民权利义务规范的特 [Characteristics of the 1954 constitution's provisions on citizen's rights and duties], <http://www.110.com/ziliao/article-273115.html>, accessed 1 March 2013.

Yan Lin (2013) Constitutional Evolution through Legislation: China's Constitution Underwent a Quiet Transition (unpublished draft).

Zhang Jun 张军 and Jiang Bixin 江必新 (eds.) (2012) *Xin xingshi susong fa ji sifa jieshi* 新刑事诉讼法及司法解释 [The new criminal procedure law and judicial interpretations], Beijing: Renmin fayuan chubanshe, pp. 352-362.

Zhang Qianfan 张千帆 (2012a) "Xianfa youyong le, gaige cai hui bian hao" 宪法有用了，改革才会变好 [Reforms will only become effective after the constitution is useful], <http://www.21ccom.net/articles/zgyj/xzmj/article_2012060461067.html>, accessed 1 March 2013.

Zhang Qianfan 张千帆 (2010b), "Guifan shangfang bushi yige falü wenti" 规范上访不是一个法律问题 [Standardizing the letters and visits system is not a legal issue], <http://www.360doc.com/content/10/0925/12/2687579_56214234.shtml>，accessed 1 March 2013.

Zhang Zhiyuan 章志远 and Gu Qinfang 顾勤芳 (2011) "Zhongguo falü wenben zhong de 'shensu' yanjiu" 中国法律文本中的 "申诉" 研究 [Research into "complaints" in Chinese legislation], in *Fazhi yanjiu* 法治研究 [Rule of law research] 8, pp. 31-36.

Gao Quanxi

The Rise of the Chinese Political Constitutionalist School[*]

The political constitutionalist school (PCS) has been on the rise in mainland China in recent years and since the ideological content combines the old with the new and is strongly rooted in reality, PCS has already attracted the attention of both national and international scholars. As one of the proponents of PCS, I have the feeling that, now, in these crucial times, when Chinese society is facing great upheavals in the political system, it is essential to sort out what is actually meant by the contested notion of the "political constitutionalist school", to reveal the reasons underlying its vigorous rise, the problems that it presents and its fundamental claims in the context of the debates of other schools of constitutionalism and the political constitutionalist school's internal debates. The next step would then be to outline the possible theoretical perspectives for the future.

The emergence of the political constitutionalist school

It must have been in 2008 that the PCS emerged as an academic school of thought. In this year, Chen Duanhong, a law professor at Peking University, published an article entitled: "On making the constitution the country's fundamental law and high-ranking law" in the *Peking University Law Journal* (Chen 2008). The publication of this article evoked wide-ranging debates and criticism among the Chinese constitutional scholars. I follow the line suggested by Chen Duanhong, with regard to the awareness of problems and methodology, but I strongly call into question his particular standpoint. Soon after the article appeared, I gave a lecture on "The political constitutionalism and judicial constitutionalism" at the salon of the Law School of Beihang University, outlining my understanding of the PCS and developing a critical analysis of Chen Duanhong's approach. After this, Chen Duanhong and I each gave many lectures and participated in discussions in the law faculties of Renmin University, Qinghua University, Peking University and Beihang University. The subjects touched upon during these lectures and discussions included a number of questions related to the PCS, for example, revolution and the constitution, the constituent power, the people's presence (*renmin chuchang* 人民出场), the relationship between the study of the constitution and political science, etc. For us, the purpose of these scholarly lectures and discussions was not merely to explain the PCS, but rather to try to enter into a dialogue with the normative constitutional school as well as with the school of constitutional hermeneutics. For this reason, we consciously launched discussions at the law institutes of Renmin University and Qinghua University, since these are China's key institutes for constitutional hermeneutics and the normative constitutional school, and issued invitations to Han Dayuan, Lin Laifan, Ren Jiantao, Yao Zhongqiu along with a number of other young scholars of law and politics, to take part. In one sense, the above-mentioned lectures and discussions did not shape a rich and constructive theory dialogue between the PCS and the normative constitutional school or the school of constitutional hermeneutics, but they certainly had a strong influence on the academic atmosphere of mainstream constitutional studies in China, revealing some important questions concerning China's constitution that always have been hidden from

---

[*] This article has been translated from Chinese by Katja Levy and Sabine Mokry.

view by mainstream constitutional approaches. If Chen Duanhong's 2008 article is taken as an indicator, the political constitutional school formally emerged in this year. However, as a kind of problem awareness in the thinking on politics and law along with the theory on constitutional methodology, its rise in mainland China started much earlier. I myself turned to considerations of the political constitutional school many years ago, after completing my earlier research on the history of Western political ideas, and discussed problems related to politics and society, constitutional politics, republican forms of government, nationalism and state interests. In 2008, my: "Five Treatises on Modern Political Systems" were published, but I had published a number of related works before this, e.g., "What kind of politics? Whose modernity?", in "My Yoke: Between Politics and Law" in 2007. For years, Chen Duanhong has been devoting himself to non-mainstream research on the study of the constitution. In 2007, he compiled and published "Constitutional Government and Sovereignty" and many of his concepts related to the PCS have been inspired by the reflections found within this book. There are also the articles authored by the young scholar, Zhai Xiaobo: "The constitution is the real rule of sovereignty" (2004) and "The highest representative authority is still the judicature" (2006). From 2008 until the present day, following the emergence and diffusion of the PCS as a school of thought along with pragmatic responses and stimulation by the one-hundred year long history of Chinese politics and law, a number of works on the PCS have been published one after another, and these contain an exciting array of related ideas and concepts. Among other representative works are: "From Extraordinary Politics to Normal Politics" (Gao 2009), "On China's System of the Constitution's Implementation" (Zhai 2009b), "The People's Constitution" (Zhai 2009a), "The Constituent Power and Fundamental Law" (Chen 2010), "The Constitutional Moment: On the Imperial Edict of the Manchu Emperor's Abdication" (Gao 2011b), as well as "Constitutional Law and Revolution: With Some Discussions of the Problem of Chinese Constitution" (Gao 2010b), "War, Revolution and Constitution" (Gao 2011c), "Wealth, Property Rights and Constitution (Gao 2011a), "On the Jurisprudence of Revolution" (Gao 2010c), "Spirit, Religion and Constitution" (Gao 2012), "State Structure and the PCS" (Gao and Chen et al. 2010), the conversation with Tian Feilong on "Problems, position and methods of the political constitutional school" (Gao and Tian 2011), and "The Gradual Evolution of the 1982 Constitution and Modern Chinese Constitutionalism" (Gao and Tian 2012). In addition, other books such as: "The Path of the Foundation of China" (Yao 2010), "China's Path to Change" (Yao 2012), "The National Interests of Modern China" (Xu Zhangrun 2011), and the article: "The unwritten provisions within the Chinese constitution–a new perspective for the understanding of the Chinese constitution" (Jiang 2009a) also belong to the PCS in a broad sense.[1]

---

[1] The discussion in China's theorists' circles and even research on the PCS is no longer limited to periodical publications; it has recently gradually started to attract the attention of academic researchers, e.g. Li Zhongxia: "Reflections on the methodology of Chinese constitutional jurisprudence", Chinese Journal of Law, 2011, No. 2; No. 3 of the Journal of Suzhou University, 2011 published several articles especially on the political constitutional school, including: "Problems, position and methods of the political constitutional school" (Gao and Tian 2011), "The ontology of the constitution: political, normative or heuristic?" (Fan and Zhang 2011), "Which era do we belong to – simple analysis of the fundamental differences between the normative study of the constitution and the political constitutional

Although the mainstream of today's research on constitutionalism in China, namely the ideological constitutional school, the constitutional hermeneutics school and the normative constitutionalist school are still dominant[2], the old original structures are nevertheless gradually being destroyed as a result of the rise of the PCS during the last few years. A new ideological and theoretical path, a conceptual system as well as a methodology, and even an awareness of problems and value orientation have begun to emerge. Some scholars hold that the PCS is of only minor significance, but there are also others who think that the PCS reveals the dullness of semantics. However, I think that the PCS with its sharply-honed ideological content and its feel for reality has revealed the academic disguise of constitutional law studies in China. It forces our scholars working in the field of constitutional law to face the reality of the Chinese constitutional system (including the complex and frustrating hundred years of the constitution), and to stop trying to hide behind the provisions of a constitution on paper to ponder over the impressions made by the constitutional norms of various Western countries (Tian 2011b). Of course, as I have stated again and again, the PCS is only one kind of problem-awareness and one methodology of constitutional law; it is one academic school of thought. This does not mean that our understanding of China's constitution is unanimous, nor does it mean that we are completely opposed to the above-mentioned three mainstream approaches to the study of the constitution. The question is somehow more complex. For example, Chen Duanhong's five great fundamental laws of China's Constitution and their order on the level of values, has some affinity with the ideological mainstream study of constitutional law. And Jiang Shigong's position on the unwritten provisions of China's constitution, in fact, defends the theory of the party state advanced by the traditional ideological school of constitutional study from a new perspective. As for my point of view, I have stressed the normativity of the PCS from the beginning. I think that modern China is undergoing a period of transformation, moving from extraordinary politics to normal politics. To analyze this country's constitutional structure together with

---

school (Zheng 2011), "On the normative nature of the constitution" (Yang 2011), "The Chinese style expression of political constitutionalism" (Wang 2011); the journal *Open Times* has recently published a series of articles on the research subject of political constitutionalist study, for example, "Fundamental problems of political philosophy (Wu 2011), "Legal order and political resolutions–critical discussions on 'the political constitutionalist school'" (Wu 2012), "The three directions of the implementation of the Chinese constitution, between political constitutionalist school, the sociological constitutionalist school and the normativist study of the constitution" (Han 2012).

It is reported that today there are already several dissertations within the fields of the study of the constitution, legal theory and political science with the political constitutionalist school as the subject of study, for example, Tian Feilong's dissertation at Peking University Law School on "Political constitutionalism – an alternative approach to the transition of China's constitutionalism". In addition, my own book "The Constitutional Moment: On the Imperial Edict of the Manchu Emperor's Abdication", takes the PCS as a theoretical foundation. During the hundred year anniversary of the Qinghai Revolution in 2011, it had a great theoretical impact. In a certain sense, it expanded the field of vision as well as the limits of the research on the history of the establishment of the Chinese constitution and triggered widespread discussion and responses.

[2] For an even more carefully elaborated analysis of the theoretical schools of the Chinese study of the constitution, refer to Tian 2009.

its intrinsic driving forces is far more meaningful than simply doing research on non-adjustable normativity.

Nevertheless, the PCS and the above-mentioned three mainstream approaches to the study of the constitution differ greatly. In my opinion, these differences are concentrated and reflected in the awareness of problems and the methodology. In other words, the PCS makes "the political constitution" the key question of Chinese constitutional law. It provides a kind of revelation of the truth about China's hundred years of constitutionalism, particularly the constitution of the People's Republic formulated by the Chinese people under the guidance of the Communist Party, by adopting a life–structuralist methodology and pursuing its future constitutional reform. This awareness of problems and methodology is the difference between the PCS and the mainstream schools of constitutional law – the ideological study of constitutional law, the constitutional hermeneutics school and normative constitutional studies. The PCS no longer pays attention to the standard interpretations of constitutional provisions, nor does it directly promote political ideology slogans or consider the reform path of the judicialization of the constitution important[3]. Instead, it focuses directly on the structure of China's constitution and on the constituent power as well as on the underlying spirit of the constitution with the intrinsic driving forces. These are the key issues of the PCS and as a result, "political nature" turns into a key concept of the PCS; the relationship between politics and constitution turns into a key question of the PCS; legislative power (and not judicial power) turns into a core question of the PCS. The people, the revolution and constituent power (not judges, judicature, rights) turn into key points of consideration for the PCS. The question of how to bring the political constitution into the organic structure of the spirit of drawing up of a modern state's constitution and to reveal the rules of its inherent occurrence, expansion and even decline, underlines the need for the PCS to adopt a holistic kind of methodology, what I call the "life–structuralist" methodology. This means that the PCS does not conceive of the constitution as a completely mechanical system, but rather sees it as a dynamic, animate system, including the passion, rationality and decisiveness of those who establish the constitution. It is the practical product of a political people (nation).

Of course, because of the ideological tensions within the PCS, deep disagreements still exist over the meaning of "political character" and "constitutional character" in the context of the "political constitution" and that of the realism and normativism of the "life–structuralist" methodology. For example, there is a great difference between Chen Duanhong's understanding of "politics" and my own; we also differ greatly on the focal points of "reality" and "normative character". Quite naturally, as a result, great differences also exist concerning a number of concepts, value orientations and even the general nature of the PCS. I would suggest that we represent the "left" and the "right" of the PCS. In a certain sense, the differences between us are actually much, much greater than the

---

[3] This is a normative pursuit of judicial constitutionalism; it is a perspective on the system that is shared by constitutional hermeneutics and the normativist study of the constitution, which under the name of "constitutional judicialization" at the beginning of this century, started a dynamic system imitation of the pattern of the "common law revolution" on the American constitutionalism model. This imitative process was not merely a scholarly appeal made by the academic community, but was also welcomed by elite judges in China's highest judicial bodies. Related typical works are Wang 2000; Huang 2001.

differences between us and the normative constitutional school and the constitutional hermeneutics school.

However, no matter what, we are still part of the PCS, because our awareness of problems is the same, and our methodology is also the same. In our view, the constitution is a "political constitution" and the hundred years of the Chinese constitution reflect the people's (nation's) political will, decisiveness and rational choice. The study of the Chinese constitution must take into account modern China's sovereignty of the people, grasp firmly the implicit, fundamentally important relationship between the people, the party and the constitution, and reveal its evolutionary path from "rule of existence" to "rule of liberty".[4] More specifically, Chen Duanhong's concept of PCS is based on the five fundamental laws of the 1982 Constitution, guiding the people that are drawing up the constitution according to the people's constituent power, and conceiving the leadership of the party as the first principle of the Chinese constitution; Zhai Xiaobo places an emphasis on the highest representative institutions of the people's constitutionalism as well as on deliberative democracy (*gongyi minzhu* 公议民主), thus rejecting the reform path towards the judicialization of the Chinese constitution within the environment of the Chinese legal system. I myself place the emphasis on "free constitutionalism" and the "constitutional moment", striving to reveal the dynamic mechanisms of the Chinese constitutional system, and seeking a constitutional path in conservative reformism from extraordinary politics to normal politics.[5]

To sum up, what critics have termed the PCS with all the related ideas on constitutionalism, as this is represented by Chen Duanhong, Zhai Xiaobo and me, (which I describe as PCS in a narrow sense), and the constitutional sociology of the party-state represented by Jiang Shigong, the Confucian theory of establishing a constitution and state-building represented by Yao Zhongqiu, as well as historical jurisprudence based on national interests (raison d'etat), represented by Xu Zhangrun (which I describe as PCS in a broader sense)[6], have become particularly dynamic during the last few years, and the authors mentioned above have put forward many opinions and viewpoints that have differed from the three traditional mainstream approaches to the study of the constitution, forming a powerful trend of constitutional thought. In my opinion, the opinions and standpoints of these people, their work and their speeches, as well as the debates and

---

[4] In the past, Chen Duanhong clearly acknowledged this evolutionary path, see Chen 2008.

[5] Chen Duanhong's "five fundamental laws" in fact formed the central norm of his PCS, containing the meaning of [Carl] Schmitt's "absolute constitution", see Chen 2008; Zhai Xiaobo was quite deeply influenced by the English PCS; his discussion on the path of political implementation of the Chinese constitution formed the trend and distinguishing feature of normalization of his PCS, see Zhai 2009b. For a good theoretical explanation and academic critical analysis of this academic intention, see Tian 2011a. My own initial research on the constitutional framework of conservative reformism formed my fundamental concern for and distinguishing feature of the PCS, see Gao 2011b.

[6] Jiang Shigong cut into research on the Chinese constitution from a background of sociology of law, typical works by Jiang Shigong include: "The unwritten provisions within the Chinese constitution–a new perspective for the understanding of the Chinese constitution", in *Open Times* 12, 2009; for Yao Zhongqiu's theory of state-building with Confucian constitutionalism, refer to Yao 2011, as well as Yao 2012; for Xu Zhangrun's historical law approach on the basis of state rationale, refer to Xu 2011.

disputes among them are continuing to strengthen the constitutional difficulties in a situation of crisis that China has not experienced in a thousand years and this is symbolic of the tremendous upheavals in politics that are about to arise.

The political constitutionalist school's awareness of problems

The current dynamic appearance of the PCS, in my opinion, is certainly no coincidence, but rather a product of its time, or to be more precise, a product of the spirit of the time (Zeitgeist) of Chinese society's transformation. The demand to constitutionalize that has been invoked by the spirit of the time has a framework of three time levels or, in other words, there are three lines of constitutional reasoning in the political tradition.

Firstly, the PCS is the product of societal appeals in the thirty years since the reform and opening up policy that have called for a change in direction from the economic to the political realm. This means that the reform of China's economic system has already come to an end after thirty years of development, and implies that the reform of the political system has become a key topic for China's reform processes. Chinese society has started to leave behind matters related to the economy and to consider the question of reforming the constitutional system, to develop "a political constitution", in the course of constructing a modern state. In fact, this question of "a political constitution" has existed since the beginning of the opening and reform policy, but the Chinese study of the constitution lacks the corresponding awareness of problems and methodology to develop an appropriate approach to the question. Instead, it has been wrapped up in the language of official ideology and, in academia, it has been dropped and completely replaced by the school of constitutional hermeneutics and the normative constitutional school. Although the language of official ideology expresses the political nature of the rule of the revolutionary party and the ruling party, it is not at all constitutional in nature. How are the political languages of different times and different political meanings, such as, the 'dictatorship of the proletariat', the 'people's democratic dictatorship', the 'three representatives', the 'harmonious society' as well as 'rule by law', 'the party's leadership', 'democratic centralism', 'socialism' and 'capitalism', etc., to be transformed into a political constitution? The methodology of the PCS is needed to deal with the systemic structure of the political constitution, in particular, while the constitutional spirit and the reformist rule of law which are contained in this political language need the political constitutional school for justification. The school of constitutional hermeneutics and the normative constitutional school avoid these fundamental questions of a political constitution; they simply use the constitutional provisions and the normativism of Western constitutional studies to interpret or conduct research on the Chinese constitution. This is why these theories are either restricted to the problems of particular side issues or limited to idealism. For example, the attention that is paid to the articles concerning rights, as well as their efforts at judicialization, are suppressed almost to invisibility in the face of the political structure of the Chinese constitution.

It is precisely because of the above-mentioned defects found in the mainstream study of the constitution that the PCS focuses directly on the issue of the people's constituent power, and deals openly with the mechanisms needed for establishing the Chinese constitutionism. Within the structure of the PCS, an effort is made to settle the question of the appropriateness of the constitution. In pursuing the reform of the spirit of the constitution, the PCS deals with issues that are concerned with sovereignty and party power, constituent power and constitutional system, revolution and counterrevolution, the people's presence and dual representation, subsistence and freedom as well as many others, thus proposing a constitutional path for the reform of the political system. In contrast to the extrinsic demands made by the school of constitutional hermeneutics and the normative constitutional school for the protection of rights, a limited constitution and judicial independence based on individualism, the PCS emphasizes the people's vital force to draw up the constitution in the Chinese constitution together with its dynamic mechanisms of change. The idea is, that today, in the course of opening and reform, the PCS has to wake the people up to take up responsibility and participate in drawing up the country's constitution; the leadership of the party and the people's mastering its own affairs have to be united. What is called the PCS is to complete the transformation from revolutionism to constitutionalism, to build a party to serve the interests of the people, to rule the country according to the constitution and to establish the rule of law of the civil society.

Of course, since the reform of China's political system has not yet been fully implemented and the drive to constitutionalize still contains entangled paradoxes, the response of the PCS with regard to dealing with the spirit of the time is still complex. There are even some reactionary viewpoints. In a certain sense, The PCS advocated by Chen Duanhong is both extremely radical and extraordinarily conservative. It is radical in the context of his single-minded drive to establish the sovereignty of the people and the revolutionary character of the participation of the people. This revolutionary radical constitutionalism continues the heritage of French political idealism following Rousseau and points towards permanent political revolution. It is conservative in the context of the five fundamental laws that he proposes for the Chinese constitution, particularly the leadership of the party as the first principle. In this way, he constrains the development of the Chinese constitution's free spirit, which he has revealed; the party's current system of rule consolidates the constitutional structure in his mind, which burdens his study of the constitution, and makes it difficult to translate theory into practice.[7] This kind of constitutional study that serves to protect the old system becomes even more apparent in Jiang Shigong's constitutional sociology. He tries to extract a set of sociological origins out of the theory of the English unwritten constitution, and as a next step brings forward evidence for the unity and appropriateness of the party state system, thus rejecting the constitutional reform of China's constitutional system (cf. Jiang 2009a; Jiang 2009b).

My own political constitutionalist line of reasoning is in opposition to these leftist paths of thought. Although I recognize the historical appropriateness of the people's revolutionary jurisprudence and the revolutionary founding of the state, I still think that the revolutionary constitutional system under the leadership of the party is by no means a fundamental feature of the PCS. The "revolutionary counter-revolution", i.e., completing the transformation from a party system state to a regular judicial constitutionalism through

---

[7] Chen Duanhong's theoretical foundation of the PCS ultimately draws on the theory of the "constituent power", see Chen 2011. There is, however, obvious tension between the radicalism of the right to draw up a constitution and the conservatism of his "five fundamental laws" in his 2008 paper. This tension confirms my analysis here. My critical evaluations of Chen Duanhong's work are mainly collected in Gao 2009.

a constitutional-political transformation, is actually the essential intention of China's constitution.[8] Within this, there is a constitutional and political state-building process and the political structure of a new people as well as the extension of the rights of the people and the citizens. It is therefore necessary to closely investigate the causes of the dynamic force, the material causes, the causes of the forming and the aims of Chinese constitutionalism[9], a glorious reformist revolution is necessary, as well as the molding of the norms of the Chinese constitution taking existentialism as a foundation. Only in this way can one achieve what Chen Duanhong has described as the spirit and character of the Chinese constitution's transition from "existence" to "freedom", but his five fundamental laws cannot penetrate into this other world.

Seen from a certain perspective, the thirty years of experience with reform and opening up have already shifted the character of the constitution away from existentialism towards a spirit of freedom. This is typically reflected in the 1982 constitution, especially in the formulation of its four amendments (cf. Zhai 2012). Of course, it is not enough to examine the rise of the PCS by looking only at the internal driving forces of social transformation during those thirty years. In fact, the awareness of the problems of the PCS also draws on another tradition, namely the constitutional tradition of the founding of the state in 1949; one can even go a little further back and follow the constitutional tradition of the Republic of China. This touches upon what I call the three time layers of the 'zeitgeist constitutionalization' (*shidai jingshen xianfahua* 时代精神宪法化): 1912, the time of the constitutional tradition of the Republic of China, is the first time layer of modern China; 1928, the tradition of the Party State of the Nationalist Party (Guomindang) and the tradition of the Party State of the Communist Party in 1949 are the second time layer of modern China; the reform and opening up in 1978 is the third time layer of modern China which is reflected in the 1982 constitution (including its four Amendments). In fact, for China today, the sense of the PCS, how to differentiate between these different historical layers, how to examine these hundred years of political and constitutional national history and to decide on the necessary criteria for such a study are crucial questions in the context of the PCS.[10] A means of differentiating between the three time layers has not yet found general acceptance in the fields of constitutional study or the study of history; at present, I can only offer a combination of various viewpoints within the PCS and the study of history which I have integrated in a new perspective. Furthermore, I have not yet even presented these viewpoints in a detailed and structured way; some tensions still exist at the theoretical level. Nevertheless, as far as the historical consciousness of my PCS is concerned, the picture is clear. In other words, the first modern China, the founding of the Republic of China, possessed a moment of constitutionalism together with an internal

---

[8] On the logic of the "counter-revolution of the revolution", I have already combined this with a detailed analysis of Chinese constitutionalism, see Gao 2010b.

[9] On Aristotle's theory of the four causes and its application in his theory of government, see Gao 2010d.

[10] Modern China in the sense of the political constitution, in my opinion, is neither the same as the one in the ordinary historical stages of the study of history nor the same as the conception of [modern China as] the transition from ancient to modern China in cultural studies and social sciences, nor does the so-called division between modern and contemporary China apply. It rather stresses the inclusion of constitutional politics or makes the establishment of the constitution and state-building the only important criteria for division, see Gao 2012a.

constitutional spirit. It gave rise to a change between the old and the new as well as the revolution and the road toward improvement that led to the drawing up of the constitution and the founding of the state; after the abdication of the Manchu emperor, a modern Republic was established.[11] However, the first Chinese Republic eventually failed and came to an end after about ten years. After the renewed outbreak of the revolution, the National Party of the National Revolution, allied with Russia and in cooperation with the Communist Party, and armed with the three Principles of the People went on the northern expedition and established a single-party-state system, following a road map of military administration, political tutelage and constitutionalism[12]. But the National Party's purging of activists betrayed the revolution, and the Communist Party started to promote the cause of independent revolution and state-building. After going through the Anti-Japanese War and then three years of bloody civil war, the Communist Party was finally victorious on the Mainland in 1949, and led the Chinese people to found the New China.[13] The Common Program and the 1954 constitution announced the foundation of the party-state under the rule of the Communist Party. The Nationalist Party retreated to Taiwan. This period can be described as the second historical phase of modern China, and here we also have the PCS problem of the foundation of the revolutionary state by "the party and the people" (cf. Gao 2010a, Gao 2010b).

This party-state system lasted for 60 years, during which time tremendous changes in the constitution and in politics took place. On the Mainland, during the completely lawless days of the Cultural Revolution, the constitution became nothing but a worthless piece of paper. Biased Taiwan had the Nationalist Party and was going through a successful transformation from autocracy to democracy and constitutionalism[14]; today, this system is still referred to as the constitution of the Chinese Republic. And the Chinese mainland went through 30 years of reform and opening up after the Cultural Revolution, including the 1982 constitution and its four Amendments. How should we see the 1982 constitution and the ensuing thirty years of constitution and politics? In my opinion, a two-dimensional perspective should be adopted to examine China's current "revolutionary" constitution: first, there is the dimension of constitutional continuity, that is to say that this constitution is nothing more than an upgraded version of the party-state system led by the Chinese Communist Party, a constitution that has still has not separated itself from the party state

---

[11] For the political constitutionalist analysis of this process, refer to Gao 2011b.

[12] The "General Plan of the Revolution" of the time of the Chinese Revolutionary League (*tongmenghui* 同盟会) contains the sequence of "military law, provisional constitution, constitution", in 1914, at the time when the revolutionary party of China was reorganized, and the doctrine of the three phases "military administration, political tutelage, constitutional government" was put forward; this was the proposition and argument of the official and systematic theory of constitutionalism and state-building, the "Outline for the establishment of a National Government" in 1923. For historical reflections on this subject and an analysis, see Wang 2003: 20-26.

[13] Another indicator for symbolization is Mao Zedong's heroic claim that "The Chinese People have risen up to their feet", put forward on October 1st, 1949 at the ceremony for the founding of the state.

[14] Jiang Jingguo played an active historical role in this process of transformation; external forces of protest (represented by the Democratic Progressive Party in its early stages) also had an important boosting function on Taiwan's transformation to democratic constitutionalism. For an analysis of the political and social experiences of this transformation process, see Zhu 2012.

system, although it imposed order on the chaos of political China during the Cultural Revolution [15]. This has to be seen in close relation with the Chinese Party State constitution in the new tradition of the Nationalist Party and the Communist Party; it is simply a part of this new tradition. There is, however, a second dimension, that is to say that this constitution is not the final product but the start of a great process of constitutional reform; it bears the seed of the future; it marks an important shift in the Chinese constitutional system, from "existence" to "freedom", from a party system to a constitutional system [16]. For this reason, it is absolutely essential to see this shift as marking the beginning of a third time layer, particularly if it is perceived from the gradual and progressive path of a conservative reformist constitution. It is only the beginning or the prelude; the main acts of the drama are still to come.

To sum up, opinions differ on how the hundred years of Chinese constitutionalism can be divided up into periods, and the criteria for distinguishing among these different periods are difficult to identify and agree upon; it is also extremely difficult to consistently define the various stages of state-building in China during which the constitution has been drawn up and to develop an understanding of the people, the revolution and the party system. However, the ability to face these questions and to develop historical awareness are precisely the features that distinguish the PCS from other constitutional theories. It can be said that the problem-awareness of PCS is closely interrelated to its awareness of history. The constitutional and political logic of the PCS along with its attempts to shed light on constitutional main topics such as sovereignty, revolution, party, people, drawing up a constitution, state-building, the constitutional structure, citizens' rights, etc., are all very closely related to China's modern and contemporary history. In other words, the PCS's awareness of problems originates from the awareness of history. It has been brought forward, expanded and developed by the hundred years of history of modern China. Understanding the history of the changes in China from the ancient to the modern, and understanding the history of the building of the modern state in China, of revolution, of drawing up the constitution, of reform, of existentialism, of freedom, are the keys to understanding the Chinese PCS and the history and real background of the rise of the Chinese PCS.

Of course, [Benedetto] Croce [1866-1952], following Hegel, said that all history is contemporary history, and the PCS's awareness of history cannot simply be separated from contemporary history. To be more precise, it cannot be separated from the contemporary history of thirty years of reform and opening in China. It could therefore be argued that the rise of the PCS stems directly from the legal and political practices of thirty years of reform and opening in China, that it follows the Chinese process of reform and opening, even to the point that it has developed out of the complexities and frustrations of this process. Why do I say this? Because we all know that this process is not simply a single economic reform process, but a whole-hearted reform that encompasses politics, economics and even society as a whole. This comprehensive reform

---

[15] Traces of the party state system can easily be identified in the account of the revolutionary history in the preamble as well as in the principles and structure of the political constitutionalism of the 1982 constitution. For a political science analysis of this inner core of the party state in a transitional system, see Ren 2012.

[16] For a theoretical analysis of the reform constitution's reform intention and prospects, see Xia 2003.

of the modern state has not advanced in time, but the fetus of the reform of the political system died a violent death[17]. The one-dimensional economic reforms, without any doubt, released unprecedented energy, a distorted economy and society developed quickly, and suddenly China became one of the world's very few great economic powers. The China model ran rampant for a while[18], but since it lacked the integration of rights and capital which would be conditioned by the constitution, it led to the development of a form of Leninist state (big wigs)-capitalism. Thus, it can be seen that the common functions of the current constitution have not been implemented effectively. The judicial constitutionalism in China is an illusion, normative constitutional studies and constitutional hermeneutics lack any solid foundations and have been reduced to a game of words. As far as the so-called improvement of the socialist system, and the construction of the socialist rule of law civilization are concerned, there seems, at a time when the socialist law system has been declared completed, to be little sign of progress. Why did such a situation develop? Does the Chinese constitution not exist? Does the Chinese constitution not have any binding force? Obviously, it is not that easy.

From the perspective of conventional studies of the constitution, especially the Western form of constitutional studies, it is hard to say that the Chinese constitution is a constitution of rich force. Whether in the context of normative constitutional studies or in the context of constitutional hermeneutics, within the framework of the Chinese constitutional system, it is difficult to obtain effective justification. No doubt our constitutional provisions include a system of vertical and horizontal divisions of state power and some clauses on safeguarding citizens' rights. However, the operation of this power structure and the implementation of citizens' rights, especially from the perspective of examining constitutional cases, are little more than empty words; the provisions are written on paper, but they are not effectively implemented in practice and what is more, there is no powerful judicial system to protect them. A great deal of debate has been provoked that has, in turn, drawn criticism and even blame, but it is not within the scope of this article to further expand on these aspects. I would contend that this is only one aspect of the problem of China's constitutional system, and by no means all of it. It should be noted that there are some institutions in China's constitution which are still being effectively implemented. Particularly after the promulgation and amendments of the Administrative Procedure Law and the Criminal Procedure Law, some so called detailed rule of law institutions started to be implemented. Although they are partial, even to the point that their progress is often one step backwards and two steps forward, on the whole, they manifest some constitutional rule of law value and possess partially structural constitutional meaning.[19] Furthermore, China's system of People's Congresses has also

---

[17] In his speech at the Lingnan Forum on the subject of "30 years of agitation: a summary of the experiences of reform and opening" Zhu Xueqin has already proposed the theory of the two stages of reform, providing a thorough analysis of the feature of tensions of the framework of reform, see Zhu 2007.

[18] The China model has become a keyword for left-wing scholars during recent years, among whom Pan Wei is an important advocate, see Pan and Ma 2010; for a focused and systematic criticism of the China model refer to Ding 2011.

[19] This touches upon the question of the evaluation framework of the rule of law in 30 years of reform. It cannot be completely negated simply because of the lagging behind of the constitutional system, neither

gradually started to show the constitutional function of the people's participation in state affairs. Of course, this is all superficial, of local character and cannot be taken as evidence that China's constitutional system is a genuine democratic constitutional government system. Seen from a normativist perspective, these are all of initial and whitewash character.

China's constitution is of whitewash character; however, China's political system is still working effectively. And this effectively working political state system also seems to be strong, it has not collapsed, society has not dissolved, the processes of the political power operations continue to function, and the economy is still expanding fast. In addition, after all, the constitution exists; there is a constitutional system. How can this actually be the case? Is there a puzzle within the Chinese system? If we define a constitution as a kind of regulation of political order, where is the origin of China's constitutional system? What are the constitutional rules of Chinese politics? Or, what is the nature of China's constitution? What is the relationship between the constitution and the regulations of power order? This set of questions is obviously the key interest of the PCS. From the perspective of studies of the constitution, these key systemic topics are to be found in the preamble to the Chinese constitution and in the integrated structure of the party and the state. As a result, in the Chinese constitution, normativism cannot be taken as a starting point, the "preamble" must come first, and the actual constitutional framework should be taken as the actual starting point. The essential center of the study of the Chinese constitution is therefore the preamble and the overall structure. With regard to this preamble and the overall structure, Chinese traditional constitutional hermeneutics seem to remain on the surface of the text, relying on the characters' superficial meaning and blindly following the ideology of the political language; there is no plan to interpret or examine the preamble or the overall structure, their study is limited to interpretations of so-called constitutional semantics and interpretations of articles. The result is the irrelevance of constitutional hermeneutics. Perhaps the curricula for the study of the constitution in other forms, after observing the above-mentioned powerlessness of hermeneutics, have simply hidden the constitution's preamble and political ideology and have taken the normativism of the Western study of the constitution and the judicial investigative systems as cases for compiling a study of the Chinese constitution. In this way, they have at least been able to avoid the corrosion of political ideology; this is said to be a "military strategy" for the study of the constitution. [20] To sum up, avoiding the political character of the Chinese constitution is a mainstream attitude in the study of the constitution in China, but it could be argued that although this kind of attitude can, without doubt, avoid the problem, resist the old political ideological language of the study

---

can one be high-handed, only because there is progress in the rule of law in some particular departments. A finer analytical framework is required. For a fairly concise reflection on this aspect, see Gao, Zhang and Tian 2012, in Chapter 5 "Transformational rule of law facing normality: reform and governance" a binary analytical framework [with the two variables] "fundamental rule of law and concrete rule of law" is established.

[20] A representative of the normative study of the constitution, Professor Lin Laifan, has used this expression before.

of the constitution[21], and provide innumerable reserves of academic theories for the study of the constitution under the conditions of real daily politics, it still has nothing to do with resolving the essential questions of the current Chinese constitution, and it is irrelevant to move mechanisms for the presentation and then resolution of China's constitutional reform. It represents a scholarly position that has abandoned reality and departed from practical rationality.

The PCS: political science or study of the constitution?

In contrast to the above-mentioned approaches to the study of the constitution, the PCS holds that the constitution's political character cannot be hidden, particularly in the context of the study of China's modern constitution. The "political constitution" is the key question; it is concentrated and realized in the preamble and structure of the Chinese constitution. The political and constitutional character is the main problem confronting the study of the Chinese constitution; it is also the fundamental question facing any modern state that is creating and interpreting its constitution. Only when the problem of the relationship between the constitutional and political character of the constitution has been resolved, will it be possible for the every-day problems of the so-called normative constitutional school and constitutional hermeneutics school to be developed and promoted.

Chen Duanhong has an unusually clear-cut awareness of the above-mentioned question of the political constitution. He has dealt with the question of the constitutional and political character in two introductory articles: first of all, "The dialog between a political scientist and a scholar of the constitution on the right to draw up a constitution" (Chen 2010) in his major work "Constituent Power and Fundamental Law"; the other article is the manuscript of a speech he delivered at Qinghua University's Law Institute, under the heading of the "Limits of knowledge in the study of the constitution".[22] One central topic that runs through Chen Duanhong's two articles and all his thinking on the study of the constitution is his insistence on the need to firmly establish the limits of the knowledge of the study of the Chinese constitution, i.e., to establish a political science foundation for the study of the constitution. And this political science, in Chen Duanhong's view, is based on the political right to draw up a constitution, or even, to put it differently, the people's (continuous) revolutionary right to draw up a constitution. According to Chen, this right to draw up a constitution is the foundation of the PCS. For this reason, he has formulated and re-established some vocabulary for the new studies of the constitution that differ from the old studies of the constitution, e.g., "the Chinese people under the leadership of the Chinese Communist Party", "the people have to emerge", "the people neither emerge nor are absent", "the constitution is a democracy's Holy Bible, the melody for the peaceful sleep of the people", etc. These are some of Chen Duanhong's central concepts of the PCS, and for a while they enjoyed a wide circulation.

---

[21] What I describe here as the old study of the constitution is the theory of the study of the constitution by the older generation of revolutionaries and constitutional theorists since the founding of the state in 1949, and theories on the study of the constitution within the system from Dong Biwu to Zhang Fawu and Chen Shuwen. For the style and features of their fundamental theories, see Zhang et al. 2003.

[22] For the record of this speech, see Chen et al. 2011.

Chen Duanhong blatantly exposes the undisguised nature of political power in the face of the PCS, regarding it as the foundation of the study of the constitution and thus assigning limits to studies of the constitution. Without doubt, this constitutes a direct attack on the weak points of constitutional hermeneutics and the normative constitutional school, exposing the ferocious side of the constitution. This naturally has an epistemological meaning, but its meaning at the political science level is even more crucial and it is therefore fully comprehensible that it has led to oral and written denouncements from within the mainstream studies of the constitution. Chen Duanhong's political constitutionalist theory, in particular, the way that he closely links the constitution and political power with political decision-making, and the fact that he does not hesitate to repeat what is written in the Party's constitution, has indubitably drawn expressions of disgust from many scholars, and even defamation by some, who regard it as a form of anti-constitutionalism, as leftist radicalism (cf. Lin Laifan's Law Blog, 09.2008). Some scholars have expressed the view that Chen Duanhong is going so far as to say that political constitutionalist theory is not jurisprudence, but political science, that it is the academic packaging of power politics. They think that political theory deals only with power politics, while legal theory deals with rights and has nothing to do with politics and power, and even if there is a relation, it is normative political power which restricts and resists political power. A constitutional government is there to guard against the unscrupulousness of political power and therefore guarantees human rights. The study of the constitution is simply normativism, so it is the hermeneutics of legal articles on the basis of normativism; it is the fight against tyranny and the guaranteeing of rights on the basis of the right to judicial investigation. The study of the constitution and the study of political theory therefore need to be strictly separated; political theory has to be left on one side and there has to be a return to the study of rights. In the opinions of the critics of Chen Duanhong, the PCS is not a study of the constitution, but political theory; it substitutes the constitution with politics, and replaces constitutional hermeneutics with political sociology. According to the standpoints of these critics, a number of articles about the constitution recently published by Jiang Shigong, particularly from what he calls the viewpoint of the unwritten constitution, in comparison to Chen Duanhong's five fundamental laws, pave the way even more openly for political power; Jiang does not hesitate to distort and use the English constitution to boost his appeal for politics and to defend China's constitution without constitutionalism. These scholars also classify some of my thoughts as political science and think that they cannot be considered as the study of the constitution, but rather belong to the history of political thought.

How should the above-mentioned theoretical dispute be perceived? In my opinion, the doubts that the proponents of the mainstream study of the constitution cast on Chen Duanhong's political constitutionalist thought derive from their study of the constitution. The study of the constitution is, as far as its normal meaning is concerned, a letter that guarantees political rights, the charter of the people, a declaration of resistance against power politics and thus political power with divisions of power and checks and balances for safeguarding and guaranteeing individual rights, defending the honor of the constitution through the judicature, ruling on constitutional disputes by investigating violations of the constitution and so forth. These are all necessary; they are all in need of constitutional hermeneutics which is given close normative attention. In this sense, the study of the constitution is not political science, what it pursues is nothing other than judicial justice; it is about the standardized binding and limitation of political power. However, the problem is that the study of the constitution also has another side to it. It needs to have political empowerment as its foundation, in other words, the constitution needs to face its origins. Where does it come from? How did its genesis, its formation and its goals come about? To answer these questions, the study of the constitution has to confront political science. It cannot easily be separated from political science, but has to deal with the relationship of the constitution and politics. Otherwise, the study of constitution will not be able to answer the above standpoints and will not be able to maintain its inherent quality of resisting power and protecting rights. The reason for the PCS's continued existence lies in the fact that it dares to face the question of political power in the study of the constitution and considers politics to be the foundation of the constitution. This school of thought holds that an everyday constitution did not fall from the sky, but that it is the result of politics, or to be more specific, it is the result of the people drawing up a constitution and building a state. The people created the constitution by exercising their sovereign powers, by putting their own will and reason into a constitution to form a state system, or a state regime. And according to political principles, the separation of power and checks and balances was implemented in the system, thus protecting the rights of every individual citizen. If there had not been any political empowerment in the beginning, it would not have been possible to create a constitution and there would be no judicial constitutionalism worth speaking of.

From the historical practice of the modern constitutional system, we can clearly see that there is a close relationship between the constitution and politics. Any part of the modern constitution stems from the process of the people drawing up the constitution. To be more specific, it all stems from the people's revolutionary state-building and political empowerment, which are all products of a highly politicized time. Mainstream approaches to the study of the constitution have only the objective of the rule of law in ordinary circumstances, not the study of the constitution in extraordinary circumstances. In contrast, the PCS pays attention to nothing but what came before and after the ordinary constitution, what is called the constitution of the "political constitution", or the political character of the constitution, especially the political nature which is created by the constitution in extraordinary times. Mainstream approaches to the study of the constitution might refuse to emphasize this, but they can neither completely disregard it or even hide it, because if there were no period before the ordinary times, their constitution would not be able to exist at all, and even if it did exist, it would remain simply a useless ornament, a worthless piece of paper, a dead constitution. We are criticizing the mainstream approaches of constitutional hermeneutics and the normative study of the constitution not because they do not undertake to study the constitution, but because they do not represent Chinese study of the constitution. They take lifeless objects for living objects; they deceive themselves as well as others by making a worthless piece of paper the object of their research and interpretations. And they have disregarded or forgotten the political character of the Chinese constitution; they have forgotten that the Chinese constitution has not yet reached the period of ordinary rule of law. Its political character is still the lifeblood of the Chinese constitution. With regard to this point, the preamble and even the structure of the Chinese constitution are found in the following clearly stated questions:

31

What is the leadership of the Communist party? What does it mean that the people are the masters of their own affairs? What is revolutionary state building? What is the people's democratic dictatorship? What are the four cardinal principles? What is democratic centralism? What is a socialist country? What is public ownership? And so on. How could these be constitutional concepts in the context of the regular rule of law? All of them are clearly political in character, all of them are products of revolutionary politics out of the extraordinary times of revolutionary state building and the people's participation; they are the political will dominating the constitution. All this shows that the Chinese constitution is a political constitution. In fact, it should be noted that every modern constitution is a political constitution or, in other words, they all possess the determination of a political constitution. For example, the Succession Act, the Right of Inheritance Act as well as the Tolerance Act all constitute the English unwritten constitution; the Federal Constitution of the United States of America and its Amendments, all constitutions of the different Republics of France, the Weimar Constitution of Germany, Japan's Meiji Restoration constitution, and even the constitution of the Republic of China. Who could deny the political character of those constitutions and the political decisions of the people who built the state and drew up the constitution? For this reason, the political constitution is not external to a modern constitution or, in other words, it is not true to say that the constitution has a constitutional character but no political character. The nature of the constitution itself is already political, namely the political character of the people drawing up the constitution. Only after experiencing revolution, war and the drawing up of a constitution and state-building, and after the political community, consolidated by a constitution, has resumed life under regular conditions, will the political character of the constitution give way to the rule of law character of the constitution and constitutional hermeneutics, in its normal sense, and judicial constitutionalism will emerge, becoming the mainstream of the study of the constitution (Gao 2009).

If the modern constitution is acknowledged as being political in character or is a political constitution, does this mean that Chen Duanhong's theory concerning the PCS is correct? Here I have my doubts: I do not follow the concept of constitutional politics put forward by Chen Duanhong and Jiang Shigong. Of course, my doubts are different from those of the mainstream approaches of constitutional hermeneutics and the normative constitutional school. I do not at all reject the political character of the political constitution, and I do not at all reject Chen Duanhong's and the others' awareness of problems, even their constitutional methodology. What I strongly doubt is their concept of constitutional politics. In my opinion, the perception and interpretation of the political character of the constitution proposed by Chen Duanhong and other scholars is nothing other than realist political science; it is the doctrine of power politics and it is not the normativism of political science. That is to say that they seriously misrepresent the political science appeals for political legitimacy; they take power politics or political strength to define the constitution and completely abandon the normativism of politics. In this sense, it is reasonable and correct that they draw criticism from those scholars who represent the mainstream studies of the constitution. That they consider it as political science and not as the study of the constitution is also reasonable, because the study of the constitution has one main feature that differs greatly from political theory. That is, the constitution is not the justification of political power; it is not an endorsement of politics, but the defense of rights; it serves to regulate normative political power. What contorts the study of the constitution is the legitimacy and appropriateness of political power. With regard to this question, the PCS that I propose differs greatly from that of Chen Duanhong's. When Chen Duanhong's outstanding work on the five fundamental laws was published, I examined it from a normativist perspective and severely criticized it. In particular, I resisted his tendency to allow various forms of political constitutionalism and changed this into one that continued the tradition of liberal political constitutionalism. Obviously, I think that Chen Duanhong overemphasizes political realism, extreme politics and the absoluteness of political resolutions, and that he tends to disregard other aspects, such as, the appropriateness of political normativism and the pursuit of justice. His political science is the political science of Machiavelli, Hobbes, and [Carl] Schmitt. It is the modern version of "whatever is reasonable is true, and whatever is true is reasonable" [Hegel, translators' note]. But this kind of brutal political science is not political science per se. Political science also has another side to it, namely legitimacy and appropriateness, i.e., real politics are nothing but power; they stem from the power of the general will of the people which has the consent of the people. Only if the so-called five fundamental laws are measured and evaluated from this perspective of righteous politics, can the essential pursuit of the PCS be followed. Therefore, with regard to the crucial question of how to perceive "PCS", Chen Duanhong and I have serious differences: we represent the left and the right of the PCS.

In my opinion, the crux of the matter when it comes to deciding whether the PCS should be seen as the study of the constitution or as an endorsement of realist political power, is whether one recognizes the normative values of the political constitution, and whether one pursues the legitimacy of politics. This legitimacy is not legality within the constitutional statutes, but is the legitimacy of the constitution, the original legitimacy, that is, its appropriateness. No matter if the appropriate comes from natural rights or is God-given or if it is derived from the mandate of heaven and popular sentiments, it cannot come from naked power. What exists is not always rational, sometimes it is evil, something that the people need to resist. The people, and that means each and every citizen, have the natural right to resist oppressive power and the right to revolution. This is the principle of Locke; it is the principle of modern constitutions; it is the principle of American constitutionalism; it is also the principle of the Chinese revolution and state building. Therefore, the political constitution cannot simply be the people's political resolution and the creation of the leadership of the revolutionary party, but also has to be a kind of political constitutionalism, that is, a control mechanism for political power. In my opinion, Chen Duanhong's PCS only moves around politics or around power, there is no constitutional government and no normativism. His articles are pervaded with the scent of brutality and the decay of political power.

The PCS must pursue normativism; it has to depart from political realism; it has to establish its own system of norms to tame power. This then is the study of the constitution; it is not political science (in the sense of realism). However, concerning the study of the constitution, I again differ from the mainstream approaches of constitutional hermeneutics and the normativist constitutional school. Concerning the aspects of problem-awareness and methodology, I still agree with the PCS. In my opinion, the fundamental problem of the Chinese constitution is not a problem of a rule of law constitution in ordinary times but is situated in extraordinary times. Or to be more precise, it belongs to a time of transition from extraordinary politics to ordinary politics. In such a period, the study of the Chinese constitution cannot be taken over by mainstream approaches, but has to be taken over only by the PCS, that is, to face the essence of the Chinese political constitution, and to create a study of the constitution for transitional constitutionalism. Therefore, the normativism of the constitution that I emphasize differs from the normative constitutional studies of ordinary times. I cannot approve of the abstract construct of a normative constitution which is not based on the Chinese political constitution and the standard of the study of the constitution. In other words, I cannot accept what have been called the norms of universal rights in the sense of the Western study of the constitution or the rights values or declaration of Western constitutions. I think that this kind of external normativism lacks strength and meaning. Of course, I pursue universal values, and I pursue the normative values of normative political power, but these norms cannot simply be transported or transplanted from outside, they can only come from the interior function of the political power of the Chinese constitution, from the historical process of Chinese constitutionalism, from the inner longing and the vital energy produced by the creativity and reform of the Chinese people, from the pursuit of the values of the Chinese political constitution and the process of institutional practice itself.

In my opinion, it is therefore esssential to differentiate among and refute two aspects simultaneously. First, I have to resist and be on guard against Chen Duanhong's strand of political realism, that is, I have to reject his claim that the constitution is based on the political science of political power or on a positivist study of the constitution, and fight to expand the normative values of political constitutionalist studies, to strive to establish the constitution on the just foundation of the normative value of tamed political power. On the other hand, however, it is necessary to justify the distinctive characteristics of the current political constitution, to differentiate between the PCS and the mainstream approaches of normative constitution and constitutional hermeneutics. At the same time, I have to emphasize the need to resist their abstract and empty idealism and their hiding of the truth of politics: I want to build the constitution on the consent of political resolution and rationality of rich vitality, to let the norms grow out of political power and not be transported or transplanted from outside. Considering the turbulence that has been produced by the above-mentioned theories, I think that the Chinese PCS is neither undisguised political theory nor a dry doctrinaire study of the constitution; it is a form of PCS that develops, grows and progresses through history and practice, and at its core, are the normative values that are sent out from the reality of politics, from realism to idealism, from existentialism to liberalism. This historical evolution of the Chinese constitution from "survival" to "freedom" is the spirit of the Chinese constitution. Therefore, there is no need to focus excessively on the question of whether "the political constitution" belongs to political science or the study of the constitution. Of course, a certain scientific intellectual boundary has to be drawn between political science and the study of the constitution, but the political constitutional school is just the political constitutional school, it belongs both to political science and to the study of the constitution, or in other words, it does not belong to political science or to the study of the constitution. The key question is, how to agree on a definition of political science and the study of the constitution. In my opinion, the fundamental questions that the PCS deals with lie between political science and the study of the constitution, in the historical evolution from political realism to constitutional normativism.

References

Chen Duanhong 陈端洪 (2007) *Xianzhi yu zhuquan* 宪治与主权 [Constitutional Government and Sovereignty], Beijing: Falü chubanshe.

Chen Duanhong 陈端洪 (2008) "Lun xianfa zuowei guojia de genbenfa yu gaojifa" 论宪法作为国家的根本法与高级法 [On making the constitution the country's fundamental and high-ranking law], in *Zhongwai faxue* 中外法学 [Peking University Law Journal] 4, pp. 485-511.

Chen Duanhong 陈端洪 (2010) *Zhixianquan yu genbenfa* 制宪权与根本法 [Constituent Power and Fundamental Law], Beijing: Zhongguo fazhi chubanshe.

Chen Duanhong 陈端洪 et. al. (2011) "Zhengzhi xianfaxue yu guifan xianfaxue 'duihuao' shilu" 政治宪法学与规范宪法学'对话'实录 [Recorded 'dialogues' between the PCS and the normativist study of the constitution], in *Gongfa yanjiu* 公法研究 [Public Law Research] 10.

Ding Xueliang 丁学良 (2011) *Bianlun "Zhongguo moshi"* 辩论"中国模式" [Criticizing the "China Model"], Beijing: Shehui kexue wenxian chubanshe.

Fan Jinxue 范进学 and Zhang Yujie 张玉洁 (2011) "Xianfa bentixing: zhengzhixing, guifanxing yihuo jieshixing?" 宪法本体性: 政治性, 规范性抑或解释性? [The ontology of the constitution: political, normative or heuristic?], in *Suzhou daxue xuebao* 苏州大学学报 [Journal of Suzhou University], No. 3, pp. 81-84.

Gao Quanxi 高全喜 (2007) "Hezhong zhengzhi? Shei zhi xiandaixing?" 何种政治？谁之现代性? [What kind of politics? Whose modernity?], in Gao Quanxi (ed.) *Wode e – zai zhengzhi yu falü zhijian* 我的轭——在政治与法律之间 [My yoke: between politics and law], Beijing: Zhongguo fazhi chubanshe.

Gao Quanxi 高全喜 (2008) *Xiandai zhengzhi wu lun* 现代政制五论 [Five Theories on Modern Political Systems], Beijing: Falü chubanshe.

Gao Quanxi 高全喜 (2009) "Zhengzhi xianfa zhuyi yu sifa xianzheng zhuyi – jiyu Zhongguo zhengzhi shehui de yi zhong lixian zhuyi sikao" 政治宪政主义与司法宪政主义——基于中国政治社会的一种立宪主义思考 [Political constitutionalism and judicial constitutionalism – reflections on a constitutionalism based on China's political society], in Gao Quanxi (ed.) *Cong feichang zhengzhi dao richang zhengzhi – lun xianshidai de zhengfa ji qita* 从非常政治到日常政治——论现时代的政法及其他 [From Exceptional to Normal Politics – Discussing Current Politics, Laws and Other Things], Beijing: Zhongguo fazhi chubanshe.

Gao Quanxi 高全喜 (2010a) "Geming yu xianfa ji Zhongguo xianzhi wenti" 革命与宪法及中国宪制问题 [Revolution and Constitution, the problem of the establishment of the Chinese constitution], in *Beida falü pinglun* 北大法律评论 [Beijing Law Commentary], Beijing: Beijing Daxue chubanshe.

Gao Quanxi 高全喜 (2010b) "Xianfa yu geming ji Zhongguo xianzhi wenti" 宪法与革命及中国宪制问题 [Constitutional Law and Revolution: With Some Discussions of the Problem of Chinese Constitution], in *Beida falü pinglun* 北大法律评论 [Beijing Law Commentary], Beijing: Beijing Daxue chubanshe.

Gao Quanxi 高全喜 (2010c) "Lun geming de falixue" 论革命的法理学 [On the jurisprudence of revolution], in *Beijing daxue yanjiusheng xuezhi* 北京大学研究生学志 [Beijing University Graduate Student Journal] 1, pp. 1-7.

Gao Quanxi 高全喜 (2010d) "Meiguo xiandai zhengzhi de 'mimi'" 美国现代政治的'秘密' [The 'secret' of modern US politics], in *Zhanlüe yu guanli* 战略与管理 [Strategy and Management] 5/6.

Gao Quanxi 高全喜 (2011a) "Caifu, caichanquan yu xianfa" 财富, 财产权与宪法 [Wealth, property rights and constitution], in *Fazhi yu shehui fazhan* 法制与社会发展 [The legal system and societal development] 5, pp. 61-71.

Gao Quanxi 高全喜 (2011b) *Lixian shike: lun "Qingdi xunwei zhaoshu"* 立宪时刻: 论"清帝逊位诏书" [The Constitutional Moment: On the Imperial Edict of the Manchu Emperor's Abdication], Guilin: Guanxi shifan daxue chubanshe.

Gao Quanxi 高全喜 (2011c) "Zhanzheng, geming yu xianfa" 战争, 革命与宪法 [War, revolution and the constitution], in *Huadong zhengzhi daxue xuebao* 华东政治大学学报 [East China University of Politics and Law Journal] 1, pp. 3-26.

Gao Quanxi 高全喜 (2012) "Xinling, zongjiao yu xianfa" 心灵, 宗教与宪法 [Spirit, Religion and Constitution], in *Huadong zhengzhi daxue xuebao* 华东政治大学学报 [Journal of the East China University of Politics and Law] 2, pp. 133-154.

Gao Quanxi 高全喜, Chen Duanghong 陈端洪 et al. (2010) "Guojia goujian yu zhengzhi xianfaxue" 国家构建与政治宪法学 [State strucuture and political constitutionalist school], in *Zhanlüe yu guanli* 战略与管理 [Strategy and Management] 11/12.

Gao Quanxi 高全喜 and Tian Feilong 田飞龙 (2011) "Zhengzhi xianfaxue de wenti, dingwei yu fangfa" 政治宪法学的问题, 定位与方法 [Problems, position and methods of the political constitutional school], in *Suzhou daxue xuebao* 苏州大学学报 [Journal of Suzhou University] 3, pp. 72-80.

Gao Quanxi 高全喜 and Tian Feilong 田飞龙 (2012) "Baer xianfa yu xiandai Zhongguo xianzheng de yanjin" 八二宪法与现代中国宪政的演进 [The gradual evolution of the 1982 constitution and modern Chinese constitutionalism], in *Ershiyi shiji* 二十一世纪 [The twenty-first century] 6.

Gao Quanxi 高全喜, Zhang Wei 张伟 and Tian Feilong 田飞龙 (2012) *Xiandai Zhongguo de fazhi zhilu* 现代中国的法治之路 [The Path of the Rule of Law in Modern China], Beijing: Shehui kexue wenxian chubanshe.

Han Xiuyi 韩秀义 (2012) "Zhongguo xianfa shishi de sang ge mianxiang – zai zhengzhi xianfaxue, xianfa shehuixue yu xianfaxue zhujian" 中国宪法实施的三个面向——在政治宪法学, 宪法社会学与规范宪法学之间 [The three directions of the implementation of the Chinese constitution, between political constitutionalist school, the sociological constitutionalist school and the normative study of the constitution], in *Kaifang shidai* 开放时代 [Open Times] 4, pp. 50-70.

Huang Songyou 黄松有 (2001) "Xianfa sifahua jiqi yiyi – cong zuigao renmin fayuan jintian de yi ge 'pifu' tanqi" 宪法司法化及其意义——从最高人民法院今天的一个"批复"谈起 [The judicialization of the constitution and its meaning – speaking of today's response of the People's Supreme Court], in *Renmin fayuanbao* 人民法院报 [People's Court Daily], 13.8.2001.

Jiang Shigong 强世功 (2009a) "Zhongguo xianfa zhong de buchengwen xianfa – lijie Zhongguo xianfa de xin shijiao" 中国宪法中的不成文宪法——理解中国宪法的新视角 [The unwritten provisions within the Chinese constitution – a new perspective for the understanding of the Chinese constitution], in *Kaifang shidai* 开放时代 [Open Times] 12, pp. 10-39.

Jiang Shigong 强世功 (2009b) "'Buchengwen xianfa': yingguo xianfaxue chuantong de qishi" "不成文宪法": 英国宪法学传统的启示 [The unwritten constitution: inspirations from English study traditions of the constitution], in *Dushu* 读书 [Reading] 11, pp. 63-70.

Li Zhongxia 李忠夏 (2011) "Zhongguo xianfaxue fangfa lun sixiang" 中国宪法学方法论反思 [Reflections on the methodology of Chinese constitutional jurisprudence], in *Faxue yanjiu* 法学研究 [Chinese Journal of Law] 2, pp. 160-172.

Lin Laifan's Law Blog (09.2008) Discussion entries posted to <http://linlaifan.fyfz.cn/art/404016.htm>, accessed 14 May 2012.

Pan Wei 潘维 and Ma Ya 玛雅 (eds.) (2010) *Renmin gongheguo liushi nian yu Zhongguo moshi* 人民共和国六十年与中国模式 [Sixty Years of the People's Republic and the China Model], Beijing: Sanlian shudian.

Ren Jiantao 任剑涛 (2012) "Guojia xingtai yu xianfa jieshi" 国家形态与宪法解释 [The shape of the country and the interpretation of the constitution], in *Zhanlüe yu guanli* 战略与管理 [Strategy and management] 3/4.

Tian Feilong 田飞龙 (2009) *Zhongguo xianfaxue lilun liupai de xingcheng* 中国宪法学理论流派的形成 [The Formation of Chinese Constitutional Theory Schools], Jinan: Shandong Daxue chubanshe.

Tian Feilong 田飞龙 (2011a) "Minsheng zhizhong yu minzhu zhihou – lun Zhai Xiaobo de xianfa minzhuhua yanjiu" 民主之中与民主之后——评翟小波的宪法民主化研究 [Within and after democracy – discussing Zhai Xiaobo's research on the democratization of the constitution], in Su Li 苏力 (ed.) *Falü shupin* 法律书评 [Law Book Review], 9th edition, Beijing: Beijing daxue chubanshe.

Tian Feilong 田飞龙 (2011b) "Bainian gonghe yu zhengzhi xianfaxue de xiongxin" 百年共和与政治宪法学的雄心 [Hundred years of the republic and the great aspirations of political constitutionalist school], in *Xin chanjing* 新产经 [New Industrial Economy] 2.

Tian Feilong 田飞龙 (2012) *Zhengzhi xianzheng zhuyi – Zhongguo xianzheng zhuanxing de ling yi zhong jinlu* 政治宪政主义——中国宪政转型的另一种进路 [Political constitutionalism – an alternative approach to the transition of China's constitutionalism], Beijing: Beijing daxue faxueyuan.

Wang Lei 王磊 (2000) *Xianfa de sifahua* 宪法的司法化 [The Judicialization of the Chinese Constitution], Beijing: Zhongguo zhengfa daxue chubanshe.

Wang Qisheng 王奇生 (2003) *Dangyuan, dangquan yu dangzheng: 1924-1949 nian zhongguo guomindang de zuzhi xingtai* 党员，党权与党争: 1924-1949 年中国国民党的组织形态 [Comrades, Control and Contention of the Kuomintang 1924-1929], Shanghai: Shanghai shudian chubanshe.

Wang Xiangsheng 汪祥胜 (2011) "Zhengzhi xianfaxue de Zhongguoshi biaoda" 政治宪法学的中国式表达 [The Chinese style expression of political constitutionalism], in *Suzhou daxue xuebao* 苏州大学学报 [Journal of Suzhou University] 3, pp. 95-100.

Wu Guanjun 吴冠军 (2011) "Zhengzhizhexue de genben wenti" 政治哲学的根本问题 [Fundamental problems of political philosophy], in *Kaifang shidai* 开放时代 [Open Times] 2, pp. 130-144.

Wu Yan 吴彦 (2012) "Fazhixu yu zhengzhi jueduan – youguan 'zhengzhi xianfaxue' de pipanxing taolun" 法秩序与政治决断——有关'政治宪法学'的批判性检讨 [Legal order and political resolutions – critical discussions on "the political constitutionalist school"], in *Kaifang shidai* 开放时代 [Open Times] 2, pp. 64-81.

Xia Yong 夏勇 (2003) "Zhongguo xianfa gaige de jige jieben lilun wenti" 中国宪法改革的几个基本理论问题 [Several theoretical issues confronting constitutional reform in China], in *Zhongguo shehui kexue* 中国社会科学 [Social Sciences in China] 2, pp. 4-17.

Xu Zhangrun 许章润 (2011) *Xiandai Zhongguo de guojia lixing: guanyu guojia jiangou de ziyou minzuzhuyi gonghe fali* 现代中国的国家理性: 关于国家建构的自由民族主义共和法理 [Modern China's National Interests: On the Republican Legal Principles of the Free Democratic State-Building], Beijing: Falü chubanshe.

Yang Chen 杨陈 (2011) "Lun xianfa de guifanxing" 论宪法的规范性 [On the normative nature of the constitution], in *Suzhou daxue xuebao* 苏州大学学报 [Journal of Suzhou University] 3, pp. 89-94.

Yao Zhongqiu 姚中秋 (2010) *Xiandai Zhongguo de liguo zhidao* 现代中国的立国之道 [The Founding Path of Modern China], Beijing: Falü chubanshe.

Yao Zhongqiu 姚中秋 (2011a) *Zhongguo biange zhidao: dangdai Zhongguo de zhili zhixu jiqi biange fanglüe* 中国变革之道：当代中国的治理秩序及其变革方略 [China's Path to Transformation: Modern China's Governance and Transformation Strategy], Beijing: Falü chubanshe.

Yao Zhongqiu 姚中秋 (2011b) "Ruijia xianfa minsheng zhuyi" 儒家宪政民生主义 [Confucian constitutional people's livelihood], in *Kaifang shidai* 开放时代 [Open Times], No. 6, pp. 26-41.

Yao Zhongqiu 姚中秋 (2012) *Huaxia zhili zhixushi (di yi quan tianxia, di er quan fengjian)* 华夏治理秩序史（第一卷·天下；第二卷·封建）[History of China's Governance Order" (First volume: Tianxia, Second volume: Feudalism)], Haikou: Hainan chubanshe.

Zhai Xiaobo 翟小波 (2004) "Xianfa shi guanyu zhuquan de zhenshi guize" 宪法是关于主权的真实规则 [The constitution is the real rule of sovereignty], in *Faxue yanjiu* 法学研究 [Chinese Journal of Law] 6, pp. 23-35.

Zhai Xiaobo 翟小波 (2006) "Daiyi jiguan zhishang, hai shi sifahua" 代议机关至上，还是司法化 [The highest representative authority is still the judicature], in *Zhongwai faxue* 中外法学 [Peking University Law Journal] 4, pp. 426-447.

Zhai Xiaobo 翟小波 (2009a) *Renmin de xianfa* 人民的宪法 [The people's constitution], Beijing: Falü chubanshe.

Zhai Xiaobo 翟小波 (2009b) *Lun woguo xianfa de shishi zhidu* 论我国宪法的实施制度 [On China's System of Constitutional Implementation], Beijing: Zhongguo fazhi chubanshe.

Zhai Zhiyong 翟志勇 (2012) "Ba'er xianfa xiuzhengan yu xin de xianzheng sheji" 八二宪法修正案与新的宪政设计 [The amendments of the 1982 constitution and new constitutional design], in *Zhanlüe yu guanli* 战略与管理 [Strategy and Management] 3/4.

Zhang Youyu 张友渔 et al. (2003) *Xianfalun wenji* 宪法论文集 (Collection of Essays on the Constitution), Beijing: Shehui kexue wenjian chubanshe.

Zheng Lei 郑磊 (2011) "Women chuyu shenme shidai – jianxi guifan xianfaxue yu zhengzhi xianfayue zhi genben fenqi" 我们处于什么时代——简析规范宪法学与政治宪法学之根本分歧 [Which era do we belong to – simple analysis of the fundamental differences between the normative study of the constitution and the political constitutional school], in *Suzhou daxue xuebao* 苏州大学学报 [Journal of Suzhou University] 3, pp. 85-88.

Zhu Xueqin 朱学勤 (2007) *Jidang sanshi nian: gaige kaifang de zhenxiang* 激荡三十年改革开放的真相 [Thirty years of agitation: a summary of the experiences of reform and opening], in *Lingnan dajiangtan* 岭南大讲坛 [Lingnan Forum], <http://www.360doc.com/content/07/1219/11/16670_907974.shtml>, accessed 10 May 2012.

Zhu Yunhan 朱云汉 (2012) *Taiwan minzhu zhuanxing de jingyan yu qishi* 台湾民主转型的经验与启示 [Taiwan's Democratic Transition: Experience and Inspiration], Beijing: Shehui kexue wenxian chubanshe.

Huang Hui[*]

Objectives and Ways of Implementation of the Normative Constitutional School[1]

Work objectives of the normative constitutional study

In the development of the Chinese Constitution and constitutional studies at the systemic level, there have been four revisions of the Constitution with 31 amendments during the last 30 years. At the academic level, there have been at least four movements of different dimensions, namely the proposal of a constitutional review system for violations of the Constitution (*weixian shencha zhidu* 违宪审查制度) in the 1980s,[2] which in parts was also called "constitutional supervision" (*xianfa jiandu* 宪法监督), the debate on "benign violations of the Constitution" (*liangxing weixian* 良性违宪) in the early 1990s,[3] which in a way treated the Constitution with much flexibility, the movement to judicialize the Constitution (and its failures) in the early 2000s, and the dispute between political constitutional study (*zhengzhi xianfaxue* 政治宪法学) and normative constitutional study (*guifan xianfaxue* 规范宪法学) which has arisen in the last few years. The objectives and standpoints of the first three academic movements can be clearly distinguished. The "theory of benign violations of the Constitution" can be roughly summarized as a "rubber band strategy" (*xiangpijin celüe* 橡皮筋策略), which contends that the Constitution can be shaped and surmounted at will. The other two academic movements put forward proposals to establish a concrete system for reviewing violations of the Constitution. This aimed at bringing the Constitution into action, exchanging passive for active. Furthermore, the recent so-called dispute among differing schools of thought has been driven and accompanied by the rapid rise of the school of political constitutionalism. For unclear reasons, this school of thought, that has placed a particular emphasis on political objectives and political structures from the beginning of its rise, made the scholars working on the level of normative constitutionalism the target of its opposition, regarding them as narrow-minded, conservative and powerless "technicians" (*jishuliu* 技术流).[4] Wittingly or unwittingly, a number of constitutional scholars who had originally been

---

[*] This article was translated from Chinese to English by Katja Levy, Sabine Mokry and Sören Vogler. German expressions in the text were added by the author, if not stated otherwise – translators' note.

[1] The author presented a paper under the same title at the international conference, "Social Change and the Constitution – a Conference on the Occasion of the 30th Anniversary of the Constitution of the PR China of 1982" at Free University Berlin. This article is based on the original text – author's note.

[2] See mainly Hu 1985; Dong and Hu 1987; Huang 1985; Cai 1989.

[3] The concept of "benign violations of the Constitution" was first put forward by Prof. Hao Tiechuan and soon afterwards debated with Tong Zhiwei; see (in chronological order) Hao 1996a; Tong 1996; Hao 1996b; Tong 1997; Hao 1997.

[4] Two important representatives of the political constitutional school are Professor Chen Duanhong 陈端洪 (Peking University) and Professor Gao Quanxi 高全喜 (Beihang University). For details on the political constitutionalist school, see, mainly, Gao 2012. It should be noted that there is no agreement at all between the representative figures of the political constitutionalist school on ideology, jurisprudential thinking, intellectual resources or scientific objectives, apart from the fact that they are all opposed to the normative constitutional study.

Chinese History and Society/Berliner China-Hefte 45 (2015), pp. 39-60

working separately on how to apply constitutional norms at the level of jurisprudence, gradually formed, under the "fighting strategy" of political constitutionalism, the so-called normative constitutional school (*guifan xianfa xuepai* 规范宪法学派). The author is one of these scholars.

The name "normative constitutional study [school]" can basically be traced back to the Qinghua University Professor Lin Laifan 林来梵 and his monograph published in 2001.[5] Professor Lin introduced Karl Loewenstein's ontological method of classifying constitutions, which according to their effectiveness in the reality divides constitutions into three types, i.e. normative constitutions, nominal constitutions and semantic constitutions (Loewenstein 1951: 191 ff.). Among these, the "normative constitution" denotes that the constitutional norms are identical with the constitution's actual effects and that these two enter a form of relationship in which they live together. "Under these circumstances, the constitutional norms control the political process; and the other way around, operations of power can also 'adapt and submit' constitutional norms" (Lin 2001: 263 ff.). To use another image to explain, a normative constitution is a constitution possessing practical effects; it can be compared to "a piece of clothing that fits the body and is frequently worn" (Lin 2001: 265). Very obviously, the normative constitution discussed here is a descriptive definition of a country's constitution at the level of effectiveness, whether or not and to what degree constitutional norms are implemented, and what is called the normative constitutional school, is then correspondingly defined as the scholarship concerning the attempt to implement constitutional norms. In order to avoid the quagmire of Kelsen's pure theory of law [Reine Rechtslehre, translators' note] which abandons the pursuit of basic values, the normative constitutional school puts forward essential requirements for constitutional norms, i.e. "In theory, firstly confirm the core value status of the rights and values within the entire constitutional norms, then secondly attempt to raise constitutional norms towards 'normative constitution'" (Lin 2001: 8). Here it is also very clear, that the Constitution dealt with by the normative constitutional school does not only call for the principles of modern constitutional government, such as democracy, rule of law and the systematic division of power by checks and balances to establish the limits of each organ of state power. It also calls for the inclusion of constitutional basic rights provisions. This, then, to the lowest degree, shakes off the moral weight at the level of value judgements. For example, the dispute between "unjust law is unlawful" [lex injusta non est lex, translators' note] and "unjust law is also law". Then the normative constitutional school can honorably plead that constitutional studies should return to constitutional norms and their implementation. This research by Professor Lin contributed to his high ranking in mainland China's constitutional studies' circles. 'Normative constitution' and 'normative constitutional' studies have become significant terms in mainland constitutional studies' research. A large number of young disciples follow its call under the broad banner of normative constitutional studies and explore the methods and techniques of China's constitutionalism to implement the Constitution.[6]

---

[5] See Lin 2001. It should be mentioned that Professor Lin still held his position at Zhejiang University when he wrote this work.

[6] See, mainly, Lin 2009. The eight contributors to this book have all studied under Professor Lin; without exception, they are specialists in the field of normative constitutionalism. Further see Bai 2009; Bai 2010; Zheng 2009; Zhai 2012.

It should be pointed out that within the dimension of normativism, in addition to normative constitutional studies, there is also the so-called theory of constitutional hermeneutics, introduced by Professor Han Dayuan 韩大元 of Renmin University's Law School. Although constitutional hermeneutics place an emphasis on taking a more open-minded approach towards interpretation methods than normative constitutionalism, by taking the "positive constitutional order" (*shiding xianfa zhixu* 实定宪法秩序), i.e. the text of the Constitution, as a starting point for work and focusing on the exploration of solid evidence for the intentions of the constitutional norms, they completely agree with each other (cf. Han/Lin et al. 2008; Lin 2010). For the sake of simplicity, this article includes constitutional hermeneutics in the normative constitutional school. And, for the same reason, the scholars who follow the normative constitutional school and those who follow the constitutional hermeneutics school are categorized under the so-called school of normative constitutional study (*guifan xianfa xuepai* 规范宪法学派).

Most of the constitutional scholars that are currently actively or passively included in the normative constitutional school have studied in Germany or Japan, or rely on the constitutional materials of the continental law countries. Precisely because of this, normative constitutional scholars are almost acting in unison: the text of the Constitution serves as the starting point for their work, in their work objectives, and in their working methods for unearthing the standard criteria of constitutional interpretations and constitutional judgments, i.e. the work objectives clearly point to constitutional implementation, the starting point for work and the methods (strategies) acknowledge the legal efficacy of the Constitution of 1982. Their work is focused on methods of constitutional implementation within the constitutional framework (see section 2 and 3) and on those interpretations and techniques for the application of constitutional norms that are required at the actual time of implementation (see section 4).

The first way of implementing the Constitution: the construction of a system of constitutional review

Any effort to pursue the Constitution's actual effects can ultimately develop into a call for a system of constitutional reviews; this is a widespread phenomenon of modern constitutional states. In other words, if the Constitution is to be "implemented wisely", the most effective measure is the setting up of a system of constitutional review. The so-called constitutional review (*xianfa shencha* 宪法审查), also described as the "investigation of violations of the Constitution" (*weixian shencha* 违宪审查), and in the US, as "judicial review" (*sifa shencha* 司法审查), points to organs, such as, the German and Austrian Constitutional Courts (Verfassungsgericht), the US Supreme Court, and the French Constitutional Council (Conseil constitutionnel) which have been specially authorized to carry out reviews on whether the behavior of the legislative, administrative or judicative state powers violates the Constitution or not, as well as whether, on the basis of the results of these reviews, to rule on this behavior's abolition or on its correction. Constitutional reviews can be divided into two types: ex ante review and ex post review. The former normally refers to the subject of review carrying out a review before the state's behaviour produces legal consequences, which has the function of preventing behavior that violates the Constitution before it happens. The latter is the common form of reviews of constitutional violations, and refers to the subject which, by following specially designated procedures, carries out the review of constitutionality for a state organ's behavior that has already had legal effects.

The Constitution that is in force in China does not refer to the expressions "constitutional review" or "review of violations of the Constitution". However, researchers working in the field of constitutional studies have already reached consensus, that the writers of the Constitution, with the systems of "constitutional supervision" (*xianfa jiandu* 宪法监督), "constitutional interpretation" (*xianfa jieshi* 宪法解释), the "committee for the investigation of particular questions" (*tebie wenti diaocha weiyuanhui* 特别问题调查委员会) and "legislative approval" (*lifa pizhun* 立法批准), have already endowed the National People's Congress (NPC) and its Standing Committee with the power to investigate violations of the constitution. This can be explained in detail by considering the following aspects:

Firstly, China implements a pluralist legislative system in which the legislations of different subjects do not only possess different hierarchical levels of effect, but are also termed differently. They form a "pyramid shaped" hierarchical system.[7] The system's specific content is as follows: the first hierarchical level is naturally the Constitution; this is at the top of the pyramid, "laws, administrative regulations and local regulations must not conflict with the Constitution", violations "must be pursued" (Constitution, Art. 3, para. 3). At the second level are the "laws" (*falü* 法律), formulated by the NPC and its Standing Committee. Among these, the so-called "basic laws" (*jiben falü* 基本法律) can only be formulated by the NPC. At the third level are the "administrative regulations" (*xingzheng fagui* 行政法规) formulated by the State Council. At the fourth level are "local regulations" (*difangxing fagui* 地方性法规), "regulations of autonomous regions" (*zizhi tiaoli* 自治条例) and "specific regulations" (*danxing tiaoli* 单行条例). The former are formulated by the People's Congresses and their Standing Committees in the provinces, municipalities directly under the central government, autonomous regions as well as "comparatively larger cities"[8]. The formulating bodies of the latter two are the autonomous regions, autonomous prefectures and the autonomous counties, but the relevant legislation requires the approval of the People's Congress Standing Committee in the province, autonomous region or municipality directly under the central government. At the fifth level are the "regulations" (*guizhang* 规章), including "department regulations" (*buwei guizhang* 部委规章) formulated by the State Council's ministries and committees, the People's Bank of China, the Audit Commission and directly subordinated organs that possess administrative functions, as well as "local regulations" (*difangxing guizhang* 地方性规章) formulated by the People's governments of provinces, autonomous

---

[7] Although an outline of the approximate contents of the pyramidal hierarchical system can be obtained from the provisions of the Constitution that stipulate the function of each state organ, more specific details can be obtained from the Legislation Law (*lifa fa* 立法法): see, in particular, Legislation Law, Art. 7; 56; 63; 71; 78. In some of these Articles, the provisions of the Constitution are stated; others contain supplements to the provisions of the Constitution.

[8] According to Art. 63, para. 4 of the Legislation Law, "comparatively larger cities" are cities "where a provincial or autonomous regional people's government is located or where a special economic zone is located, or a city approved as such by the State Council." They can "formulate local regulations", but need the approval of the respective People's Congress Standing Committee of the province or autonomous region (para. 2).

regions, municipalities directly under the central government and comparatively larger cities. Art. 5, para. 3 of the Constitution stipulates: "No laws, administrative regulations or local regulations may contravene the Constitution"; and para. 4, sentence 2 provides: "All acts in violation of the Constitution or other laws must be investigated". These two provisions serve as the foundation for a system of reviews of violations of the Constitution.

Secondly, the typical review of violations of the Constitution mainly refers to reviews of legislation, in particular, to a review of constitutional violations of the "law(s)" (*falü* 法律), i.e. the review of violations of the Constitution of "laws" formulated by the NPC and its Standing Committee. With this as a starting point, the review mechanisms for violations of the Constitution can be further observed and studied. Art. 62, para. 2 and Art. 67, para. 1 of the Constitution each stipulates that the National People's Congress and its Standing Committee bear responsibility for "supervising the implementation of the Constitution" (*jiandu xianfa de shishi* 监督宪法的实施). Since there are no other provisions being related, the function of "supervising the implementation of the Constitution", can be seen as taking over the function of the Constitutional review. In other words, in having the framework of the Constitution, the National People's Congress and its Standing Committee can possibly serve as organs of constitutional review. However, from the point of view of feasibility, it would be impossible for the National People's Congress, with its single annual meeting that lasts for around two weeks, to carry out such review function. Therefore, if one of the two organs has to be chosen to review violations of the Constitution, it has to be the NPC's Standing Committee. Evidence for this judgment can be found in the Constitution's text: the provision on the function of the NPC, namely Art. 62, does not touch upon how to deal with legislation that violates the Constitution,[9] but the provision on the functions of the People's Congress' Standing Committee, i.e. Art. 67, stipulates that the tasks to be performed by the Standing Committee of the People's Congress include "to annul those administrative regulations, decisions or orders of the State Council that contravene the Constitution or other laws" (para. 7) and "to annul those local regulations or decisions of the organs of state power of provinces, autonomous regions, and municipalities directly under the Central Government that contravene the Constitution, other laws or administrative regulations" (para. 8). As a result, it may be concluded that the Constitution tends to point to the "review of violations of the Constitution" as a task for the Standing Committee of the People's Congress. However, one problem soon becomes apparent: from Art. 67, it can be seen quite clearly that the Standing Committee of the People's Congress has the powers mentioned and also the right "to decide on the ratification or abrogation of treaties and important agreements concluded with foreign states" (para. 14). However, there is nothing in the wording at all that could be seen as granting the Standing Committee the authority to investigate "laws" formulated by the NPC and itself. And to a certain extent, the carrying out of

---

[9] Art. 62, para.11 of the Constitution stipulates: "to alter or annul inappropriate decisions of the Standing Committee of the National People's Congress". Here, a "decision" (*jueding* 决定), due to its context, should not include legislation, but of course the inclusion of a "legislative decision" (*lifa jueding* 立法决定) by interpretation cannot always be avoided; such an understanding would hardly find consensus among scholars.

constitutional reviews in the parliamentary legislation can be used to judge whether a country fulfills the criteria for the constitutional review.

Apart from the text of the Constitution, the Legislation Law (*lifa fa* 立法法), which was promulgated and put into effect in 2000 by the NPC, exclusively regulates the system of legislation. It stipulates the hierarchical pyramidal structure of the law and its protection mechanisms in detail. The provisions that refer to the review of legislation should be included in the targets of the observation and study of the Chinese constitutional review. Art. 88 of the Legislation Law firmly stipulates the system to be applied for revoking legislation. Compared with Art. 62 and Art. 67 of the Constitution, the main difference lies in the first stipulation that the NPC has the power to revoke laws that have been "improperly stipulated" by its Standing Committee. The expression "improper" here should include but should not be limited to circumstances of "violations of the Constitution". In other words, the Legislation Law, here, has clearly added one clause, namely that the NPC can carry out revisions of laws that have been stipulated by the NPC Standing Committee, despite the fact that this rule stands little chance of being implemented. Apart from this, with regard to the NPC's Standing Committee's function of reviewing constitutional violations, Art. 88, para. 2 of the Legislation Law mentions only that it has the authority to repeal regulations below NPC law which violate the Constitution, that is administrative regulations, local regulations and regulations in autonomous regions and special regulations approved by the People's Congresses at provincial level. And Art. 90 stipulates how the review procedure is to be started.[10] To sum up, the Legislation Law does not provide a further normative foundation to sustain the NPC to carry out constitutional reviews at the level of "laws".[11]

---

[10] Article 90 of the Legislation Law stipulates "When the State Council, the Central Military Commission, the Supreme People's Court, the Supreme People's Procuratorate and the standing committees of the people's congresses of the provinces, autonomous regions and municipalities directly under the Central Government consider that administrative regulations, local regulations, autonomous regulations or separate regulations contradict the Constitution or laws, they may submit to the Standing Committee of the National People's Congress written requests for examination, and the working offices of the Standing Committee shall refer the requests to the relevant special committees for examination and suggestions. When State organs other than the ones mentioned in the preceding paragraph, public organizations, enterprises and institutions or citizens consider that administrative regulations, local regulations, autonomous regulations or separate regulations contradict the Constitution or laws, they may submit to the Standing Committee of the National People's Congress written suggestions for examination, and the working offices of the Standing Committee shall study the suggestions and shall, when necessary, refer them to the relevant special committees for examination and suggestions."

[11] In the author's opinion, at the methodological level of jurisprudence (*faxue fangfalun* 法学方法论, Juristische Methodenlehre), the stipulation, "No laws or administrative or local rules and regulations may contravene the Constitution" (Art. 5, para. 3 of the Constitution), may be seen as justifying action being taken to recognize and identify the loopholes in the Legislation Law, in the provisions that are related to dealing with laws that violate the Constitution which the Legislative Law is designed to protect. To deduce whether the norms in the lower legal hierarchical violate the Constitution, one can apply the Art. 90 of Legislation Law in analogy, which would mean that the subjects that are listed in the first paragraph, can *request* starting the procedure of review of violations of the Constitution (*shenqing qidong weixian shencha chengxu* 申请启动违宪审查程序), while the subjects listed in para. 2 can *suggest* starting this procedure (*tichu qidong zhi jianyi* 提出启动之建议). Of course, because the

Thirdly, although direct evidence in support of the idea that the NPC's Standing Committee can carry out legislative reviews (*lifa shencha* 立法审查) of laws is not found either in the Constitution or in the Legislation Law, many scholars, including this author, still maintain that the NPC's Standing Committee has the power to carry out reviews of violations of the Constitution.[12] There are two reasons for this: one is the special situation in China, where a great deal of the legislation that is closely related to the national economy and people's livelihoods takes the form of administrative and local regulations. Therefore, although it can be seen as a shortcoming of the system that the NPC Standing Committee does not have the authority to review the question of whether laws violate the Constitution, the review system for suspected violations of the Constitution still should not be abandoned, because if, by this means, problems arising from violations of the Constitution by administrative and local regulations can be resolved with, this is equal to completing the greater part of the legislative review work. The second reason is, that Art. 71, para. 1 of the Constitution stipulates: "The National People's Congress and its Standing Committee may, when they deem it necessary, appoint committees of inquiry into specific questions and adopt relevant resolutions in the light of their reports." In addition, although there are no detailed regulations on the organizational structure and work procedures of the investigation committees, nevertheless, such a meaning can certainly be identified, namely, that if the Standing Committee – based on an application of the relevant authority organ or an appeal of the society's public opinion – thinks that with regard to its own laws or even laws promulgated by the NPC, it is necessary to carry out a review of a potential violation of the Constitution, then it could certainly use the investigation committee mechanism to launch the procedure for reviewing the violation of the Constitution. Although this is not an ideal model for the review of suspected violations of the Constitution, it is nevertheless better than nothing, and can serve as a way of acquiring experiences related to the review of violations of the Constitution.

Lastly, it must be acknowledged that although the NPC Standing Committee possesses a certain – albeit not complete – power to review violations of the Constitution, in reality, the Committee still has not taken on the duty of reviewing violations of the Constitution. This first becomes evident in that none of the agents mentioned in Art. 90, para. 1 of the Legislation Law, i.e. State Council, Central Military Commission, Supreme People's Court, Supreme People's Procuratorate and the members of the People's Congresses at provincial and municipal levels directly under the central government, has ever put

---

methodology of jurisprudence in China's legal education and practice has yet not at all spread, it is hard to reach a consensus on the above mentioned interpretation within a short period of time.

[12] Some of those with opposing views claim that the Constitution and the Legislation Law have no support; others maintain: "one cannot supervise oneself". They therefore deny that the NPC and its Standing Committee can supervise the laws that they themselves have stipulated. This judgment does not lack reason, but it does not seem to be in accordance with real life experience. It can be compared with a situation where students are supposed to check their work themselves one or two times before handing in an exam paper. Although this might not be as effective as having a third party doing the review, it is also possible that the student will rectify at least some if not all of the mistakes. In the author's opinion, therefore, "one cannot supervise oneself" cannot and should not be the reason for denying the NPC Standing Committee the power to review violations of the Constitution. The key question is how to include this stipulation within the existing institutional framework, see Huang 2012.

forward an appeal to carry out a legislative review on administrative regulations or local regulations. Secondly, concerning the significant number of "proposals" (*jianyi* 建议) raised by "subjects from among the people" (*minjian zhuti* 民间主体), such as, professors of colleges and universities, persons engaged in the protection of rights and ordinary citizens according to Art. 90, para. 2, to launch a review of violations of the Constitution, the Standing Committee of the NPC, up to now, has never formally accepted or heard a case. One explanation for this could be that the related procedures are not reasonable and specific enough; it is also possible that the representative organs do not have the skills required for such reviews and, naturally, it is also possible that the authority at the highest policy making level is not sincere about this.

This said, to conclude that the review system of China's representative system of government only exists on paper, solely because the Standing Committee of the NPC does not carry out its responsibility with regard to the so-called ex post legislative review of violations of the Constitution according to the stipulations of the Constitution and Legislation Law, is also not a fair judgment. For in addition to the ex post legislative review, there is also the so-called ex ante review. This kind of review appears as an "approval" system ("*pizhun*" *zhidu* "批准" 制度) in the Constitution, i.e. when the lower level legislative organs promulgate legislation they have to obtain "approval". Furthermore, the NPC Standing Committee uses the method of "inquiry and reply" (*xunwen dafu* 询问答复) since the 1954 Constitution on – its essence can be understood as the NPC Standing Committee carrying out Art. 67, para. 4 of the Constitution, which stipulates the function of "constitutional interpretation" – to conduct the work of ex ante review.[13] Here we can cite the famous Reply, the NPC Standing Committee's "first constitutional interpretation" as an explanation. Art. 37 of the 1954 Constitution stipulated: "No deputy to the National People's Congress may be arrested or placed on trial without the consent of the National People's Congress or, when the National People's Congress is not in session, of its Standing Committee."[14] The Tianjin Intermediate Court was once uncertain about the usage of the provision during a civil case and therefore asked the NPC Standing Committee to give an interpretation. On November 6, 1957, the NPC Standing Committee General Office (*quanguo renda bangongting* 全国人大常委会办公厅) issued its "Reply to the question as to whether a delegate of the National People's Congress can or cannot be summoned to court when he is the subject of charges in a civil lawsuit" (关于全国人民代表大会因民事纠纷被诉法院可否传唤问题的答复):

> After discussions, the NPC's Legal Commission came to the conclusion that Art. 37 of China's Constitution stipulates that the personal freedom of the delegates of the NPC is not to be infringed, in order to ensure that the delegates are able to fulfill their duties. However, since a civil case does usually not involve the restriction of personal freedom, it does not fall within the scope of the

---

[13] E.g. Art. 116 stipulates: "The regulations on the exercise of autonomy and other separate regulations of autonomous regions shall be submitted to the Standing Committee of the National People's Congress for approval before they go into effect. Those of autonomous prefectures and counties shall be submitted to the standing committees of the people's congresses of provinces or autonomous regions for approval before they go into effect, and they shall be reported to the Standing Committee of the National People's Congress for the record." Unfortunately, the author has not been able to locate any material related to how the organs under the "approval"-mechanism implement the constitutional review.

[14] For the NPC Standing Committee's constitutional interpretations before 1982, see Zhou 2004.

regulation of Art. 37 of the Constitution. Due to the fact that the delegate, Bi Mingqi, is the defendant in a civil case, the court can, according to the law, issue him with a summons; the permission of the NPC Standing Committee is not required.

This is a very skillful constitutional interpretation derived from the original intention of the legislation: according to a literal understanding of Art. 37 of the 1954 Constitution, the "hearing of a civil case" also belongs under the category of "hearing a legal case", but the specific case that the Tianjin Intermediate People's Court encountered, allowed doubts to emerge about the results of such literal interpretations. The NPC Standing Committee, on the basis of the original intention of the legislation, i.e. "not to hinder delegates from carrying out duties", reduced the meaning of "trying a case" to "the restriction of personal freedom by trying a case". In fact, this blocked a unique opportunity to obtain a judgment on a violation of the Constitution from a judicial organ.

To sum up the above, seen from the framework for the review of violations of the Constitution provided by the Constitution and the Legislation Law, China has already built up control mechanisms of constitutional implementation in various forms. Among these, the ex ante "approval" aimed at the legislation - along with the a-typical "inquiry and reply" mechanism - and the ex post system of "revocation" have built up the review structure for violations of the Constitution "with Chinese characteristics". Although in constitutional practice, the systems have not yet been implemented sufficiently, this is still better than nothing; against this background, scholars of the normative constitutional school can examine ways to further strengthen and implement both review systems for violations of the Constitution[15]. In this sense, for the normative constitutional school, the issue has become easier: on the one hand, this school of research has to think about how to encourage the NPC Standing Committee, within the framework of bearing responsibility for "supervising the constitutional implementation", to take responsibility for reviewing violations of the Constitution in its true meaning, i.e. ex post review of violations of the Constitution. On the other hand, there is also the aspect which is even more a specialty of the normative constitutional school, that is, to examine and accumulate skills on how to carry out the review of violations of the Constitution.

The second way of implementing the Constitution: constitutional interpretation within the framework of the judicialization of the Constitution

Within the framework of China's current system, another means of implementing the Constitution is the so-called judicialization of the Constitution. The "judicialization of the Constitution" (*xianfa sifahua* 宪法司法化) is a legal term of special significance in jurists' circles in Mainland China. According to its literal meaning, it should be understood as the organs of the judicature – the constitutional court or common courts – implementing the Constitution, but since China does not have a constitutional court, the judicialization of the Constitution refers to the system whereby the people's courts hear

---

[15] The legal expert and scholar of the constitutional scholars' circle, Xu Chongde 许崇德, insisted that on the basis of the existing system of constitutional supervision, the contents of other conventions of constitutional review should also be introduced see Xu 2006. With regard to the implementation, constitutional scholars have always put forward the suggestion that the NPC Standing Committee establish a permanent constitutional organ in the form of a commission (Constitutional Commission or Constitutional Supervisory Commission). See, mainly, Dong and Hu 1987; Hu 1997; Liu 2010.

common judicial cases implementing the Constitution. For this, the normative constitutional school has to question the Constitution and related laws on how to regulate this system, and how to put it into practice. But before providing firm answers to this and an analysis, it is first necessary to understand the "constitutional judicialization movement" and the famous "Qi Yuling Case" (*Qi Yuling an* 齐玉苓案) as the trigger of this movement. The essence of this case was that the Supreme People's Court wanted to follow the experience of the American Marbury vs. Madison Case, two hundred years ago, i.e. to use the opportunity presented by the official judicial "Response" (*pifu* 批复)[16] in the Qi Yuling case to achieve the goal that each level of People's Courts should be able to refer to the Constitution when trying individual cases and that, ultimately, the Supreme People's Court will be able to carry out the function of the constitutional review.[17]

The "Qi Yuling Case" occurred in the City of Tengzhou (滕州) in Shandong Province at the beginning of the 1990s. The protagonist of the case was Qi Yuling, a girl from the countryside. In the early summer of 1990, the 17-year old Qi Yuling graduated from high school and was accepted by the Jining Business School (济宁商校) as a student of finance and accounting after taking the national unified university entrance exam. The "admission notice" was sent to Qi's high school, High School No. 8 of Tengzhou City (滕州八中). Qi's classmate, Chen Xiaoqi (陈晓琦), took the "admission notice", counterfeited a personal I.D. and a number of official documents and letters and then took up her studies in the name of Qi Yuling at Jining Business School. After graduation in 1993 she was assigned a workplace at the Ximenkou Savings Bank Branch of the Bank of China (中国人民银行西门口储蓄所). Qi Yuling, at that time, believed that she had failed the exam, and because the family was in financial difficulties, she returned to the countryside to work as a peasant, which was exactly what every student from the countryside would like to avoid by taking the university entrance exam; afterwards, she left the countryside again and became a migrant worker. Later, she spent 6,000 yuan on an urban registration (*chengshi hukou* 城市户口) in order to attend Zoucheng Technical School (邹城技工学

---

[16] The NPC Standing Committee issued the "Resolution on strengthening the legal interpreting work" (关于加强法律解释工作的决议) in 1981. The second point stipulates: "Interpretation of questions involving the specific application of laws and decrees in court trials shall be provided by the Supreme People's Court" [English translation provided by ChinaLawInfo: <http://www.lawinfochina.com>, accessed 7 July 2014]. Accordingly, the Supreme People's Court issues different forms of judicial interpretation, i.e. "interpretation" (*jieshi* 解释), "stipulation" (*guiding* 规定), "response" (*pifu* 批复) and "resolution" (*jueding* 决定), to tackle different kinds of questions (the title of the document shows the kind of judicial interpretation to which it belongs). The "response" is the judicial response, which is stipulated for the requests from the Higher People's Courts and the Liberation Army's Military Courts to give advice on questions concerning the specific application of the law in specific case; the "Response in the Qi Yuling Case" is precisely an example of this kind. For details of the types of judicial interpretations and the drafting procedure, see "Provisions of the Supreme People's Court on the Judicial Interpretation Work" (最高人民法院关于司法解释工作的规定) issued 2007 by the Supreme People's Court, which took the place of "Several Provisions of the Supreme People's Court on the Judicial Interpretation Work" (最高人民法院关于司法解释工作的若干规定) issued 1997.

[17] The "Judicialization of the Constitution", as a concept, was first put forward by Professor Wang Lei 王磊 (Beijing University) in his book "Judicialization of the Constitution" (cf. Wang 2000). As a result of the discussions following the Qi Yuling Case, this became part of the common discourse in legal experts' and scholars' circles and beyond. About this movement, see Jiang 2003.

校). After graduating from this technical school, she was formally employed as a worker in a factory but was forced to leave when the factory reduced its personnel. In order to make a living, she took on the job of selling breakfast snacks and fast food. In short, her life was extraordinarily hard. In 1998, Qi Yuling accidentally found out that Chen Xiaoqi had stolen her university admission notice and had taken her place by assuming her name. On January 29, 1999, she succeeded in filing a lawsuit at the Intermediate People's Court in Zaozhuang, Shandong (山东省枣庄市中级人民法院), against Chen Xiaoqi and her father, Chen Kezheng, High School No. 8 of Tengzhou City, Jining Business School and the Education Committee of Tengzhou (山东省滕州市教育委员会), stating that the accused had practiced fraud together and facilitated the acceptance of the accused, Chen Xiaoqi, at Jining Business School to study under her name, which had resulted in the violation of her right to her name, the right to education and other related rights, requesting the court to impose a sentence on the defendants to stop the violations, to make a formal apology, and to pay compensation of 160,000 Yuan for Qi's economic losses and 400,000 Yuan for mental suffering. In May 1999, the Intermediate People's Court in Zaozhuang, Shandong, ruled that the defendant, Chen Xiaoqi, had to stop the violation of the plaintiff Qi Yuling's right to her name, and that the five accused together make a formal apology to Qi Yuling, take over the legal fees of 825 Yuan, and pay compensation of 35,000 Yuan for mental suffering. The court rejected other claims in this lawsuit. Qi Yuling then appealed to the Shandong Province Higher People's Court (山东省高级人民法院), which requested the Supreme People's Court for an interpretation of this case. On July 24, 2001, the Judicial Committee of the Supreme People's court issued the "Supreme People's Court's response on the question of whether someone violating the con-stitutionally-protected fundamental right of a citizen to receive education by means of violating rights to the person's name should bear civil liability" (hereafter: "Response in the Qi Yuling Case"):

> After due consideration, we hold that on the basis of the facts in this case, Chen Xiaoqi and others have violated the fundamental right to receive education stipulated in the Constitution enjoyed by Qi Yuling by means of violating rights to a person's name. As this violation has resulted in actual damages, they have to bear the corresponding civil liability.

According to this response, the Shandong Province Higher People's Court made its final judgment on August 13, 1999. In the judgment, Art. 46 of the Constitution was quoted, that is, the right to receive education, and the "Response in the Qi Yuling Case". The court decided that Qi Yuling's constitutionally-protected right to receive education had been violated, and affirmed that the defendants must pay compensation of 7,000 Yuan for direct losses, 41,045 Yuan for indirect losses and 50,000 Yuan for mental suffering.

The "Response in the Qi Yuling Case" was interpreted by the legal profession as the Supreme People's Court instructing the Shandong Province Higher People's Court to judge the Qi Yuling Case on the basis of the provisions in the Constitution – in the author's opinion, this reading was not accurate, but it does not fall within the scope of this article to go deeply into this matter – and initiated a broad and persistent discussion in legal circles regarding ways of implementing China's Constitution. A further question, moreover, is whether this topic under discussion gradually focused on the two so-called issues of "judicialization of the Constitution", namely, whether courts may or may not make direct use of the Constitution in their judgments and whether the Supreme People's

Court may or may not enjoy the right to review violations of the Constitution. The Qi Yuling Case became known as the "first case of judicialization of the Constitution" and this wide-ranging discussion in which the legal profession and academic circles were mutually linked was called the "constitutional judicialization movement".[18] Nevertheless, this constitutional movement, which brought together the ideal of a constitutional government and the rule of law with the wish to expand power, which came with so much force and, even today, has not yet been outdone in its scope and influence by any other constitutional theory or movement, only obtained short term success, because the Supreme People's Court in 2008 annulled the "Response in the Qi Yuling case" without announcing any reason, thus declaring the judicialization movement, which had lasted for almost eight years, a failure.[19] In a certain sense, it was certainly reasonable for the Supreme People's Court to put an end to the "constitutional judicialization" movement of its own accord, because one of the important aims of the movement was to urge the Supreme People's Court to exert firm control over reviews of violations of the Constitution, and this – as mentioned above – would not have fitted within the existing constitutional framework. This approach, following a pattern of violating the Constitution to pursue the implementation of the Constitution can certainly be perceived as violating the spirit of the rule by law and should not get sympathy. What is regrettable is that the abolition of the "Response in the Qi Yuling Case" did not only restrain the behaviour of the Supreme People's Court with regard to violating the Constitution to inappropriately covet the power to review violations of the Constitution, but also put an end to any possibility of the People's Courts' using the Constitution in ordinary lawsuit procedures – which does conform to the constitutional framework. This is mainly reflected in the fact that, since the current constitution was promulgated in 1982, although there was a serious shortage of reserves of understanding and knowledge on the side of the legal profession on the question of whether and how to use the Constitution, the Supreme Court (and also the common courts) has nevertheless cited provisions of the Constitution in special cases – because the strict use of ordinary laws would lead to judgment results that were in serious violation of justice in individual cases[20] –, and this has never been opposed by legal academic circles. However, since the abolition of the "Response in the Qi Yuling Case", the People's Courts at every level and their judges have generally been of the opinion that, in an ordinary lawsuit procedure, any form of use of the Constitution should

---

[18] For the contents of the judicialization of the Constitution movement, see, mainly, Jiang 2003.

[19] On December 18, 2008 the Supreme Court issued the "Resolution regarding the annulment of all resolutions concerning judicial interpretations issued before the end of 2007 (seventh batch)" (关于废止 2007 年底以前发布的有关司法解释 (第七批)的决定) (this Resolution came into effect on December 24, 2008); the "Response in the Qi Yuling Case" of 2001 was one of these resolutions. In the "reasons for annulment", explanations such as, "situation has changed" or "replaced by new law" were not given, but merely the expression "application already stopped" (*yi tingzhi shiyong* 已停止适用).

[20] Wang Yu 王禹 (2005) published "Judicialization of the Constitution: Critical Analysis of Precedents". This book presents a collection of 33 cases which used citations of the Constitution's basic rights in their judgments. Careful reading reveals that among these cases, there are some in which the constitution's basic rights' provisions are the basis of the judgment or the basis for the reasoning, but in others, it is only the litigants who mention that their aim is to obtain protection under the Constitution, but the court does not agree and sometimes disregards this.

be banned unconditionally.[21] The practice of judicializing the Constitution seems to have reached an impasse, and as yet there is no sign of any way out in the near future.

What is inspiring is that the reactions of the judicial circles were not all the same. The 'shilly-shallying' of the Supreme Court did not at all hinder the constitutional scholars from exploring the ways of judicializing of the Constitution, and also urged the scholars to attach even more importance to the opportunities that were available within the existing framework of the system. On the one hand, scholars reflected again on the problems that were inherent in the "constitutional judicialization movement" itself. They realized that the first appeal for the judicialization of the movement, namely, that the Supreme Court exercises the power of the constitutional review, violated the political framework firmly established by China's Constitution. Therefore, a considerable number of the scholars devoted themselves to appealing in all kinds of ways for a Commission for Constitutional Supervision to be established under the Standing Committee of the NPC.[22] On the other hand, although the failure of the judicialization movement almost put an end to any chance of that the judges would make direct use of the Constitution in their judgments on individual cases – making the constitutional norms the basis of a claim (Anspruchsgrundlage), it nevertheless also inspired the scholars to consider the notion that the judges could use the Constitution indirectly – using the norms of the Constitution as explanations and arguments. This was an exact match with the theory of the interpretation of constitutionality (*hexianxing jieshi* 合宪性解释) which was referred to in various ways by many scholars at that time. And they also found out that the interpretation of constitutionality in reality was only a synonym of "indirect application". Therefore, around the year 2008, the interpretation of constitutionality was the third method of judicialization and became a hot topic of discussion in the constitutional studies area.[23] According to the theory of the interpretation of constitutionality, the judges at all levels of courts in their judicial judgments are obliged to consider the interpretation of constitutionality, i.e. when carrying out the interpretation of the laws and regulations that they apply, they should consider the constitutional principles and the spirit of the Constitution in the discussions. In the most likely interpretation, they should in any case, make it a priority to select and apply the one that best conforms to the constitutional principles (cf. Huang 2014). The legal foundation for the interpretation of constitutionality is stipulated in Art. 5, para. 4 of the Constitution: "All state organs, the armed forces, all

---

[21] High-level leaders of the Supreme Court use similar words, see Luo and Wu 2010.

[22] See footnote 15 above.

[23] For the theory of the interpretation of constitutionality, see the Mainland constitutional scholars' perspective. 2008 was a particularly important year. Zhang Xiang 张翔 published an article named "Two kinds of constitutional cases – the possible impact of the Constitution on the judicature seen from the interpretation of constitutionality" (cf. Zhang 2008), which generated a massive impact. He pointed out that, apart from "genuine constitutional cases" on the level of "reviewing violations of the Constitution" there is a second type of "non-genuine constitutional case", i.e. "the interpretation of the constitutionality of laws". Shangguan Piliang 上官丕亮 published "Ways and methods of the judicialization of China's current Constitution" (cf. Shangguan 2008); in this article, the interpretation of the constitutionality was called 'the third form of judicial interpretation' for the first time. For legislative development, legal foundations, the current situation and development bottleneck of the Mainland constitutional scholars' interpretation of constitutionality, see Huang 2014.

political parties and public organizations and all enterprises and institutions must abide by the Constitution and the law."[24] Here, "all state organs" of course include the People's Courts. And the phrase that the People's Courts "respect the Constitution" which, in common language, transforms into "apply the Constitution", naturally means that, at the core of their duties, that is, in the ruling of cases, they conform to the Constitution.

Although constitutional scholars have only fairly recently started to undertake research on the theory of the interpretation of constitutionality, in the case of the judicature, early in the 1980s, the judicial organs have already started to practice the interpretation of constitutionality, without a proper name for it and without the guidance of a clear-cut theory, because the legislation and related legal doctrines were flawed or the results of judgments according to law obviously violated judicial fairness.[25] The most famous case was the "Clause of non-responsibility for work-related injury" (*gongshang gai bu fuze an* 工伤概不负责案) that occurred in Tianjin in 1988.[26] The situation was basically as follows: the accused employer had a contract for a project involving the demolition of a factory building. Due to the breaking of regulations, an accident happened during the construction work and a labourer was injured. After this employee was hospitalized, he contracted septicaemia and died. The relatives of the deceased demanded that the employer pay compensation. However, the accused had signed a "Clause of non-responsibility for work-related injury" with the deceased and therefore refused to pay the compensation. In the end, this case went to the Higher People's Court of Tianjin (天津高级人民法院). The court expressed the opinion, on the one hand, that the principles of the freedom of will and the freedom of contract in the "General Principles of the Civil Law" (*minfa tongze* 民法通则) which had just been put into practice on January 1, 1987, should be upheld. On the other hand, the court held the opinion that the counter-plea of the accused to "have no responsibility under any circumstances" which was based on the work contract would represent a violation of social justice. Therefore, the Higher Court asked the Supreme People's Court for instructions.

On this issue, the Supreme People's Court issued its "Response on the question of whether a hiring labour contract should execute the laws and regulations for labour protection to the letter" (关于雇工合同应当严格执行劳动保护法规问题的批复) (in the following: "Response to the Clause of non-responsibility for work-related injury") on October 14, 1988:

---

[24] The last two sentences of the Constitution's preamble stipulate similarly: "This Constitution, in legal form, affirms the achievements of the struggles of the Chinese people of all nationalities and defines the basic system and basic tasks of the state; it is the fundamental law of the state and has supreme legal authority. The people of all nationalities, all state organs, the armed forces, all political parties and public organizations and all enterprises and institutions in the country must take the Constitution as the basic standard of conduct, and they have the duty to uphold the dignity of the Constitution and ensure its implementation."

[25] In the author's opinion, the 33 precedents quoted in Wang 2005 (see also footnote 20) can generally be defined as having the quality of constitutional interpretation cases.

[26] The judicial rulings of this case are published in "Supreme Peoples' Court Bulletin" 1989, No. 1. The title is "The case of the compensation damages dispute involving Zhang Lianqi and Jiao Ronglan, who are suing Zhang Xuezhen" (张连起, 焦容兰诉张学珍损害赔偿纠纷案).

After consideration we hold that to implement labour protection for the labourer is already stipulated clearly in China's Constitution; it is the right that the labourers enjoy […]. (The clause) 'no responsibility will be borne in case of injuries suffered during the job' […] then does not conform to related legal regulations, and seriously violates social justice and morality; it should belong to civil behaviour that is null and void. As for the questions of the legal consequences of and compensation for this behaviour has been acknowledged as null and void, your court is asked to deal with this case appropriately on the basis of the general principles of the Civil Law in combination with the specific circumstances of this case.

The final result of the case was that the persons involved in the mediation of the Tianjin City Tanggu District's People's Court (天津市塘沽区人民法院) arrived at an agreement on compensation. In its response, the Supreme Court, on the basis of the provision on labourers' rights [27] in the Constitution acknowledged that the agreement "that non-responsibility for work-related injury" belongs to behaviour which is null and void in Civil Law – here there is no discussion of the question as to whether the citing of the Constitution in this "response" is necessary and correct, and how the invalidity of a legal transaction (*wuxiao jizhi* 无效机制) should work; with regard to the purport of this article, this is a very typical interpretation of constitutionality.

For a very long period of time, the methods employed by the judges in a few cases to consider Articles of the Constitution as a basis for their judgments or as a basis for their reasoning did not by any means lead to any considerable reaction from academic circles. The reason is probably, on the one hand, that the focus of attention of legal scholars is on legislation, not on judicial practice – this phenomenon can still be seen today. On the other hand, the knowledge of legal scholars with regard to whether and how to apply the Constitution is extremely limited. However, at the beginning of this century, when the Supreme People's Court gave its "Response in the Qi Yuling Case", the situation was no longer the same. One important reason was that the legal scholars were already familiar with some theories on the application of the Constitution, for example, a large number of legal scholars held that a constitution is public law and cannot be applied to civil cases like the "Qi Yuling Case". Another group of the scholars, especially those familiar with the German theory of the third-party effects of basic rights (*jiben quanli di san ren xiaoli lilun* 基本权利第三人效力理论; Theorie der Drittwirkung der Grundrechte), would also think that the Constitution can be applied [directly] in civil law cases, but they basically all accept the German theory of indirect application. The second aim of the "constitutional judicialization movement", however, was the direct application of the Constitution. The judicialization of the Constitution was therefore welcomed at the conceptual level of the constitutional government, but in legal theory and in the debate on techniques it met with resistance.[28] Furthermore, the Supreme People's Court's expressed its ambitions of power expansion too obviously in the movement to judicialize the Constitution, at that time – under the linkage of the academic judicialization school – on the one hand reprimanded the NPC standing Committee's "non action" (*bu zuowei* 不作为), but at the same time also made a reckless attempt to consolidate its power to review violations of the Constitution

---

[27] Clearly hinting at Art. 42. Para. 2 of the Constitution: "Through various channels, the state creates conditions for employment, enhances occupational safety and health, improves working conditions and, on the basis of expanded production, increases remuneration for work and welfare benefits."

[28] See, mainly, Tong 2001; Tong 2008; Liu 2009.

with its "Response in the Qi Yuling Case". This probably led simply to the opposing reaction of the legislation organs. The extreme political tension that resulted from this again forced the Supreme Court into a situation in which there was absolutely no reason for it to explain the annulation of the "Response in the Qi Yuling Case". In the end, this brought about the current situation that judicial circles universally reject the application of the Constitution in any form.

Just as stated above, within the current constitutional framework, judicial organs can and must carry out the interpretation of constitutionality, when hearing a case, i.e. apply the Constitution indirectly. The author holds that, if the Supreme Court after the promulgation of the Constitution in 1982 had indicated that the courts of all levels should apply the Constitution if necessary, to counter the serious lagging behind of the legislation of that time – whether this would have resulted from the demands of judicial practice or from wild ambitions based on coveting the power to review violations of the Constitution – then, on the basis of the political and legal environment at that time, the NPC Standing Committee, under most circumstances would have allowed the indirect application of the Constitution and would probably not have considered the direct application as a "violation of the Constitution".

However, the Supreme Court has already missed this historic opportunity. Moreover the problems of whether the courts at all levels have the authority to apply the Constitution and whether they need to differentiate between the direct and the indirect applications have become legal academic issues. This has brought together many different standpoints and theories. Therefore, the constitutional interpretation which is the third form of constitutional judicialization has already become a mainstream subject in the work of constitutional scholars. The lack of mutual theoretical understanding received some clarification when the constitutional hermeneutics unfolded. But unfortunately this highly potential constitutional implementation mechanism which conformed to the spirit of the "1982 Constitution" was, on the level of judicial practice, not able to make any progress. The general opinion among legal scholars is that it is very difficult to persuade the judges at all levels to overcome the traditional mentality of "the official sitting [far away] in the county seat can't order people around like one sitting right here" (*xianguan buru xianguan* 县官不如现管). Unless the Supreme Court accepts the interpretation of constitutionality and calls the courts at all levels to act in response and is successful in this endeavour, there is political work necessary in advance.[29]

---

[29] The author suggests that the constitutional scholars' circles might then enter a phase focusing on the substantial promotion of the Constitution's implementation. The reason is that the new government fully underlines the importance of the Constitution and its implementation. For example, the China Communist Party Central Committee Secretary and Chairman of the Central Military Commission, Xi Jinping, in his speech at the "Conference commemorating the 30th anniversary of the promulgation of the current Constitution" on December 4, 2012, pointed out that "The life of the Constitution is in its implementation and its authority is also in its implementation. We have to unremittingly make great efforts to implement the Constitution. We want to lift the complete implementation of the Constitution onto a new level." What is even more important is that the third Plenum of the 18th Party Congress (which closed on November 12, 2013) passed the "CCP Central Committee Resolution Concerning Some Major Issues in Comprehensively Deepening Reform", emphasizing again that "the legal authority of the Constitution shall be protected".

The normative constitutional school's working method of "individual case model" – instead of a summary

The normative constitutional study has to take the norms of the Constitution and their application as the starting point for work; the general objective of the work is to implement the Constitution, i.e. as Art. 5, para. 4 of the Constitution stipulates, to ensure that "All state organs, the armed forces, all political parties and public organizations and all enterprises and institutions must abide by the Constitution and the law. All acts in violation of the Constitution or the law must be investigated." However, a standpoint is not the same as an operation. Effective operation certainly depends on the approach and method employed for the operation. As mentioned in the second and third chapters above, within the framework of the current Constitution, the review mechanism under the leadership of the NPC Standing Committee for violations of the Constitution and the interpretation of constitutionality by the judicial organs are two ways of implementing the Constitution which are readily available. Nevertheless, although these two methods of constitutional implementation have already been thoroughly validated by academic analysis, they have not yet been truly unfolded at the practical level, for many subjective and objective reasons. Faced with this situation, the normative constitutionalists who are devoting themselves to the implementation of the Constitution must ask themselves: apart from the call for the NPC Standing Committee and the Supreme Court to deal seriously with the Constitution and to establish and perfect specific implementation mechanisms as quickly as possible, what else can and do we have to do?

In fact, some ideas are already emerging from the debate on how to establish and complete the review mechanism for violations of the Constitution and the interpretation mechanisms for constitutionality. If scholars really want to promote the construction of a system, then they must go further than preaching general concepts; only if they are willing to venture deep into the specific system mechanisms that conform to the constitutional framework and have a feasible system design, will the scholars' call carry conviction. For the same reason, since they take the implementation of the Constitution as their mission, on the question of specific implementation, the normative constitutionalists have to produce practical implementation techniques. A comprehensive look at the literature of mainland constitutional scholars reveals that those scholars who are classified as belonging to the normative constitutional school, especially the young generation, are already aware of the importance of the interpretation and application techniques of constitutional norms. Their works are permeated with phrases that pointing the direction of legal application techniques, such as the "interpretation of the Constitution", "application of the Constitution", "constitutional techniques", "constitutional dogmatics" and "constitutional methodology". [30] Among these, one phenomenon merits close attention: more and more constitutional scholars do not only pay close attention to drawing conclusions from summaries of the constitutional application techniques, but rather go deep into the technical details of constitutional cases, following specific problems that have arisen in the individual cases and interpreting constitutional norms that are probably applicable.

---

[30] For example, see Lin 2008; Zhang 2013; Huang 2009; Du 2011; Wang 2008; Li 2011.

The existing literature and the research trends of mainland constitutional scholar shows that the research on individual constitutional cases can roughly be divided into three situations: the first is simply to introduce foreign constitutional precedents. Among these, the decisions of the US Supreme Court and the German Federal Constitutional Court are given first place. In recent years, scholars have attached growing importance to German constitutional dogmatics (Verfassungsdogmatik), and scholars with a background of training in German legal dogmatics are beginning to systematically introduce German constitutional cases.[31] The second kind are purely Chinese constitutional cases. Since 2006, the People's University Law School, annually and at year-end, selects that year's ten most important constitutional cases, organizes scholars to analyse them critically and edits them. By comparing the precedents of several years, one can see that although the analysis of the precedents is not completely focused at the level of "constitutional norms", more and more importance is being attached to the interpretation and analysis of the applications of related constitutional norms.[32]

The third kind is the so-called "case-related constitutional comparison" (*ge'an yindao xia de xianfa bijiao* 个案引导下的宪法比较; fallbezogener Verfassungsrechtsvergleich) put forward by the author. In other words, first put order into the legal reality and the legal claims in Chinese constitutional cases – generally precedents touching upon citizens' basic rights –; and then purposefully look for a related constitutional precedent from a "model state of constitutional government", and focusing on the interpretation of constitutional norms and the expounding and proving of judgments, make a legal comparative evaluation. The most important aspect of this comparison method is that the comparison's purpose is not for the sake of summarizing the similarities – and differences in Chinese and foreign law, but to improve and perfect the scheme for resolving Chinese constitutional cases. Practice has proved this to be very effective.[33]

---

[31] For example, Zhang Xiang has edited a set of selected German constitutional cases; the first volume has already been published. Altogether he has selected 12 decisions of the German Federal Constitutional Court, including the Elfes case, the Lueth case and the Pharmacy case, which had a great impact on the structure and development of the German theory on basic rights. Each critical explanation of a precedent consists of the seven elements' "case names" (including the German Name and its Chinese translation) and the cases' number in the "Decisions of the German Federal Constitutionals Court" (Entscheidungen des Bundesverfassungsgerichts), "keywords", "details of the case", "gist of the judgement", "reasoning and expounding and proving of the judgment", "important theoretical questions that are touched upon" and "later influence and significance". See: Zhang 2012.

[32] Professor Han Dayuan 韩大元 from Renmin University has edited five volumes of "Research on China's Constitutional Instances" (*Zhongguo xianfa shili yanjiu* 中国宪法事例研究) in 2005, 2008, 2009, 2010 and 2011 (Beijing: Falü chubanshe); Professor Hu Jinguang 胡锦光 edited together with Liu Feiyu 刘飞宇 "Critical Analysis of Typical Constitutional Instances in 2007" (*2007 nian zhongguo dianxing xianfa shili pingxi* 2007 年中国典型宪法事例评析) (Beijing: Zhongguo renmin daxue chubanshe); Hu and Wang Kai 王锴 edited and published a volume of zhongguo shida xianfa shili pingxi 中国十大宪法事例评析 [Critical Analysis of China's ten great constitutional instances] (Beijing: Falü chubanshe) every year. It should be noted that because some cases did not go through the litigation process and did not become canonical "cases", they are called "constitutional instances" (*xianfa shili* 宪法事例).

[33] On February 5 and 6, 2010, the author, Philip Kunig and Detlef Leenen organized the two-day "Seminar on Chinese Media Cases" at the Law Department of Free University Berlin. Twelve cases were selected that had received broad media attention in recent years, and the students used German legal theories and

To sum up, the normative constitutional study (school) has already become the main stream of China's constitutional studies. The scholars of this school accept the legal effecacy of the existing Constitution; in particular, they accept that it contains many basic rights articles of a universal nature. Normative constitutional scholars do not only have the above-mentioned working position, but have already explored methods that effectively promote their work, i.e. by using constitutional precedents to go deeply into the particulars of constitutional interpretation and application. Research that centres on the norms that are unfolded by constitutional precedents has already shown the effectiveness of this work, and there is every reason to believe that this will become the main approach for research of normative constitutional school; this is a development to be welcomed.

References

Bai Bin 白斌 (2009) "Xingfa de kunjing yu xianfade jieda – guifan xianfa xue shiye zhong de Xu Ting an" 刑法的困境与宪法的解答——规范宪法学视野中的许霆案 [The predicaments of criminal law and the Constitution's answers – the case of Xu Ting from the perspective of the normative constitutionalist studies], in *Faxue yanjiu* 法学研究 [Chinese Journal of Law] 4, pp 108-121.

Bai Bin 白斌 (2010) "Lun fa jiaoyi xue: yuanliu, tezheng ji qi gongneng" 论法教义学: 源流, 特征及其功能 [Discussing legal doctrine: origins and development, characteristics and functions], in *Huanqiu falü pinglun* 环球法律评论 [Global Law Review] 3, pp. 5-7.

Cai Dingjian 蔡定剑 (1989) "Woguo xianfa jiandu zhidu tantao" 我国宪法监督制度探讨 [Discussion of China's system of constitutional supervision], in *Faxue yanjiu* 法学研究 [Chinese Journal of Law] 3, pp. 25-31.

Dong Chengmei 董成美 and Hu Jinguang 胡锦光 (1987) "Woguo xianfa shencha de zuzhi jigou chutan" 我国违宪审查的组织机构初探 [First explorations on an institutional framework for constitutional review in China], in *Zhongguo renmin daxue xuebao* 中国人民大学学报 [Journal of Renmin University of China] 1.

Du Qiangqiang 杜强强 (2011) "Jiben quanli de guifan lingyu yu baohu chengdu" 基本权利的规范领域与保护程度 [The normative domain of fundamental rights and the degree of protection], in *Zhongwai faxue* 中外法学 [Peking University Law Journal] 1, pp. 3-14.

Gao Quanxi (2012) "Zhengzhi xianfa xue de xingqi yu shanbian" 政治宪法学的兴起与嬗变 [The rise and evolution of political constitutionalism], in *Jiaoda faxue* 交大法学 [SJTU Law Review] 1, pp. 22-43.

Han Dayuan 韩大元, Lin Laifan 林来梵 and Zheng Lei 郑磊 (2008) "Xianfa jieshi xue yu guifan xianfaxue de duihua" 宪法解释学与规范宪法学的对话 [Dialogue of Constitutional Hermeneutics and Normative Constitutionalist Studies], in *Zhejiang xuekan* 浙江学刊 [Zhejiang Academic Journal] 2, pp. 134-143.

---

methods to analyse the cases. During the seminar, the author obtained particularly meaningful insights into China's current problems. Furthermore, the author conducted a comparison using the "Decision on investment assistance" (Investitionshilfe-Entscheidung) and the "Pharmacy Decision" (Apotheken-Entscheidung) of the German Federal Constitutional Court which was aimed at the great debate in China on the "Property Law violating the Constitution Case". One of the core problems discussed in this debate was how to explain the stipulation of Art. 15, para. 1 of the Constitution, which states "The State practises socialist market economy." This comparison came to the conclusion that China, with regard to the problem of the provisions concerning the economy (Wirtschaftsverfassungsklausel), had used a different approach. It is therefore impossible to draw conclusions from the German experience. See Huang 2009.

Hao Tiechuan 郝铁川 (1996a) "Lun liangxing weixian" 论良性违宪 [On benign violations of the Constitution], in *Faxue yanjiu* 法学研究 [Chinese Journal of Law] 4, pp. 89-91.

Hao Tiechuan 郝铁川 (1996b) "Shehui biangeng yu chengwenfa de juxianxing – zai tan liangxing weixian jian da Tong Zhiwei tongzhi" 社会变更与成文法的局限性——再谈良性违宪兼答童之伟同志 [Social change and the limitations of written law – a new discussion of benign violations of the Constitution and a reply to comrade Tong Zhiwei], in *Faxue yanjiu* 法学研究 [Chinese Journal of Law] 6, pp. 23-24.

Hao Tiechuan 郝铁川 (1997) "Wenrou de dikang – guanyu 'liangxing weixian' de jidian shuoming" 温柔的抵抗——关于"良性违宪"的几点说明 [Gentle resistance – a few explanations on "benign violations of the Constitution"], in *Faxue* 法学 [Legal Studies] 5, p. 18.

Hu Jinguang 胡锦光 (1985) "Lun xianfa jiandu zhidu" 论宪法监督制度 [Discussing the system of constitutional supervision], in *Zhongguo faxue* 中国法学 [China Legal Science] 1, pp. 72-79.

Hu Jinguang 胡锦光 (1997) "Zhongguo xianfa de sifa shiyongxing taolun" 中国宪法的司法适用性探讨 [Discussion on the judicial applicability of the Chinese Constitution], in *Zhongguo renmin daxue xuebao* 中国人民大学学报 [Journal of Renmin University of China] 5, pp. 58-63.

Huang Hui 黄卉 (2009) "Xianfa jingji zhidu tiaokuan de falü shiyong – cong deguo jingji xianfa zhi zheng tanqi" 宪法经济制度条款的法律适用——从德国经济宪法之争谈起 [The legal application of the Constitution's articles on the economic system – starting the discussion from the German constitutional controversy on economy], in *Zhongwai faxue* 中外法学 [Peking University Law Journal] 4, pp. 559-573.

Huang Hui (2012) "Guifan xianfaxue de fangxiang: gai ba er xianfa zhi bei dong wei zhudong" 规范宪法学的方向: 改八二宪法之被动为主动 [Trends of the normative constitutional theory: Transforming the 1982 Constitution from passive to active], in *Du shu* 读书 [Reading] 12.

Huang Hui 黄卉 (2014) "Hexianxing jieshi ji qi lilun jiantao" 合宪性解释及其理论检讨 [Discussion on the interpretation of constitutionality and its theory], in *Zhongguo faxue* 中国法学 [Chinese legal studies] 1, pp. 285-302.

Huang Mingli 黄明利 (1985) "Shilun woguo weixian shencha zhidu de neirong he tedian" 试论我国违宪审查制度的内容和特点 [On content and characteristics of China's system of constitutional review], in *Falü kexue* 法律科学 [Law Science] 3, pp. 21-25.

Jiang Shigong 强世功 (2003) "Xianfa sifahua de beilun – qian lun faxuejia zai tuidong xianzheng zhong de kunjing" 宪法司法化的悖论——兼论法学家在推动宪政中的困境 [The paradox of judicialization of the Constitution – discussing the predicament of legal scholars promoting constitutional government], in *Zhongguo shehui kexue* 中国社会科学 [Social Sciences in China] 2, pp. 18-28.

Loewenstein, Karl (1951) "Reflexions on the value of constitutions in our revolutionary age", in Zurcher, Arnold J. (ed.) *Constitutions and Constitutional Trends after World War II*, New York: New York University Press, pp. 191-224.

Li Zhongxia 李忠夏 (2011) "Zhongguo xianfaxue fangfalun fansi" 中国宪法学方法论反思 [Rethinking the methodology of Chinese constitutional studies], in *Faxue yanjiu* 法学研究 [Chinese Journal of Law] 2, pp. 160-172.

Lin Laifan 林来梵 (2001) "Cong xianfa guifan da guifan xianfa – guifan xianfa xue de yi zhong qianyan" 从宪法规范到规范宪法 [From Constitutional Norms to Normative Constitution – An Introduction to Normative Constitutional Studies], Beijing: Falü chubanshe.

Lin Laifan 林来梵 (2008) "Ren de zunyan yu renge zunyan - jian lun zhongguo xianfa di 38 tiao de jieshi fang'an" 人的尊严与人格尊严——兼论中国宪法第 38 条的解释方案 [Human dignity and personal dignity: on interpretation scheme of no. 38 of the PRC Constitution], in *Zhejiang shehui kexue* 浙江社会科学 [Zhejiang Social Sciences] 3, pp. 47-56.

Lin Laifan 林来梵 (ed.) (2009) *Xianfa shencha de yuanli yu jishu* 宪法审查的原理与技术 [The Principles and Techniques of Constitutional Review], Beijing: Falü chubanshe.

Lin Laifan 林来梵 (2010) "Zhongguo xianfa xue de xianzhuang yu zhanwang" 中国宪法学的现状与展望 [The current situation and direction of development of China's Constitution], in *Faxue yanjiu* 法学研究 [Chinese Journal of Law] 6, pp. 20-22.

Liu Songshan 刘松山 (2009) "Renmin fayuan de shenpan yiju weishenme bu neng shi xianfa – jian lun woguo xianfa shiyong de tedian he qianjing" 人民法院的审判依据为什么不能是宪法——兼论我国宪法适用的特点和前景 [Why the Constitution can't be the basis of the People's Courts' trials – on the special characteristics and prospects of the application of China's Constitution], in *Faxue* 法学 [Legal Studies] 2, pp. 28-37.

Liu Songshan 刘松山 (2010) "1981 nian: taidong er wei xing de xianfa weiyuanhui sheji" 1981 年: 胎动而未形的宪法委员会设计 [1981: The Constitutional Commission's design is still shapeless], in *Zhengfu luntan* 政府论坛 [Tribune of Political Science and Law] 5, pp. 94-106.

Luo Dongchuan 罗东川 and Wu Zhaoxiang 吴兆祥 (2010) "'Guanyu caipan wenshu yinyong falü, fagui deng guifanxing falü wen jian de guiding' de lijie yu shiyong" "关于裁判文书引用法律, 法规等规范性法律文件的规定"的理解与适用 [On the understanding and the application of the "Provisions of the Supreme People's Court on Citation of Such Normative Legal Documents as Laws and Regulations in the Judgments"], originally published in Xiong Xuanguo 熊选国 (ed.) (2010) *Xingshi shenpan cankao* 刑事审判参考 [Reference for Criminal Trials] 71, pp. 100-112.

Shangguan Piliang 上官丕亮 (2008) "Dangxia zhongguo xianfa sifahua de lujing yu fangfa" 当下中国宪法司法化的路径与方法 [Ways and methods of the judicialization of China's current Constitution], in *Xiandai faxue* 现代法学 [Modern legal studies] 2, pp. 3-16.

Tong Zhiwei 童之伟 (1996) "'Liangxing weixian' bu yi kending – dui Hao Tiechuan tongzhi youguan zhuzhang de butong kanfa" "良性违宪"不宜肯定——对郝铁川同志有关主张的不同看法 ["Benign violations of the Constitution" ought not to be accepted – a different perspective on comrade Hao Tiechuan's position on the matter], in *Faxue yanjiu* 法学研究 [Chinese Journal of Law] 6, pp. 19-21.

Tong Zhiwei 童之伟 (1997) "Xianfa shishi linghuoxing de dixian – zai yu Hao Tiechuan xiansheng shangque" 宪法实施灵活性的底线——再与郝铁川先生商榷 [The bottom line of the flexibility of constitutional implementation – a new discussion with Mr. Hao Tiechuan], in *Faxue* 法学 [Legal Studies] 5, pp. 15-17.

Tong Zhiwei 童之伟 (2001) "Xianfa sifa shiyong yanjiu zhong de jige wenti" 宪法司法适用研究中的几个问题 [Some questions in the research on the judicial application of the Constitution], in *Faxue* 法学 [Legal Studies] 11, pp. 3-8, 51.

Tong Zhiwei 童之伟 (2008) "Xianfa shiyong ying yixun xianfa benshen guiding de lujing" 宪法适用应依循宪法本身规定的路径 [The application of the Constitution should follow and abide by the Constitution's own stipulations], in *Zhongguo faxue* 中国法学 [Chinese legal studies] 6, pp. 22-48

Wang Lei 王磊 (2000) *Xianfa sifahua* 宪法司法化 [Judicialization of the Constitution], Beijing: Zhongguo zhengfa daxue chubanshe.

Wang Kai 王锴 (2008) "Xianfa shiyixue de wenti yu qianjing" 宪法释义学的问题与前景 [The issues and prospect of constitutional hermeneutics], in *Jiangsu xingzheng xueyuan xuebao* 江苏行政学院学报 [The Journal of Jiangsu Administration Institute] 4, pp. 115-118.

Wang Yu 王禹 (2005) *Xianfa sifahu: anli pingxi* 宪法司法化: 案例评析 [Judicialization of the Constitution: Critical Analysis of Precedents], Beijing: Beijing daxue chubanshe.

Xu Chongde 许崇德 "Xianfa sifahua zhiyi" 宪法司法化质疑 [Challenging the judicialization of the Constitution], in *Zhongguo renda* 中国人大 [The People's Congress of China] 11, pp. 44-45.

Zhai Guoqiang 翟国强 (2012) "Xianfa panduan de zhengdanghua gongneng" 宪法判断的正当化功能 [The legitimating function of constitutional judgements], in *Faxue yanjiu* 法学研究 [Chinese Journal of Law] 1, pp. 77-87.

Zhang Xiang 张翔 (2008) "Liang zhong xianfa anjian – cong hexianxing jieshi kan xianfa dui sifa de keneng yinxiang" 两种宪法案件——从合宪性解释看宪法对司法的可能影响 [Two kinds of constitutional cases – the possible impact of the Constitution on the judicature seen from the interpretation of constitutionality], in *Zhongguo Faxue* 中国法学 [Chinese legal studies] 4, pp. 110-116

Zhang Xiang 张翔 (ed.) (2012) *Deguo xianfa anli xuanze: jiben quanli zonglun* 德国宪法案例选释: 基本权利总论 [Selection of German Constitutional Cases: General Introduction to Basic Rights], Beijing: Falü chubanshe.

Zhang Xiang 张翔 (2013) "Xianfa jiaoyi xue chujie" 宪法教义学初阶 [The primary phase of constitutional dogmatics], in *Zhongwai faxue* 中外法学 [Peking University Law Journal] 5, pp. 916-936.

Zheng Lei 郑磊 (2009) "Shouhu xianfa: dui falü jinxing xianfa shencha de jieshi fang'an – yi xianfa wenben jiqi yange wei jichu de kaoliang" 守护宪法: 对法律进行宪法审查的解释方案——以宪法文本及其沿革为基础的考量 [Defending the Constitution: an interpretation design for implementing constitutional review on laws – considerations on the basis of the original text of the Constitution and its evolution], in *Huadong zhengfa daxue xuebao* 华东政法大学学报 [ECUPL Journal] 5, pp. 3-10.

Zhou Wei 周伟 (2004) "1982 nian xianfa yiqian de xianfa jieshi yu weixian shencha anli zhi qishi" 1982 年宪法以前的宪法解释与违宪审查案例之启示 [Inspirations from the constitutional interpretations and cases of constitutional review before the 1982 Constitution], in *Sichuan shifan daxue xuebao* 四川师范大学学报 [Journal of Sichuan Normal University] 1, pp. 28-35.

Chen Hsien-wu and Lin Po-wen

The Rule of Law in Taiwan's Constitution[*]

Formally, Taiwan's Constitution is still the 1947 Constitution of the Republic of China, but after the imposition and lifting of martial law, historical changes were made to Taiwan's Constitution in the direction of free and democratic development. In addition, the strengthening of the function of the Judicial Yuan's Grand Judges with regard to explaining and interpreting fundamental constitutional rights in the context of individual cases in response to formal requests for constitutional interpretations[1], has generated a decision-making function for the court similar to that of the German Federal Constitutional Court. If the activity of Taiwan's constitutional interpretation is compared with the emphasis on judicial restraint (*sifa jiezhi* 司法節制) in mature Western countries, or with the theory of judicial minimalism discussed by the American constitutional scholar, Sunstein, (*sifa jixiao zhuyi* 司法極小主義)[2], then Taiwan's Judicial Yuan's Grand Judges, as protectors of fundamental rights, should be perceived as active protectors of the Constitution (*Hüter der Verfassung*) (cf. Papier 2004: 411-429). As for the constitutional government system, within the framework of which the organisation of the government and the dynamic balance of power can be observed, this rather takes the path of heavy judicial restraint.

The Constitution in Taiwan is therefore developing in the direction of the democratic constitutional state (*demokratischer Verfassungsstaat*) described by German constitutional scholars[3]. However, this kind of development of a democratic constitutional state – namely, the establishing of strong and effective safeguards of the constitution within the constitutional state system – has not yet been universally acknowledged or even understood by the people, which has led to a considerable lack of confidence in the judicature. To study the development of the rule of law (*fazhi* 法治) in Taiwan, at this time and within the given constitutional framework, is of great practical interest (*praktisches Interesse*).

In Taiwan, the discussion on the rule of law (*fazhi* 法治) is always mingled with discussions on the rule by law (*fazhi* 法制)[4] and the rule of man (*renzhi* 人治). So what

---

[*] This text was translated from Chinese by Katja Levy, Sabine Mokry and Sören Vogler. The translators would like to thank Georg Gesk for his support during the translation process. If not otherwise stated, all German expressions were inserted in the original text by the authors, Chen and Lin.

[1] Regarding this point, the former President of Taiwan's Judicial Yuan, Weng Yueh-sheng, has conducted special research on the history of Taiwan's judicial activism and provides a detailed discussion on the continuous development of the constitutional control method of the Judicial Yuan's Grand Judges. See: Weng 2004, pp. 1219-1243; see, especially, the statistical illustrations on pp. 1230 f. and p. 1242.

[2] For Sunstein's judicial minimalism, see Sunstein 1999. Throughout the book, it is argued that a judge is to handle one case at a time. Wide-ranging discussions should only take place in exceptional situations; only minimal, relevant arguments are required to resolve the issues in specific cases.

[3] The key to understanding the democratic constitutional state, according to Alexy, is found in the existence of constitutional bodies which investigate violations of the Constitution (Alexy 1998: 262 f.).

[4] The English term "rule by law" that is used here, is the author's own formulation; the literal translation would be "legal system" – translators' note.

exactly is the true content of the rule of law (*zhi* 治)[5]? What is the content of the rule of law principle (*Rechtsstaatprinzip*)? The main aim of this paper is to clarify this 'aggregated concept' (*juhe gainian* 聚合概念).

The search for rule of law in the original text of Taiwan's Constitution

The term "rule of law state" (fazhiguo 法治國, Rechtsstaat) does not appear in the Constitution of the Republic of China or in its Amendments. However, in academic works and in the media, the term "principle of the rule of law state"[6] is very often found. How to deal with the multitude of possible meanings of the terms is a complex issue.

In his habilitation thesis entitled "Das Rechtsstaatprinzip", Philip Kunig, after exploring historical developments as well as constitutional doctrine (*Verfassungsdogmatik*) and governance and public policy studies (*Staatswissenschaften*)[7], states that, in his opinion, the rule of law state principle (cf. Kunig 1986: 8) should not be considered an aggregated concept simply because it is frequently used. The term 'rule of law state principle' (*fazhiguo yuanze* 法治國原則) should be referred to as the 'special characteristics of rule of law state' (*fazhiguo texing* 法治國特性) (cf. Kunig 1986: 457) so that the wide diversity and breadth of the meaning of the term 'rule of law state' can be reduced to the relatively specific term "special characteristics of rule of law state" in order to avoid the principles of the rule of law state being included in all constitutional principles.

Katharina Sobota, in her habilitation thesis entitled "Das Prinzip Rechtsstaat", on the principle of the rule of law state, shows that the principle of rule of law state consists of 17 key elements[8] and according to Philip Kunig, the special characteristics of the rule of law state principle should be reduced to the standpoint of the special characteristics of rule of law state (*Rechtsstaatlichkeit; fazhiguo texing zhi lichang* 法治國特性之立場); although 27 years have passed since this notion was first postulated, it is still valid. Kunig also argues that the rule of law state (*Rechtsstaat*) is a concept of type (*Typusbegriff*) (Kunig 2009: 1). This conceptual analysis of constitutional dogmatics (*xianfa shiyixue* 憲法釋義 學) deserves support. In addition, Helmut Schulze-Fielitz found that constitutional dogmatics (*Verfassungsrechtsdogmatik*) and the rule of law state (*Rechtsstaat*), at the normative level, contain interpretations of rules (*Regel*), basic rules (*Grundsatz*) and

---

[5]   The English term "rule of law" that is used here, is the author's own formulation; the literal translation would be "governance" – translators' note.

[6]   Instead of the more common translations of "rule of law principle" or "principle of the rule of law", which are usually associated with the similar but not equal concept in Anglo-American legal thought, the term "rule of law state principle "or "principle of rule of law state" will be used throughout this text in order to emphasize the relative similarity of this principle in Taiwan's legal system to the German concept of "Rechtsstaat" – translators' note.

[7]   For a clear and incisive analysis of the principle of the rule of law state and the special characteristics of the rule of law state, see: Kunig 1986: 309 f.

[8]   In her reconstruction of the principle of the rule of law state, Sobota differentiates between artificial essential elements, standard level essential elements, and relational essential elements, altogether 17 different elements. In this article, in light of the previous understanding, in the constitutional interpretations of the Judicial Yuan's Council of Grand Judges of the Republic of China, it is not possible to use such broad and detailed classifications of properties to carry out the inductive research. See Sobota 1997: 517 f.

principles (*Prinzip*) (Schulze-Fielitz 2006: marginal no. 41 f.), which together with Kunig's concept of type can be employed to clarify both concepts, so that the rule of law state is highlighted in its *form* rather than as a blurred aggregated concept.

Kunig points out that 'the rule of law state' is not mentioned in the wording of Article 20 of the Basic Law [which deals with constitutional basic principles – translators' note], but that the decisive elements of the rule of law state (*rechtsstaatliche Determinanten*) can be ascertained in other regulations of the Basic Law and those changes of the Constitution that did not change its original text (*Verfassungswandlung*), mainly resulting from the decisions of the Federal Constitutional Court (*Bundesverfassungsgericht*) (Kunig 2009: 6 f.). These achievements in the research on German constitutional jurisprudence can actually guide the research on Taiwan's constitutional changes with regard to the decisive elements of the special characteristics of the rule of law state.

A thorough word-by-word search, by the author of this article, of the original text of the Constitution of the Republic of China and its Amendments failed to find the term 'rule of law state'. This is in contrast to the specific wording of Article 13 of the Amendments to the 1982 Constitution of the People's Republic of China from 1999, which is as follows:

> In Article 5 of the Constitution, a paragraph is added which becomes the first paragraph of this article. It stipulates: The People's Republic of China governs the country according to law and makes it a socialist country under rule of law.

However, the statement of reasoning for the principle of the rule of law state provided in Interpretation No. 525 by the Grand Judges of the Judicial Yuan also contains the following description:

> A state governed by the rule of law (Rechtsstaat) is one of the fundamental principles of the Constitution. The paramount principle of a state governed by the rule of law (Rechtsstaat) is the protection of the people's rights, maintenance of legal order and adherence to the principles of honesty and goodwill.[9]

Interpretations Nos. 574 and 629 contain similar phrases.

Consequently, this shows that in the opinion of the Grand Judges, the principle of the rule of law state is one of the fundamental principles of the Constitution, but the Grand Judges have not yet discussed in further detail either the connotations of principles and *fundamental* principles or their differences. The special character of Alexy's theory on the principles of fundamental rights, that is, the optimization requirement (*Optimierungsgebot*), is not yet implemented. But by extending the instantiation of this kind of key element, namely the safeguarding of the people's rights, the stability of the legal order and the principle of legitimate expectation, it can be inferred that the principle of the rule of law state is the 'basic principle of the Constitution' and the principle of legitimate expectation is a 'constitutional principle under the basic principles' (*jiben yuanze xia zhi xianfa yuanze* 基本原則下之憲法原則).

In addition, in the statement of reasoning provided for Interpretation No. 520, it is pointed out that "[u]nder the rule-of-law principle, even substantive appropriateness is no substitute for due process"[10]. So we see that the principle of the rule of law state

---

[9] Official translation by Wei-Feng Huang for the Judicial Yuan of the Republic of China, <http://www.judicial.gov.tw/constitutionalcourt/EN/ p03_01.asp?expno=525> – translators' note.

[10] Official translation by Professor Andy Y. Sun for the Judicial Yuan of the Republic of China, <http://www.judicial.gov.tw/constitutionalcourt/EN/ p03_01.asp?expno=520> – translators' note.

encompasses legal procedures. Interpretation No. 585 states that the Legislative Yuan can set up a Special Commission to conduct an investigation into the truth that can command public prosecutors to press charges and cause the unification of the legislative and the executive powers. This is a serious violation of the division of powers in the Criminal Procedure Law and the rule of law state principle which can be understood as stating that, in the division of powers, the cores of the executive, the legislative and the judicative must not infringe upon each other. Should one power infringe upon the core of another power, this has to be considered as a violation of the principle of separation of powers and also as a violation of the rule of law state principle. The interpretations of the Grand Judges do not delve very deeply into the issue of how to set apart the separation of powers and the rule of law state principle and this certainly needs to be dealt with more thoroughly. Legal certainty has always been interpreted as a sound manifestation of the principle of the rule of law state; it is still the most evident key element. The next part of this article provides a summary of the individual decisive elements of the special characteristics of the rule of law.

Overview of the decisive elements of the rule of law state's special characteristics

The decisive key elements of the rule of law state's special characteristics in the Interpretations of the Judicial Yuan's Grand Judges have been identified as follows:

- The core area of the organs of the constitutional government and lawful legal procedures
- The binding force of the law
- The reservation of the law, the structural hierarchy of the law and the priority of the law
- The principle of legal certainty
- The stability of the laws, the protection of legitimate expectations, and the prohibition of the retroactive application of law
- The principle of proportionality
- The effective remedy[11] (*quanli youxiao jiuji* 權利有效救濟)

These elements are explained by the Grand Judges of the Judicial Yuan in their main documents and statements of reasoning as follows:

Special decisive key elements of the special characteristic of the rule of law state	Nos. of Grand Judges' Inter-pretations	Details and intentions of Interpretation	Standard Articles of reference
Dynamic equilibrium of the powers of the constitutional government organs	585	The Legislative Yuan's Regulation of the Special Commission on the Investigation of the Truth	Article 19, Basic Law of the Federal Republic of Germany; Article 80; Article 23, [Taiwan's] Constitution
	520	Halt to construction of the No. 4 Nuclear Power Plant	
	614	Enforcement Rules of the Public Functionaries Retirement Act	

---

[11] German: wirksamer Rechtsbehelf – translators' note.

Binding force of the law; legislation is bound to the Constitution; administration according to the law; principle of jurisdiction according to the law	371	Article 5 para. 2 and para. 3 of The Regulations for the Constitutional Interpretation Procedure Act and the court's right to request a constitutional interpretation	Article 20 para. 3, Basic Law of the Federal Republic of Germany; Article 171; Article 174; Article 78; Article 79 para. 2; Article 80, [Taiwan's] Constitution.
	572	"prerequisite issue" (*xianjue wenti* 先決問題), "provide specific reasons (*juti liyou* 具體理由) for objectively believing the unconstitutionality of the statute", and request […] an interpretation [of a statute's] constitutionality (*sheng qing shi xian an* 聲請釋憲案)	
Hierarchy of the reservation of the law; the hierarchic structure of the law and the priority of the law	443	Hierarchy of the reservation of the law and the principle of proportionality; draftees going abroad and fundamental rights.	Article 80, Basic Law of the Federal Republic of Germany; Articles 9 to Article 18, 21, 22, 23, [Taiwan's] Constitution
Principle of legal certainty; specificity of authorization	432, 491, 521, 524, 594, 602, 671, 623, 692, 674, 657, 650, 640	Professionals must be able to predict which of their deeds or non-deeds constitutes a violation of their duties and the corresponding punishment (432); Is Article 31 of the National Health Insurance Act consistent with the principle of legal certainty? (524); Investigation criteria for the ' specificity of legal authorization' of the administrative decrees of the tax offices (650)	
The principle of the rule of law state values the stability of the laws, protection of legitimate expectations, and prohibition of retroactive application of the law.	636	Sections of the Act for Eliminating Hoodlums violate the Constitution.	Article 23 of [Taiwan's] Constitution; Articles 17 to 20 Administrative Procedure Act
	432	Are the regulations of the Certified Public Accountant Act concerning the standards for certified accountants, due diligence and the scope of punishment in violation of the Constitution?	
	525	Is the interpretation that reservists shall enjoy preferential treatment in the civil service entrance examination in violation of the legitimate expectation principle?	
	699	Does the regulation "which punishes a vehicle driver who refused to take the sobriety test by suspending his driver's license, prohibiting him from taking the driver's license test within a period of three years, and suspending all classes of vehicle licenses"[12], violate the Constitution?	

[12] Official translation by Spenser Y. Hor for the Judicial Yuan of the Republic of China, <http://www.judicial.gov.tw/constitutionalcourt/EN/p03_01.asp?expno=699> – translators' note.

The three phase examination of the means and ends of the principle of proportionality, the introduction of the low, middle and high standard criteria of examination density in US law, and the legacy of Alexy's weighting formula	690	"Is the "necessary dispositions" provision of Article 37 para. 1 of the Communicable Disease Control Act, including compulsory quarantine, unconstitutional?"[13]	Article 23, [Taiwan's] Constitution
Effective remedy	689, 243, 369, 418, 653, 684	Does Article 89 para. 2 of the Social Order Maintenance Act that restricts the act of stalking by a journalist violate the Constitution? The so-called legal principle of 'when there are rights there are remedies' (*you quanli ji you jiuji zhi fali* 有權利即有救濟之法理) underlines the right of the people to appeal to the courts for remedy; this is the core content of the guarantee of litigation and is not easy to remove (243). For example, "if the decisions or measures infringe the student's right to education or other constitutional rights, even if the decisions or measures are not expulsions or similar decisions, based on the mandate that where there is a right, there is a remedy under Article 16 of the Constitution, the student whose right has been infringed shall be allowed to bring administrative appeal and litigation and there is no need to place special restrictions" (684).[14]	Article 16, [Taiwan's] Constitution

Core area of the constitutional government organs and the legitimate legal order, and the influence of the rule of law state on the organisation and order of the state
In Taiwan's Constitution there are five powers. In addition to the executive, the legislative and the judicative powers (with their separation, checks and balances), there are two other powers: examination and supervision. The supervisory power oversees administrative supervision, with correcting, impeaching, censuring and investigating as the content of the supervisory performance.

---

[13] Official translation by Huai-Ching R. Tsai for the Judicial Yuan of the Republic of China, <http://www.judicial.gov.tw/constitutionalcourt/EN/p03_01.asp?expno=690> – translators' note.

[14] Official translation by C. L. Chen for the Judicial Yuan of the Republic of China, <http://www.judicial.gov.tw/constitutionalcourt/EN/p03_01.asp?expno=684> – translators' note.

According to the thoughts of Sun Yat-sen, the five powers form one part of the power of the government. And there was another 'state power' (*zhengquan* 政權), belonging to the National Assembly. This system is different from the system of powers in England and the USA. But it is quite similar to the power structure of the Peoples' Congress in the Constitution of Switzerland and the 1982 Constitution of the PR China – one government and two courts as the executive body. However, in constitutional practice, in the Republic of China, the Constitution has constantly been changed and the National Assembly has already been abolished in Taiwan.

As a result, Taiwan's constitutional organs have developed into the constitutional government system of five powers. The dynamic equilibrium between the constitutional power organs, in particular, should be seen as the core of the practice of Taiwan's rule of law state. However, in the original text of the Constitution, although there is no core area of fundamental rights and no specific formulation similar to "In no case may the essence of a basic right be affected" as in Article 19 of German Basic Law, the idea of the core area of fundamental rights in Germany is still cited in the interpretation of the Taiwanese Constitution as an example, and applied to the dividing boundaries of the constitutional organs' powers. This form of dividing boundaries of powers is mainly established by the Interpretations of the Council of Grand Judges, who, by presenting their arguments and citing the 'rule of law state principle', define the core areas of the constitutional organs' powers. Most importantly, a dispute over the competencies of constitutional organs emerged for the first time in Interpretation No. 520 of the Council of Grand Judges. In the interaction of the administrative and legislative powers, it is necessary to put the rightful order into practice and Interpretation No. 585 of the Council of Grand Judges finally acknowledged that the legislative power possesses the right of investigation, but should not violate the operation of the investigative power of the Control Yuan and the operation of the judicial power of the Judicial Yuan. Interpretation No. 585 thoroughly investigates the Regulation of the Special Commission on the Investigation of the Truth, which has been passed by the Legislative Yuan. It declares only those provisions which are in conflict with the Constitution to be unconstitutional, not the entire regulation. From this, it can be seen that the Interpretations of the Council of Grand Judges are self-controlled and deeply committed to the rule of law state principle – even in cases where opinions may differ. For example, the Grand Judge Hsu Tsong-li holds that many provisions in the Regulation of the Special Commission on the Investigation of the Truth are in conflict with the Constitution, which make the matter more difficult, and that the entire regulation is simply unconstitutional. This deviating view allows the legislators to re-consider the matter and provides an opportunity to introduce new legislation. [15] From these two

---

[15] Grand Judge Hsu Tsong-li's dissenting opinion in Interpretation No. 585 points out: "According to my opinion, under these circumstances, instead it should be directly proclaimed that it violates the constitution. The legislators should have the chance to rethink it or choose a step towards changing it, while continuing to pursue its original legislative goal. Or it shall choose to make a fresh start and completely consider making a new law or straightforwardly abandoning the making of a new law. This alone would show real respect for the legislators. Taking this case as a starting point for discussion, it is obviously the core intention of the Regulation of the Special Commission on the Investigation of the Truth to exercise the criminal investigation power to find out the truth about the 3-19 incident [Translators' note: The 3-19 incident refers to the assassination attempt on Chen Shui-bian, who was President at the time,

interpretations it can be seen that the Grand Judges specify the idea of the separation of the high powers and of checks and balances as a principle norm in each case, so that the governance of the constitutional state is more likely to have a regulated character. Only in this way, through the interpretation of the Constitution, can the development of the rule of law be further consolidated.

The principle of the rule of law state therefore lies in the separation of powers and the balance of powers in the constitutional organs, in the acknowledgement of the core areas of the executive power and the legislative power and their being protected against violation, namely, citing the principle of the rule of law state. Firstly, in Taiwan's democracy, after the elections in 2000, the first change of Taiwan's governing parties took place. At that time, the governing party had not even gained a majority in the Legislative Yuan, but formed a minority government; it was in the difficult situation of the so-called "small dynasty in a big wilderness" (*chao xiao ye da* 朝小野大). The Executive Yuan then unilaterally announced that construction of the No. 4 Nuclear Power Plant would be terminated. As a consequence, the Budget Law, which had been passed by the Legislative Yuan, could not be implemented; this created tensions between the legislative and the executive. In the end, the Legislative Yuan (the Nationalist Party's Parliamentary Group) applied to the Council of Grand Judges for an Interpretation. On January 15, 90 [2001][16] the Council of Grand Judges released Interpretation No. 520 on the Budget Law for the construction of No. 4 Nuclear Power Plant and, for the first time, the rule of law state

during his election campaign on March 19, 2004]. At the time of the oral statements the representative of the Legislative Yuan and the legal representative of the election candidate also pledged and pointed out that the Special Commission on the Investigation of the Truth is not a subordinate organ of the parliament exercising the parliament's power of investigation and that there is no relation at all with the Legislative Yuan. However, the majority of opinions avoided the legislative intention and the legislators' own experiences that appear objectively in the Regulation of the Special Commission on the Investigation of the Truth. They deviate from the core of this regulation. They want to remould the Special Commission on the Investigation of the Truth from a type of organization that exercises independent public prosecution powers, as was originally planned by the legislators, into a type of organization that exercises the investigation powers of the parliament, as has never been intended by the legislators beforehand. And then on the basis of its being a subordinate organ of the parliament, they declare that the Special Commission on the Investigation of the Truth is not allowed to exercise its core official power, the criminal investigation power. There are even up to 16 reasons why it is not a subordinate organ of the parliament and needs to either be declared as violating the constitution or in other ways to be given an explanation why it should conform to the constitution or an amendment needs to be discussed thoroughly. The Special Commission on the Investigation of the Truth has gone through this forced adaptation remould of its organisation; no doubt was it able to obtain that the organization still is in accord with the constitution. It only needs to conclude procedural amendments and corrections. But the old bottle even though it went through repair and could maintain itself in whole, does not contain old wine anymore, but it's the new wine that the judicature has produced." The above-described deviating opinion of the Grand Judge, Hsu Tsung-li, can, in fact, contribute important source material on the debate of methodology in the constitutional interpretation, especially on the question of the efficacy of the control of abstract laws and regulations. In the future, its importance will exert even more influence.

[16] The author uses the Taiwan Calendar Years; the Western Calendar Years are added in brackets by the translators here and below – translators' note.

principle was clearly announced in a statement of reasoning. Explanations were given regarding the checks and balances of power for the organs of the executive and the legislative, and also regarding the legal order that must be put into practice which can be summarized as follows:

> Democratic governance is governance by public opinion. The path to realize the governance of public opinion is the election of the President and members of the Legislative Yuan as their terms expire. It is indeed a common occurrence in partisan politics that an elected presidential candidate seeks to promote what was promised during the campaign, so that the President, through his appointed Premier of the Executive Yuan, may change previously existing policies or orientation not [necessarily] consistent with his political views. Regardless of the change in ruling political party or reorganization of the Executive Yuan, however, any change of policy direction or critical policy should nevertheless abide by the checks and balance of powers upon which the constitutional order is based. Under the rule-of-law principle, even substantive appropriateness is no substitute for due process.[17]

This means that, according to the principle of rule of law state, the Executive Yuan's suspension of the Budget for the No. 4 Nuclear Power Plant should be seen as "changes in critical policies". In such a case, it would therefore be required that the President of the Executive Yuan and the heads of the related ministries and commissions complete the procedures of reporting to the Legislative Yuan in a timely manner and of being asked for an explanation as quickly as possible. After the Executive Yuan had issued the report and received the support of the majority of the legislators, it would then be able to implement the related budget, which had been previously blocked. Should the Legislative Yuan raise objections or formulate different resolutions, negotiations would have to be conducted to resolve the stalemate.

On 15th December 93 [2004], the Council of Grand Judges' Interpretation No. 585 analysed the 'Regulation of the Special Commission on the Investigation of the Truth'. First of all, the Legislative Yuan's right of supervision was acknowledged. The core competencies of other constitutional organs, however, could not be derogated. To put it briefly:

> Under Article 13-I and III, the SCIT [Special Commission on the Investigation of the Truth in Respect of the 319 Shooting – translators' note] not only has the jurisdiction over a specific criminal case, but also may instruct a prosecutor in carrying out prosecution, thus combining the legislative power with the executive power and weakening the principle of separation of powers as to criminal procedure and Rechtsstaat (a state governed by rule of law).[18]

In addition, Article 13 para. 3 of the Regulation of the Special Commission on the Investigation of the Truth provides that in the event that the outcome of the investigation conducted by this Commission differs from the facts as determined by a court in its final and conclusive judgment, the opinion maintained by the Commission shall be the standard. This already violates the core of judicial independence and obviously violates Article 18 of the Constitution, since it amounts to an infringement of the core area of the Judicial Yuan.

---

[17] Official translation by Andy Y. Sun for the Judicial Yuan of the Republic of China, <http://www.judicial.gov.tw/constitutionalcourt/EN/p03_01.asp?expno=520> – translators' note.

[18] Official translation by Vincent C. Kuan for the Judicial Yuan of the Republic of China, <http://www.judicial.gov.tw/constitutionalcourt/EN/p03_01.asp?expno=585> – translators' note.

On July 28, 95 [2006], Interpretation No. 614 of the Council of Grand Judges gave an explanation of the question "Are the provisions of Article 12-III of the Enforcement Rules of the Public Functionaries Retirement Act unconstitutional?":

> The modern principle of a constitutional state is specifically manifested by the principle of legal reservation under the Constitution. Not only does it regulate the relations between the state and the people, but it also involves the division of powers and authorities between the executive and legislative branches. If the people's freedoms and rights are not restricted by a measure related to Leistungsverwaltung [expense administration, translators' note] there should be no violation of the principle of legal reservation under Article 23 of the Constitution, which concerns the restriction of fundamental rights of the people. If, however, any significant matter is involved, e.g., public interests or protection of fundamental rights of the people, the competent authority, in principle, should not formulate and issue any regulation without express authorization of the law.[19]

The binding forces of the law: the legislature is bound by the Constitution; administration and judicature are bound by the law

In Taiwan's Constitution, there is also no formulation similar to Article 20 para. 3, sentence 2, of German Basic Law, which states that the constitutional organs (executive, legislative and judicative) are bound by legality and legitimacy (*Gesetz und Recht*). Therefore, generally speaking, only the executive and judicative powers are bound by the laws, but the Council of Grand Judges reviews concrete and abstract violations of the Constitution. For the legislators a free space had developed. But this free space, however, is still bound by the Constitution, meaning that the Constitution is not to be violated. When applying the law, the judicative power does its best to formulate interpretations of the laws in accordance with the Constitution, and this allows the judges to suspend a trial and ask for an interpretation of the Constitution whenever they have profound doubts and believe that there may be a violation of the Constitution. The rule of law state principle starts from the Constitution and the laws which emphasize legality and legitimacy (Gesetz und Recht) as the operational bases for state power. Expressed in terms of the executive, legislative and judicative powers of the Republic of China, it should rather include the direct binding forces of the powers of examination and supervision. Of course, the legislators only have to bear in mind the framework order of the Constitution and the basic order, but the executive and judicative powers, apart from the framework order and basic order of the Constitution, also have to be given the direct binding force of the laws that have been passed by the legislative, i.e. the so-called principles of "administration according to the law" of the executive and of "trials according to the law" of the judicative. Interpretation No. 371 of the Council of Grand Judges states that:

> The Constitution is the state's highest legal authority. Any statute that contradicts the Constitution shall be null and void. Whether a given statute contradicts the Constitution shall be interpreted by the Grand Justices of the Judicial Yuan. The above statement is obvious from Articles 171, 173 and 78, and Article 79, Paragraph 2, of the Constitution. In addition, Article 80 of the Constitution clearly provides that judges shall only try cases in accordance with law. In trying a case, a judge shall base his decision on statutes that have been promulgated and effective in accordance with the legal procedure. A judge shall have no capacity to hold a statute unconstitutional, and shall not

---

[19] Official translation by Vincent C. Kuan for the Judicial Yuan of the Republic of China, <http://www.judicial.gov.tw/constitutionalcourt/EN/p03_01.asp?expno=614> – translators' note.

refuse to apply a statute for that reason. Nonetheless, since the Constitution's authority is higher than the statute's, judges have the obligation to obey the Constitution over any other statutes. Therefore, in trying a case where a judge, with reasonable assurance, has suspected that the statute applicable to the case is unconstitutional, he shall surely be allowed to petition for interpretation of its constitutionality. In the abovementioned situation, judges of different levels may suspend the pending procedure on the ground that the constitutionality of the statute is a prerequisite issue. At the same time, they shall provide concrete reasons for objectively believing the unconstitutionality of the statute, and petition to the Grand Justices of the Yuan to interpret its constitutionality. The provisions of Article 5, Paragraphs 2 and 3, of the Constitutional Interpretation Procedure Act which are inconsistent with the above decision shall no longer be applied.[20]

The Council of Grand Judges' Interpretation No. 572 explains:

When deciding a case, if the judge reasonably believes that the applicable statute may conflict with the Constitution, each instance of court should regard this as a prerequisite issue, suspend the litigation procedures, provide concrete reasoning of its objective belief that the statute violates the Constitution, and petition the Grand Justices for constitutional interpretation pursuant to [Judicial Yuan] Interpretation No. 371. The matter, when the court presiding over the pending case believes that the law at issue violates the Constitution and may clearly affect the ruling of the case, is called the 'prerequisite issue'. 'To provide concrete reasons for objectively believing the unconstitutionality of the statute' signifies that in the petition, the petitioning court is required to describe in detail its interpretation of the statute that violates the Constitution, explain the standard used to interpret the Constitution, and accordingly, provide evidence that it believes the statute is unconstitutional and is objectively without obvious mistakes. If the petitioner only has doubts about whether the statute is unconstitutional or the statute may possibly be reconciled with the requirement for requesting a constitutional interpretation, this is not sufficient to constitute concrete reasons for objectively believing that the statute is unconstitutional.[21]

The hierarchy of the reservation of the law (Vorbehalt des Gesetzes), the hierarchic structure of the law, and the priority of the law (Vorrang des Gesetzes)

The legal structure theory of the hierarchization of law, which was advocated by the representative scholars of the Vienna School of Jurisprudence (*Wiener rechtstheoretische Schule*) H. Kelsen, A.J. Merkl and A. Verdross and its practice in Taiwan by the constitutional interpretation of the Council of Grand Judges is the substantiated hierarchized reservation of law. Although the Council of Grand Judges does not mention the Vienna School of Jurisprudence, legal scholars are well aware that it is written up following the theory of the hierarchization of law. Firstly, on December 26, 86 [1997] the Council of Grand Judges' Interpretation No. 443 put forward the hierarchized reservation of law and the principle of proportionality.

The range of freedom and rights of the people stipulated in the Constitution is very broad. Any freedom and right, which is not in contravention of the order of the society and the public interest, is protected by the Constitution. Nevertheless, not every freedom and right is protected in the same way in the Constitution. The physical freedom of the people is stipulated in detail in Article 8 of

---

[20] Official translation by Jaw-Perng Wang for the Judicial Yuan of the Republic of China, <http://www.judicial.gov.tw/constitutionalcourt/EN/ p03_01.asp?expno=371> – translators' note.

[21] Official translation by Wei-Feng Huang for the Judicial Yuan of the Republic of China, <http://www.judicial.gov.tw/constitutionalcourt/EN/p03_01.asp?expno=572> – translators' note.

the Constitution, in which those rights reserved in the Constitution shall not be limited even by the legislative authority (See J. Y. [Judicial Yuan] Interpretation No. 392), whereas freedom and rights under Articles 7, 9-18, 21 and 22 may be limited by the law upon meeting the conditions stipulated in Article 23 of the Constitution. The determination of which freedom or right shall be regulated by law or by rules authorized by the law shall depend on regulated intensity. Reasonable deviation is allowed considering the party to be regulated, the content of the regulation, or the limitations to be made on the interests or freedom. For instance, depriving people's lives or limiting their physical freedom shall be in compliance with the principle of definitiveness of crime and punishment and stipulated by law; limitations concerning people's other freedoms shall also be stipulated by law, in the case where there is authorization by the law to the administrative institutions to make supplemental rules, the authorization shall be specific and precise. The competent authority, on the ground that such limitations shall not be inconvenient for the people, may make only those limitations concerning details and technical matters of law enforcement. For policies concerning benefit to the people, the law governing such policies may be constructed more loosely compared to laws governing limitations on people's rights. Nevertheless, in the case where such policies are related to major public interests, they shall be made by law or rules authorized by law.[22]

The hierarchized reservation of law in the Council of Grand Judges' Interpretation No. 443 does not only shape the hierarchized legal structure of the rule of law state, but also forms the principle of the structuredness of the Republic's legal system. The influence of this Interpretation pervades the essential conditions which central and local organs at all levels have to take into consideration when stipulating laws.

The principle of legal certainty and specificity of legal authorization [23]
The principle of legal certainty, at the methodological level, pays attention, first of all, to the concepts that are used in the laws. These all comply with the requirements of sufficient and necessary conditions. However, this requirement of the strict concepts in the legal discipline, except in cases that use numeral notions and exact concepts of the natural sciences, probably cannot be fulfilled. Instead, for essential factors of the concept of type (*Typusbegriff*), varying degrees of accuracy have to suffice, and this also applies with regard to satisfying the sufficient and necessary conditions for the conceptual definition. However, the concept of type is not only an important concept in German civil law. As already mentioned, Kunig states that the rule of law state is a concept of type. Therefore, in constitutional law and administrative law, the concept of type is used. In addition, in constitutional law and in administrative law, evaluative legal concepts and indeterminate legal concepts are also used. What does this mean? In the practical affairs of the Council of Grand Judges of the Republic of China, ideas are gradually developed on how indeterminate legal concepts can comply with the requirement of legal certainty. In other words, under which conditions the use of evaluative and indistinctive concepts sufficiently conforms to the requirement of legal certainty becomes an important problem. The requirement of legal certainty is also a decisive factor in a rule of law state concerning the requirement of the stability of the law. The statement of reasoning for the above-

---

[22] Official translation by Chi-chang Yu for the Judicial Yuan of the Republic of China, <http://www.judicial.gov.tw/constitutionalcourt/EN/p03_01.asp?expno=443> – translators' note.

[23] In German: 'Bestimmtheitsgrundsatz' and 'Grundsatz der Normenklarheit' – translators' note.

mentioned Interpretation No. 443 on the hierarchized reservation of law points out, quite unequivocally, that the specificity of authorization is a concept which is guided by the distinctiveness of the law. Methodologically speaking, the legislators do not only use 'sufficient' and 'necessary' legal concepts, but also the 'concept of type' and, in administrative law, even more indeterminate legal concepts. Many Interpretations of the Council of Grand Judges state the conditions that are necessary for indeterminate legal concepts when applying the principle of legal certainty. To put it in simple terms, the meaning of the indeterminate legal concepts that appear in the important documents formed by these legal articles can be understood, and the legal effects of the legal articles can also be predicted. If there is a conflict, the judicial organs can set up an investigation into the potential scope of use of the indistinctive legal concepts. These indistinct legal concepts therefore conform to the principle of legal certainty. Since the Grand Judges have expressed this opinion in many Interpretations, it has become a tradition. For example, in the statement of reasoning for Interpretation No. 636, there is the standard expression:

> In accordance with the rule of law, when statutes are used to restrict people's rights, the statute's constitutive elements shall conform to the principle of legal certainty. This enables the regulated person to foresee the legal consequences of his behaviour in order that the fair notice function of the law is ensured. It further creates clear standards for enforcing the law so as to ensure that the statutory purpose can be achieved. According to this Council's past Interpretations, the concepts used in a statute do not violate the principle of legal certainty if their meanings are not difficult for regulated persons to understand through the statute's text and legislative purpose, and further if the meanings can be confirmed through judicial review (see Interpretations Nos. 432, 491, 521, 594, 602, 617, 623).[24]

The Council of Grand Judges' Interpretation No. 432 on July 11, 86 [1997] marked the first occasion when the principle of legal certainty appeared in the Grand Judges' Interpretations and it can be summarized as follows:

> When professionals are subject to disciplinary measures due to their breach of duties that are required in the practice of professional services, the principle of legal certainty (Rechtsbestimmtheitprinzip) is observed only if there is a predictability regarding which acts or omissions constitute breach of duty and the corresponding disciplinary measures. Even though the legal requirements of disciplinary measures may be expressed in abstract terms, the principle of legal certainty (Rechtsbestimmtheitprinzip) shall still be maintained where indefinite concepts or general clauses are used. The requirement of legal certainty is not meant to be a formal requirement that all legal terms must be definite and exhaustive. During legislation, the legislators may apply indefinite concepts or general clauses to address the complexity of social activities (to be regulated by the law) and the adequacy of the application of the law in specific cases. With respect to the use of abstract terms in the codes of conduct and disciplinary laws governing professionals, the aforementioned principle is not violated if: the meanings of the abstract terms are not incomprehensible, they are predictable for the regulated persons, and they could be scrutinized and defined by the judiciary.[25]

---

[24] Official translation by Jaw-pern Wang and Margaret K. Lewis for the Judicial Yuan of the Republic of China, <http://www.judicial.gov.tw/constitutionalcourt/EN/p03_01.asp?expno=636> – translators' note.

[25] Official tranlsation by Pijan Wu for the Judicial Yuan of the Republic of China, <http://www.judicial.gov.tw/constitutionalcourt/EN/p03_01.asp?expno=432> – translators' note.

However, the tax authorities often violate people's property rights on the basis of administrative decrees to fulfil their basic duty to levy taxes. This goes beyond the content, goal and scope of the legal authorization and increases the limit beyond the law. The Grand Judges have therefore developed the standard criterion of *specificity of legal authorization* in many Interpretations. For example, Interpretation No. 692 of the Council of Grand Judges holds that

> [i]f a taxpayer in Taiwan has children who are twenty years old and studying at the universities in mainland China that are not recognized by the Ministry of Education, the taxpayer may not claim the tax exemption for supporting dependents when filing a final consolidated income tax return.[26]

To limit the application of the income tax law and to add [other] obligations of taxes and levies which are not mentioned in the law violates the principle of taxation by law of Article 19 of the Constitution.

Interpretation No. 674 of the Council of Grand Judges points out:

> The [...] administrative orders [of the Ministry of Finance and the Ministry of Internal Affairs] created additional requirements not provided under the statute concerning the application of agricultural land tax levy to urban odd-shaped lands that cannot be used as building sites by law for construction, but are still used for agricultural purpose contravenes the principle of taxation by law under Article 19 of the Constitution.[27]

Interpretation No. 657 of the Council of Grand Judges explains: Article 82, Paragraph 3 of the Enforcement Rules of the Income Tax Act (Internal Revenue Code) [and] Article 108-1 of the Guidelines for the Audit of Income Taxes on Profit-seeking Enterprises stipulate

> [t]hat profit-seeking enterprises shall convert and list unpaid expenses or losses having exceeded two years from account payables to [the heading of] other revenues under the above-stated regulations so that the income and taxable revenue of that enterprise is increased for the year is obviously not a detailed or technical enforcement issue, and has usurped the authorization of the Income Tax Act, thereby violating the principle of taxation by law under Article 19 of the Constitution. The [provisions in question] should be invalidated no more than one year since the issuance of this Interpretation.[28]

Interpretation No. 650 of the Council of Grand Judges explains:

> [Since the regulations in] Article 36-1, Paragraph 2 of the Guidelines for the Audit of Income Taxes on Profit-Seeking Enterprises, as amended and promulgated on January 13, 1992 [...] lack [...] clear and specific authorization from the Income Tax Act, increases the tax obligation which does not legally exist for tax payers, and contradicts the meaning and purpose of Article 19 of the Constitution, it shall be invalid as of the date this Interpretation is issued.[29]

The Grand Judges' Interpretation No. 640 expounds point seven of the Outline for Simplified Tax Audits of Businesses, Cram Schools, Kindergartens and Nursery Schools which

---

[26] Official translation by Nigel N. T. Li and Jeffrey J. F. Li for the Judicial Yuan of the Republic of China, <http://www.judicial.gov.tw/constitutionalcourt/EN/p03_01.asp?expno=692> – translators' note.

[27] Official translation by Spenser Y. Hor for the Judicial Yuan of the Republic of China, <http://www.judicial.gov.tw/constitutionalcourt/EN/p03_01.asp?expno=674> – translators' note.

[28] Official translation by Lawrence L. C. Lee for the Judicial Yuan of the Republic of China, <http://www.judicial.gov.tw/constitutionalcourt/EN/p03_01.asp?expno=657> – translators' note.

[29] Official translation by Andy Y. Sun for the Judicial Yuan of the Republic of China, <http://www.judicial.gov.tw/constitutionalcourt/EN/p03_01.asp?expno=650> – translators' note.

was issued on May 23, 86 [1997] by the Ministry of Finance, Bureau of Revenue, Northern District of Taiwan:

> Key Point 7 of the Outline provides, 'When conducting paper reviews, the tax agents may examine a random sample of ten percent of the tax returns and further audit taxpayers' bookkeeping records and receipts.' This random audit of individual taxpayers whose income tax filing amount has exceeded the standard income level for a particular kind of business established by the tax collection agency is contrary to Article 80, Paragraph 3, first portion, of the Income Tax Law. It imposes a procedural burden on the tax payer not authorized by the statutes and violates the doctrine of taxation per legislation mandated by Article 19 of the Constitution. Therefore, said Key Point 7 shall become null and void no later than one year from the date of publication of this Interpretation.[30]

The many above-mentioned interpretations of the Grand Judges of the Judicial Yuan show that the principle of legal certainty and the principle of specificity of legal authorization have already matured to become the fundamental standard for the specific characteristic of decisiveness of rule of law state. The Judicial Yuan's Grand Judges are of the opinion that the principle of specificity of legal authorization is a concept that derives from the concept of legal certainty in accordance with the legal principle of the hierarchy of the law. Without the framing order of the legal hierarchy, there would be no such reasoning structure. From the perspective of legal explanation and proof, this kind of discourse formalization at once becomes an important question in the research on the logic of law. The principle of specificity of legal authorization originates in Article 80 of German Basic Law. It was introduced to Taiwan by scholars; Taiwan's Grand Judges were influenced by academia. The principle of specificity of legal authorization was formally introduced in Interpretation No. 313 and has since then found wide application.

In Taiwan's Constitution, a clear explanation is found in Article 5 and Article 150, para. 2, of the Administrative Procedure Act; the related regulations will be explained here in turn. The definition of specificity of authorization is stipulated according to the related regulations in the Administrative Procedure Act and the Interpretations; according to Article 5, the contents of the administrative behaviour should be clear-cut. According to Article 150 para. 2, orders in laws and regulations shall clearly list the basis of their legal authorizations. They are not permitted to go beyond the scope of this legal authorization and the spirit of their legislation. Interpretations No. 313, 602, 604 and other related Interpretations state that, if the law concerning its important components authorizes an order to complement a regulation, the contents and scope of the authorization must be specific and clear; only then will it conform to the intention to restrict people's rights by law as stipulated in Article 23 of the Constitution. From the above, it can be seen that the principle of specificity of legal authorization means that when the Legislative Yuan uses the law to authorize administrative organs to formulate regulations and orders, the "aims, contents and scope" of the authorization must be specific and clear. The standard for deciding whether the legal authorization violates this principle follows the intention of the statement of reasoning of Interpretation No. 443, which is the basis for deciding this principle. The authorization of the related organs derives from the specificity of legal

---

[30] Official translation by Huai-Ching Tsai for the Judicial Yuan of the Republic of China, <http://www.judicial.gov.tw/constitutionalcourt/EN/p03_01.asp?expno=640> – translators' note.

authorization, again, to supplement laws and regulations with legal orders; these should not, however, be substituted solely by administrative rules.

The text of Interpretation No. 524 by the Grand Judges can be summarized as follows:

> National health insurance, having to do with the welfare of all citizens, is a kind of compulsory social insurance; therefore, the rights or obligations relating to the insurance should be clearly defined and regulated by the doctrine of legal reservation. If the enabling statute stipulates the supplementation of its rules in regulations on the contents of insurance relations, the stipulation should be concrete and clear and should be foreseeable by the insured. Furthermore, if the enabling statute authorizes the relevant authority the promulgation of regulations according to some specified procedure to fill the gaps in the statute, the agency should abide by this procedure – it should avoid the form of regulations with administrative rules which have validity only within the administrative organization to substitute for the regulations. If the enabling statute does not provide for further authorization, the agency cannot authorize its subordinate agencies to promulgate those related rules.[31]

The principle of the rule of law state attaches importance to the stability of the law and the protection of legitimate expectations and the prohibition of the retroactive application of the law

The subjective level of the protection of legitimate expectations emerges in the "Principle of the Protection of Legitimate Expectations" which is stated in the Council of Grand Judges' Interpretation No. 525:

> Once an administrative ordinance is proclaimed effective, the authority responsible for drafting or proclaiming such regulation shall protect the legitimate expectations of subjects affected by the regulation when seeking to amend or abolish such regulation pursuant to legal procedures. So unless the regulation has a predetermined period for application or there is a change of circumstance which leads to its ineffectiveness, in which instance there is no legitimate expectation, authorities seeking to abolish or amend the regulation for public interest, to the effect that such action abridges the privileges of those who had a legitimate expectation of enjoying these privileges, shall provide reasonable measures of remediation or transition period clauses with a view to minimize loss, thus complying with the Constitution's objective to protect the people's rights.[32]

At the same time, the Administrative Procedure Act [contains the following regulations concerning legitimate expectations]: Article 117 of the [Administrative Procedure Act] stipulates:

> The authority rendering an unlawful administrative disposition may withdraw ex officio the disposition in whole or in part upon the lapse of the statutory period of remedy; the same may be done by its superior authority; provided, however, that no withdrawal may be made under any of the following circumstances:
> 1. Where withdrawal will result in serious jeopardy to the public interest;
> 2. Where the beneficiary has not done any of the acts specified in Art. 119 hereof, making him deserves no protection of his reliance, and the benefit granted him by the administrative

---

[31] Official translation by Tze-Shiou Chien for the Judicial Yuan of the Republic of China, <http://www.judicial.gov.tw/constitutionalcourt/EN/p03_01.asp?expno=524> – translators' note.

[32] Official translation by Wei-Feng Huang for the Judicial Yuan of the Republic of China, <http://www.judicial.gov.tw/constitutionalcourt/EN/p03_01.asp?expno=525> – translators' note.

disposition because of his reliance is obviously greater than the public interest intended to be protected by way of withdrawal of the disposition.[33]

Article 118 of the Administrative Procedure Act reads:

An unlawful administrative disposition shall become null and void retroactively upon withdrawal; provided that, a different date of annulment may be specified by the authority ordering the withdrawal for the purpose of protecting the public interest or preventing property loss of the beneficiary.[34]

And Article 19 of the Administrative Procedure Act stipulates:

A beneficiary who has done any of the following acts deserves no protection of his reliance:

1. Causing the administrative authority to render an administrative disposition by way of fraud, coercion or bribery;

2. Furnishing incorrect information or making incomplete statement, thereby causing the administrative authority to render an administrative disposition based on such information or statement; and

3. Having knowledge that the administrative disposition is unlawful or failing to know that it is unlawful due to his gross negligence.[35]

As a result of the Grand Judges' Interpretations mentioned above, under the rule of law state, the people do not only trust that the administrative organs' behaviour of administration will be according to the law, but are also able to have confidence in abstract laws. Therefore, the protection of legitimate expectations is a most important argument for the people if they find reason to believe that their rights are violated by administrative organs. Following the widening application of the protection of legitimate expectations, the Grand Judges have further developed their Interpretations of individual cases and this is the active protection of the citizens' rights. However, since there are provisions for the protection of legitimate expectations in the Administrative Procedure Act, the Highest Administrative Court can also use the developed and active protection of rights. Here, the division of labour for human rights can be observed between the constitutional court and the ordinary courts. This has become a topic of hot debate in recent years in Germany. In Taiwan, we should also consider this kind of division.

The three phase examination of the means and ends of the principle of proportionality, the introduction of the low, middle and high standard criteria of examination density in US law, and the legacy of Alexy's weighting formula

Article 23 of the Constitution of the Republic of China stipulates the restriction of fundamental rights. It is possible to add restrictions in order to "prevent infringement upon the freedoms of other persons, to avert an imminent crisis, to maintain the social order or to advance the public welfare".[36] During the martial law period, the Grand Judges showed a relaxed attitude towards the constitutionality of the restriction of fundamental rights. They seemed to be of the opinion that, based on the consideration and discussion of one of the above-mentioned four conditions, it was possible to restrict fundamental rights. However,

---

[33] Official translation: <http://db.lawbank.com.tw/Eng/FLAW/FLAWDAT0201.asp> – translators' note.

[34] Official translation: <http://db.lawbank.com.tw/Eng/FLAW/FLAWDAT0201.asp> – translators' note.

[35] Official translation: <http://db.lawbank.com.tw/Eng/FLAW/FLAWDAT0201.asp> – translators' note.

[36] Official translation by Fuldien Li for the Judicial Yuan of the Republic of China, <http://www.judicial.gov.tw/constitutionalcourt/EN/p03_01.asp?expno=497> – translators' note.

after the lifting of martial law and following the three stages of examination of the aims and measures of German law and the three stages of examination density in US Law, the examination of the proportionality principle was strengthened. Thus, in many Interpretations, it was stated that the principle of proportionality of law and, with this, the Constitution, had been violated. Recently, with regard to Interpretations No. 699 and 689, although the law that had been examined did conform to the principle of proportionality and was therefore constitutional, its scope of application had already been enormously restricted due to the strict demands of the principle of proportionality. Interpretation No. 699, for example, states that

> Article 35, the preceding part of Paragraph 4 of the Road Traffic Management Penalties Regulation states that motor vehicle operators who refuse to accept the sobriety test of alcohol concentration according to the first Paragraph, first Subparagraph, of the same Article, will be suspended of their driver's license. Article 67, the preceding part of Paragraph 2, of the Road Traffic Management Penalties Regulation further stipulates that motor vehicle operators who violate Article 35, the preceding part of Paragraph 4 will be suspended of his or her license, and be prohibited from taking/receiving a driver's license for three years. As promulgated and amended on December 14, 2005, Article 68 of the same Regulation furthermore states that a motor vehicle operator whose license was suspended due to Article 35, the preceding part of Paragraph 4, would be suspended of all classes of vehicle licenses. The above provisions do not contravene the principle of proportionality of Article 23 of the Constitution, and do not violate the constitutional safeguards of people's freedom of movement and right to work.[37]

Another example is Article 68 of the same regulation which was amended and promulgated on December 14, 94 [2005], which further stipulates that all the driving licences held by a motor vehicle operator whose license has been suspended in accordance with the preceding part of paragraph 4 of Article 35, should be revoked.

The above provisions are not yet in conflict with the principle of proportionality or Article 23 of the Constitution, nor do they violate the intention of the constitutional protection of people's freedom of movement and right to work. Interpretation No. 690 reads:

> Article 37, Paragraph 1 of the Communicable Disease Control Act, revised January 30, 2002, provides: 'Any person who had physical contacts with patients of contagious diseases, or suspected of being infected, shall be detained and checked by the competent authority, and if necessary, shall be ordered to move into designated places for further examinations, or to take other necessary dispositions, including immunization, etc.' As far as the provision of necessary dispositions is read to include compulsory quarantine, hence deprivation of personal freedom, said provision neither violates the principle of legal certainty, nor the principle of proportionality implicit in Article 23 of the Constitution. It also does not violate the due process requirement of Article 8 of the Constitution.[38]

Interpretation No. 689 can be summarized as follows:

> Article 89, Paragraph 2 of the Social Order Maintenance Act aims to protect a person's freedom of movement, freedom from bodily and mental harms, freedom from intrusion with reasonable expectation in the public space and the right to autonomous control of personal information, and to

---

[37] Official translation by Spenser Y. Hor for the Judicial Yuan of the Republic of China, <http://www.judicial.gov.tw/constitutionalcourt/en/p03_01.asp?expno=699> – translators' note.

[38] Official translation by Huai-Ching R. Tsai for the Judicial Yuan of the Republic of China, <http://www.judicial.gov.tw/constitutionalcourt/en/p03_01.asp?expno=690> – translators' note.

punish a stalking behaviour which has been urged to stop yet continues without any legitimate reason. We find the Provision at issue does not violate the principle of legal certainty. A journalist's following in person shall be considered to have legitimate reasons and shall not be subject to penalty by the aforementioned provision if judging from the facts a specific event is of concern to the public, of public interest, and newsworthy, it is not intolerable under the general social standard. Within this scope, although the aforementioned provision places a limit on the behaviour of newsgathering, it is appropriate and proportionate and does not contradict the freedom of newsgathering provided by Article 11 of the Constitution or people's right to work guaranteed by Article 15 of the Constitution. Furthermore, the provision at issue delegating the power of sanction to police authorities also does not violate the principle of due process of law. The purpose of enacting the Provision at issue is not to restrict the behaviour of newsgathering. If the indirect restriction on freedom of newsgathering aims to pursue important public interests and the applied method is substantively related to achieve the objective, it is not contradictory to the principle of proportionality.[39]

All of these are appropriate examples.

Furthermore, the Interpretations of the Grand Judges apply the principle of proportionality. It is forbidden to apply the principle of proportionality outside the statutory objectives. For example, they point out that fingerprint filing, although it does not specifically mention the rule of law state principle, still emphasizes the practice of the principle of proportionality in the protection of data privacy. They state that the required protection measures must be implemented in organizations and procedures, and give a clear explanation in a standard form of the high examination density of the proportionality principle. The organizational and procedural functions of fundamental rights under German law are also introduced as an important factor under the rule of law state principle. The state is based on the objectives of specially designated "public goods". The necessity for large scale [data] collecting, compiling records of people's fingerprints and establishing material databases requires a law that clearly states the objectives of the large – scale collection of data. The collecting of such data must be necessary for and closely connected with the accomplishing of public objectives and its use outside the statutory objectives must be prohibited. The authorities concerned should, above all else, combine contemporary scientific and technological development and employ methods which are sufficient to guarantee that the information is accurate and safe. With regard to the collected fingerprint records, they should undertake the necessary organizational and procedural protection measures in order to conform to the original intention of the Constitution to guarantee the data privacy of the people. The decisive elements of the specific characteristic of the rule of law state in German Law all contain the proportionality principle. According to Alexy's theory on the principles of fundamental rights, the proportionality principle is a weighting model of means and ends for resolving fundamental rights conflicts and a solution model for conflicting fundamental rights, i.e. it is a weighting model for the principle of proportionality. Under the circumstances that two fundamental rights are in conflict with each other, a weighting of the proportionality prin-ciple can produce a standoff situation. In this kind of standoff situation, Alexy expresses the opinion that, in accordance with the rule of law state as the forming structure

---

[39] Official translation by Hsiaowei Kuan for the Judicial Yuan of the Republic of China: <http://www.judicial.gov.tw/constitutionalcourt/EN/p03_01.asp?expno=689> – translators' note.

principle, the fundamental rights' values that are proposed by the legislators enjoy preferential application. His standpoint is that the rule of law state principle and the proportionality principle appearing in the legal debate can produce the decisive function of value judgement in cases when fundamental rights are in a standoff situation.

Effective remedy

In recent years, the prevailing view of scholars has been that, according to Article 16 of the Constitution, the people have the right to appeal and the right to administrative lawsuits, i.e. "where there is a right, there is a remedy". This is the idea of the modern Constitution. Therefore, special power relations should be brought into the domain of law, so that in legal disputes, the administrative court's judgements are accepted. The rights and interests that people enjoy in particular power relations are not in any way inferior to those that exist in ordinary power relations.

For example, the positions and pensions of government employees and the academic degrees awarded to them by educational organs are not comparable in any way to ordinary property rights. While ordinary property rights do not go through cautious legal procedures and [still] "give the involved person an opportunity of account or of relief" and must not be taken away, the former particular rights should be given even more opportunity of relief.

Interpretation No. 684 says:

> When a university makes administrative decisions or other public authority measures for realizing educational purposes of seeking academic truth and cultivating talents or for maintaining the campus order, if the decisions or measures infringe the student's right to education or other constitutional rights, even if the decisions or measures are not expulsions or similar decisions, based on the mandate that where there is a right, there is a remedy under Article 16 of the Constitution, the student whose right has been infringed shall be allowed to bring administrative appeal and litigation and there is no need to place special restrictions.[40]

Interpretation No. 653 explains:

> Based on the principle - where there is a right, there is a remedy, when a person's right is infringed, the state shall provide such a person an opportunity to institute legal proceedings in court, to request a fair trial by due process of law, and to obtain timely and effective remedies. This is the core substance safeguarded by the right of action [...], which shall not be deprived of by reason of the status of a detainee [...]. When weighing factors such as type and nature of cases, policy and purposes of litigation, effective distribution of judicial resources, for enacting laws to impose limitation on the tier of courts for appeal, procedures, and relevant requirements to be followed in seeking remedy through lawsuit or authorizing a government agency to issue administrative orders for the same purpose, the Legislature should do in compliance with the requirements of article 23 of the Constitution so as not to contradict the intent contemplated by the Constitution in guaranteeing people's right to sue.[41]

---

[40] Official translation by C. L. Chen for the Judicial Yuan of the Republic of China, <http://www.judicial.gov.tw/constitutionalcourt/EN/p03_01.asp?expno=684> – translators' note.

[41] Official translation by Huai-Ching Tsai for the Judicial Yuan of the Republic of China, <http://www.judicial.gov.tw/constitutionalcourt/EN/p03_01.asp?expno=653> – translators' note.

Interpretation No. 418 cites Article 16 of the Constitution:

> The issue of whether a relief to a lawsuit should be sought in accordance with the ordinary litigation proceedings or in accordance with the administrative litigations is a matter to be formulated by the legislative authorities taking into account the nature of the lawsuit and the functions of the existing litigation system. Article 87 of the Act Governing the Punishment of Violation of Road Traffic Regulations stipulates that if the offender is dissatisfied with the punishment imposed by the competent authority for traffic violations, the offender may raise an objection to the competent district court, and may appeal the ruling rendered by the district court to the High Court in the event that the offender is dissatisfied with the ruling; however, the offender may not further appeal to the Supreme Court.[42]

This procedure, since it already gives the involved persons the opportunity to defend themselves and to bring forward evidence, conforms with the proper legal procedure. There is also Interpretation No. 396 which explains the people's right to litigate:

> The right of the people to institute legal proceedings under Article 16 of the Constitution is an entitlement to systematic safeguard of relief which is available when their rights are violated. The actual content of such right can only be affected through stipulation of laws relating to the organization of courts and the litigation procedures by the legislative authorities. Since the safeguarding of the people's right to litigation lies at the core of the Constitution, and is a basic prerequisite for the right to litigation, any lack whereof shall conflict with the intent of Article 16 of the Constitution in relation to safeguarding of the people's right to litigation.[43]

According to Interpretation No. 243[44], the legal principle that where there is a right, there is a remedy, means that the core contents of the guarantee of right to litigate lies in the demonstration of the people's right to appeal to legal courts of justice for relief and that this right cannot easily be taken away. The system of the levels of trial which guarantees the right to litigate must be decided by the legislative authorities overseeing the nature of each kind of lawsuit. As their employment relations are in the sector of public law, public functionaries must face disciplinary action when their conduct violates the Constitution or

---

[42] Official translation by David T. Liou for the Judicial Yuan of the Republic of China, <http://www.judicial.gov.tw/constitutionalcourt/EN/p03_01.asp?expno=418> – translators' note.

[43] Official translation by Baker & McKenzie for the Judicial Yuan of the Republic of China, <http://www.judicial.gov.tw/constitutionalcourt/EN/p03_01.asp?expno=396> – translators' note.

[44] Summary of Interpretation No. 243: "An administrative decision made by either a central or a local government authority to remove a public functionary from his office pursuant to the provisions of the Public Functionaries Merit Evaluation Act or other applicable laws and/or regulations has a direct impact on the constitutionally guaranteed right of such public functionary to hold public office. Therefore, such jpublic functionary may, as a matter of course, exercise his right to file an administrative appeal or right to sue as provided for under Article 16 of the Constitution. Such public functionary has petitioned the competent authorities and the personnel authorities, respectively, for a review and a second review of the decision at issue pursuant to relevant laws and, by doing so or resorting to other similar procedures to petition for relief, an administrative appeal and re-appeal proceeding should be deemed to have been sought. If such public functionary is not satisfied with the decisions of the aforesaid authorities, he should be allowed to institute an administrative litigation so as to bring the matter in line with the legal principle that there is a remedy where there is a right" (Official translation by Vincent C. Kuan for the Judicial Yuan of the Republic of China, <http://www.judicial.gov.tw/constitutionalcourt/EN/p03_01.asp?expno=243>–translators' note).

when they neglect their duties. The Constitution clearly defines the scope of the judicial power. The resolution of the Committee on the Discipline of Public Functionaries on a punishment case, although the Public Functionaries Discipline Act stipulates otherwise, is still not the final decision, because the system for the appeal for relief has still not yet been established. It could be argued that this violates Article 16 of the Constitution. In line with the doctrine of 'where there is a right there is a remedy', to avoid the piling up of appeals, meaning yearlong law suits that can last over generations (*liulang fating 30 nian* 流浪法庭 30 年) and to facilitate the overcoming of the past which is expressed in the compensation for miscarriages of justice (criminal compensation), further implementations of the rule of law state principle are required, such as, immediate and effective administrative relief (by lodging a complaint against a lower government organization with a higher one; compensation) and (full) judicial relief. And the legislation of the Criminal Speedy Trial Act, in recent years, also demonstrates the implementation of the rule of law state principle.

Conclusion: Future challenges to the principle of the rule of law state in Taiwan

The decisive elements of the special characteristic of the rule of law state are mainly the 'understanding of', the 'faith in' and the 'appropriateness of' the law and the 'effective remedies'. These key elements mentioned above are implemented step-by-step, so that they become part of the common knowledge of the people.

However, the determining factor of the special characteristic of the rule of law state is actually that of forming an outline by using the induction method. In ordinary discussions, the people and the legal scholars have a gap in their understanding of the special characteristics of the rule of law state. This gap derives from the Grand Judges' Interpretations which cite the hermeneutics of German constitutional studies and the quintessence of the US constitutional studies in legal comparisons which are formed by them. This kind of influence will still continue in Taiwan's future constitutional Interpretations. At the current stage, the author of this article has observed the following challenges to the future of the rule of law state in Taiwan:

1. With regard to the aspect of the division of powers, it is necessary to continue the reflective thinking and the reform of the constitutional system as well as the dynamic equilibrium of the checks and balances of powers. For example, the power of administrative legislation should not belong to the government and should not be united with it, because this leads to a lack of clarity regarding the function of legislation and the slowing down of policy implementation by the administrative power. In addition, with regard to the aspect of the supervision of the administration, the Control Yuan must be strengthened to ensure that administrative supervision does not become only a powerless instrument for rectification and impeachment only a formality.

2. The requirement of the stability of law and the complete trust of the people in the law can be extended to their faith in the judicature. However, in Taiwan at the present time, the judicature has low credibility among the public. According to Luhman's system theory, the connection of the structures of the judicature and the political system and their interactive communications need to be strengthened. Taiwan's present judicial system is

extremely tightly closed, which can easily lead to its perceiving itself as perfect[45] and to the fossilization of the system. The judicial system must therefore broaden its collective 'mind' and become more active. This means that the Judicial Yuan, which currently has the task of socializing the judicature, must take care not to overdo its own self-reproduction, which would lead to a judicature which has no emotions, which is far away from the feelings of the people and which is not able to gain the people's trust.

3. The understanding of the dual nature of the essential idea of law,[46] that is, the reality and validity of law, the legality and legitimacy of law, should be matched more closely together. Therefore, with regard to the requirement of legal certainty, at the academic level, it will be even more necessary to focus the attention of legal studies on analyses of the achievements of scientific theories and philosophical hermeneutics.

4. The importance of promoting communication in the constitutional dialogue between Taiwan and the PR China. From the perspective of Smend's constitutional integration theory (*Integrationslehre*)[47], the positive development of the Constitution will bring about a positive integrating function. The constitutional academic exchange will enhance the mutual understanding of the similarities and differences in the two Constitutions. Supported by a comparative study of the European and US Constitutions, the contact between the two sides and the enhanced understanding of the two Constitutions could give rise to opportunities for change and integration.

5. The discussion on the democratic rule of law state and the democratic constitutional state of Taiwan, due to the interpretation system of the Judicial Yuan's Grand Judges, has already reached appropriate levels in the working standards of the constitutional organs and the protection of human rights, and therefore conforms to the democratic constitutional state advocated by Alexy.

Of course, according to Alexy, under the rule of law state principle, in cases of doubt, the legislators have priority, which means that the law of the legislators should have priority. But in Taiwan, in cases of doubt, the Grand Judges' Interpretations will have effective priority. The above analysis shows that the constitutional interpretation of judicial power still takes into consideration the special characteristics of the rule of law state; it maintains an active stance towards the interpretation of the Constitution in the context of fundamental rights, but in the context of the interpretation of the Constitution within the organization

---

45 The most important work in Luhmann's Sociology of Law is "Law as a Social System" (Das Recht der Gesellschaft). Luhmann describes, in particular, the closedness of the legal system's operations. Although the external environment influences the legal system, the content of the law can only be decided within the legal system. In other words, stimuli from the external environment must be transformed into signs of the legal system itself, only then can they become a part of the legal system. Luhmann's description of the legal system conforms, to a great extent, to the present conditions of Taiwan's judicative system. For reference, see Luhmann 1993: 38 ff. For the application of Luhmann's system theory to fundamental rights, see Aulehner 2011: 79 ff.

46 For reference, see Alexy 2011: 389-404.

47 For Smend's viewpoint on constitutional integration theory, see Wu 2004: 10 f. On the whole, integration theory touches upon the substance of the state. According to Smend's integration theory, the state is not to be seen as an organization, but as a psychological entirety. The integrated system: 1. The entire state is constantly in a process of renewal. 2. The consciousness of community renews the concretizing process. See Smend 1994: 136 f.

of a constitutional government, it is self-restricting. At the same time, however, the contributions of the Constitution and the law on stability and continuity have caused the long term containment of Taiwan's administrative and legislative powers. Taiwan's rule of law is still developing but already serves to uphold fundamental rights and ensures the protection of the Constitution.

References

Alexy, Robert (1985) *Theorie der Grundrechte*, 1. Edition, Baden-Baden: Nomos Verlagsgesellschaft.

Alexy, Robert (1988) "Die Institutionalisierung der Menschenrechte im demokratischen Verfassungsstaat", in Gosepath, Stefan and Georg Lohmann (eds.) *Philosophie der Menschenrechte*, Frankfurt am Main: Suhrkamp, pp.244-264.

Alexy, Robert (2003) „Die Gewichtsformel", in Jickeli, Joachim, Peter Kreutz and Dieter Reuter (eds.) *Gedächtnisschrift für Jürgen Sonnenschein*, Berlin: De Gruyter, pp. 771-792.

Alexy, Robert (2011) "Die Doppelnatur des Rechts", in *Der Staat* 50, pp. 389-404.

Aulehner, Josef (2011) *Grundrechte und Gesetzgebung*, Tübingen : Mohr Siebeck.

Badura, Peter and Horst Dreier (eds.) (2001) *Festschrift 50 Jahre Bundesverfassungsgericht*, Tübingen : Mohr Siebeck.

Kunig, Philip (1986) *Das Rechtsstaatsprinzip : Überlegungen zu seiner Bedeutung für das Verfassungsrecht der Bundesrepublik Deutschland*, Tübingen : Mohr Siebeck.

Kunig, Philip (2001) "Der Rechtsstaat", in Badura, Peter and Horst Dreier (eds.) *Festschrift 50 Jahre Bundesverfassungsgericht*, Tübingen : Mohr Siebeck.

Kunig, Philip (2009) Rechtsstaatliche Determinanten des deutschen Verwaltungsrechts unter Berücksichtigung europäischer Einflüsse (*Ouzhoufa yingxiang xia zhi deguo xingzhengfa de juedingxing yaosu* 歐洲法影響下之德國行政法中法治國的決定性要素), Lecture in Taipei, 27.3.2009, pp.1-17.

Luhmann, Niklas (1993) *Das Recht der Gesellschaft*, Frankfurt am Main: Suhrkamp.

Papier, Hans-Jürgen (2004) "Das Bundesverfassungsgericht als 'Hüter der Grundrechte'", in Brenner, Michael, Peter Huber and Markus Möstl (eds.) *Der Staat des Grundgesetzes – Kontinuität und Wandel, Festschrift für Peter Badura zum siebzigsten Geburtstag*, Tübingen: Mohr Siebeck, pp.411-429.

Schulze-Fielitz, Helmuth (2006) "Art. 20 (Rechtsstaat)", in Dreier, Horst (ed.) *Grundgesetz-Kommentar*, Vol. 2, 2. edition, pp. 170-277.

Smend, Rudolf (1994) "Verfassung und Verfassungsrecht", in Smend, Rudolf (ed.) *Staatsrechtliche Abhandlungen und andere Aufsätze*, 3. Edition, Berlin: Duncker&Humblot, pp. 119-276.

Sobota, Katharina (1997) *Das Prinzip Rechtsstaat: Verfassungs- und verwaltungsrechtliche Aspekte*, Tübingen : Mohr Siebeck.

Sunstein, Cass R. (1999*) One Case at a Time: Judicial Minimalism on the Supreme Court*, Cambridge, Mass.: Harvard University Press.

Weng, Yueh-sheng (2004) "Die Verfassungskontrolle durch richterliche Fortbildung, die Geschichte von Taiwan's Judicial Activism", in Brenner, Michael, Peter Huber and Markus Möstl (eds.) *Der Staat des Grundgesetzes – Kontinuität und Wandel, Festschrift für Peter Badura zum siebzigsten Geburtstag*, Tübingen: Mohr Siebeck, pp .1219-1243.

Wu Geng 吳庚 (2004) *Xianfa de jieshi yu shiyong* 宪法的解释与使用 [The Interpretation and Application of the Constitution], 3. Edition, Taipei: San Min.

Wu Geng 吳庚 (2008) *Xingzhengfa zhi lilun yu shiyong* 行政法之理论与实用 [The Theory and Application of Adminstrative Law], 10. Edition, Taipei: San Min.

Zhu Yi

Forum: Who's Afraid of the "Big Bad" Criminal Procedure Law? – Public Participation in China's Legislation

Big bad wolf or Virginia Woolf? – ambivalent perception of the Criminal Procedure Law Amendment

The Criminal Procedure Law (CPL) Draft Amendment was released in August 2011 and approved in March 2012. It aroused heated debates in China's public sphere, especially the Internet, where negative terms abounded: secret detention, enforced disappearance, police-state, retrogression in constructing rule of law, etc. Article 73 of the CPL (which, in essence, referred to "secret detention") was the sixth most searched for keyword in March 2012 on Baidu, China's most popular search engine. Apart from Article 73, the other keywords of the Baidu ranking list were more generally comprehensible, for example, the "legal age for marriage", "social security", "what 10 yuan can buy", etc.[1] The image of the CPL amendment was like that of the "big bad wolf" in the Disney cartoon, which everybody loves to hate.

The debate surrounding this Amendment is worth further study, because amendments to the laws are usually too specialized to become a common topics of discussion. For example, the Amendment to the Civil Procedure Law in the same year drew far less attention than the Criminal Procedure Law. Actually, the opposite should be the case, since ordinary Chinese people do not tend to regard themselves as potential defendants in criminal proceedings.

According to an article in people.com in March 2012, 97.2% of the Microbloggers stated that they were concerned about the CPL amendment in a survey launched by sina weibo, China's most used social media tools. However, 65% said that they "don't completely understand" or "don't really understand" the contents of the CPL, 20% said that they were only "bystanders", and only 9% said that they "have been studying CPL" (People.com.cn 03.2012). In this respect, CPL is like the works of Virginia Woolf in that few people can understand them either. This being the case, how has the amendment of the CPL become a popular topic? Who has been the main force of the agenda-setting in the public debate? How will Internet discussions influence China's legislation or other political decision-making processes? These questions are the focus of this essay.

Premise for the public debate: public participation in legislation and the development of Internet

Open act is the premise for a public debate on law amendments. The first law that was put out for public comment after Reform and Opening was the 1982 Constitution, but, here closer inspection reveals, the discussion actually was led top-down. According to Wang Hanbin, who was, at that time, the director of the NPC Legislative Affairs Office, "under the leadership of party committees, the people's congresses at various levels organized symposia to preach and discuss the draft" (Wang 2011). Ordinary Chinese people had few opportunities for active participation, and could express their ideas only if they were invited and "organized" into the discussion.

---

[1] See <http://hot.baidu.com/201203/index.html#n1.>, accessed 10 May 2012.

Since 2000, the Chinese public sphere has been undergoing profound changes. The rise of the commercial media and the Internet has facilitated and lowered the cost of accessing information and provided opportunities for people to express their opinions. Meanwhile, demands for participation in the decision-making processes and for the protection of individual interests have been steadily increasing, particularly in the media and Internet.

The 2000 Legislation Law includes the provision that legislation should ensure people's participation in the lawmaking process through various channels. In January 2001, the Amendment to the Marriage Law was published on the NPC website for public comment, and received more than 4,000 comments from the public, which marked the highest share of public participation at that time and was the first time that the Chinese people were able to participate in legislation via the Internet.

The draft version of the Property Law in 2005 received more than 10,000 comments. According to media reports at that time, most people involved themselves in the legislation via the Internet. The Amendment to the Labor Contract Law in 2006 received more than 200,000 comments. The Amendment to the Tax Law in 2011 received more than 230,000 comments, which was clearly an unprecedented result.

In 2008, the NPC Standing Committee's Meeting of Chairmen resolved to publish all law drafts that were to be examined by the NPC, in principle, on the NPC website for public comment. In this way, open act has been institutionalized and recognized by the public.

Changes in social structure in the public sphere and changes in the role played by experts

In contrast to Marriage Law and Tax Law, the CPL is so specialized that any discussion on it must be led by experts. The experts who played an active role in the CPL-debate fall into 3 categories: firstly, experts within the system (*tizhinei zhuanjia* 体制内专家), secondly, experts from outside the system, that is, legal professionals and journalists as one group, and thirdly, Deputies to the People's Congress.

Experts within the system

The authorities assumed that by inviting experts to the closed-door symposia, they had already achieved "public participation". These experts may have felt it an honor to be acknowledged by the authorities and they might have believed that some of their suggestions would be adopted. However, they may also have noticed that they could wield more influence in the public sphere via the media. For example, Professor Chen Guangzhong: As President of China University of Political Science and Law, he played a leading role in the discussions on the proposal to amend the CPL in 1996 and has attended symposia on the CPL Amendment on four occasions. On August 17, 2011, prior to the release of the CPL Amendment, Chen introduced the highlights of the amendment and the obstacles to it, in an interview with *Southern Metropolis Daily* (Chen 2011). He also cautiously indicated that the "practical departments" were the reasons for obstacles. The content of the draft amendment released on August 30 was far beyond people's expectations and led to critical discussions on the Internet and in the media. Simultaneously, Chen Guangzhong's comments became more clear and critical: such phrases as "I don't agree"; "this is retrogression" were frequently used in his interviews to express his critical opinion of the Amendment. In March 2012, with a front-cover story entitled "A ten-year battle:

legislator vs. enforcer" (Yao 2012), the *China Economic Weekly* published an interview with Chen and other experts, who had also been invited to the symposia on the CPL Amendment that were organized by the authorities. In the interview, the law-enforcing departments were criticized for their backwardness in comparison to the legislation experts. The report even unveiled the power struggle between the public security department and the Procuratorate.

At the end of 2011, the NPC's Standing Committee undertook a second examination of the draft and replaced "Reviewing the death penalty cases, the Supreme People's Court **should** interrogate the defendant" with "The Supreme People's Court **can** interrogate the defendant", which met with fierce criticism from Chen. He stated in various interviews and TV talks that this was the "greatest retrogression". Finally, the word "can" was changed back to "should" in the approved version.

Journalists, lawyers, and the experts from outside the system (public intellectuals)
This group of experts is the most important force in pushing forward China's civil society and social justice, because they have professions and have a platform for disseminating information. Meanwhile, since they are outside the system, they often need to support each other and "fight jointly". A good example is the case of Sun Zhigang in 2003[2].

Some media practitioners suffered official retaliation and were jailed for reporting the case of Sun Zhigang (obviously the trial had violated the CPL). Lawyers are also among the vulnerable groups in China's judicial system: article 306 of criminal law, under which lawyers can be accused of perjury, has become the lawyers' "Sword of Damocles", and article 38 of the CPL echoes this. Public intellectuals who criticize the authorities mainly via the media and the Internet are taking risks under the current political system. They still remember Ai Weiwei's being taken into custody illegally in April 2011. These three professional groups are therefore most aware of the CPL amendment; they are also the most active players in the Internet discussion, because they are aware of the dangers inherent in any expansion of state power.

On August 30, the draft CPL was published; on August 31, Wang Heyan, a famous investigative journalist belonging to the Caixin media group, wrote a report called "The revision of Criminal Procedure Law to set back the wheel of history", leading to his "secret arrest". Spread and reproduced by many websites, this article became the most influential of the day. On that same day, Lei Yi, a history scholar, under the subject heading of "Too Terrible", criticized the clauses related to secret arrest in his *sina* microblog. This microblog was forwarded 20,000 times and commented by 7,000 people within 24 hours. The negative image of the draft of the CPL was established in one day, while the efforts of officials to produce a "progressive image" have been weakened.

A great number of journalists, lawyers and scholars now voice their opinions via blogs and microblogs, among them are famous opinion leaders such as the journalist Chen Baocheng, the poet Ye Kuangzheng, the lawyers Chen Youxi and Si Weijiang, the

---

[2] Sun Zhigang was detained and beaten to death in police custody in Guangzhou as he didn't take his ID card with him. Media reports on this tragedy caused national outcry. Lawyers and legal intellectuals sent open letters demanding a review of the so called *Detention and Repatriation System*. Under the huge public pressure, China's State Council abolished the regulation on the "Custody and Repatriation of Vagrants and Beggars in Cities".

scholars He Weifang and Xiao Han, who all have tens and hundreds thousands of fans. Every remark they make has a profound influence.

Representatives of the Two Sessions (NPC and CPPCC)
The representatives entered the game in the final stage of the revision of the draft–before the vote. It is well-known that 70% of China's National People's Congress (NPC) representatives are party members. The representatives that I am going to refer to are special cases, however, and their actions deserve special mention.
On March 7, the lawyer Chi Susheng, an NPC representative, wrote on her microblog, "I have finally got hold of the draft of the revised CPL." This drew a quick reaction on the Internet: people believed that the procedure violated Article 15 of the Legislation Law, which requires the representatives to obtain draft laws and amendments one month in advance of the convening of the Congress.
On March 8, Chen Zhilun, a Chinese People's Political Consultative Conference (CPPCC) representative, told the media: "The CPPCC does not have the right to make laws, but can't we even make suggestions? Many representatives know nothing about the draft. Some of them have submitted a joint protest letter to the NPC."
On March 11, the legal scholar Wang Mingwen, an NPC representative, put out an entry on his microblog during the conference, "The revised draft CPL was reviewed in the morning; the crucial points have not been changed in this version."
On the same day, the journalist Chen Baocheng and the Non-Governmental Organization member Xiong Wei, argued on a website that the procedure was in violation of the Legislation Law and appealed for a postponement of the vote on the draft law. The investor Xu Manzi launched a poll on *sina* microblog, in which more than ten thousand people participated: 93% of them voted to "delay the NPC decision". However, in spite of all these efforts, the revised CPL was passed on March 14, with 2,639 affirmative, 160 negative and 57 abstention votes.
The entire process of the CPL debate reveals the lack of conformity between the social structures in the public sphere and reality. In China's real society, the public authorities, NPC representatives and experts within the system comprise a tight-knit circle, which can make decisions and ignore opinions coming from outside. As the lawyer Ding Jinkun mocked in his blogs: the revision of the CPL was "proposed by functional departments, polished by experts, adopted by representatives and decided by leaders" (Ding 2011). It was "a big victory for the public security departments". However, scholars both within the system and outside it, jointly with journalists, lawyers and some representatives, worked closely together and tried to enhance their influence through the mass media. Supported by netizens, they have continued to express their opinions loudly. In contrast, the voices of public security and state prosecution organs are rarely heard throughout the process. This consolidated their negative image of being stubborn and backward and left them in the position of marginalized groups in the debate. Even when they voiced an opinion, it was expressed in a clumsy and irrelevant way. For example, the revised CPL provides the relatives of criminal suspect with "witness immunity", which no longer requires them to "place righteousness above family loyalty." This has been seen as an enormous advance by all sides. However, the People's Public Security Newspaper still published an article under the heading of "Placing righteousness above family loyalty needs further

encouragement". The discussion on the revised CPL could be described as a communication disaster for the law enforcement agencies, in particular, the public security departments.

Results and Future Outlook

It is fully comprehensible that people who have devoted time and effort to the discussion are disappointed. Hu Yong, media professor at Beijing University, wrote in his blog,

> In general, state power is not more restrictive now than it was in the past, but it has been expanded by some key clauses. The revised law shouts out the slogan of guaranteeing human rights, but the emphasis is still on strengthening the power of specific departments. Citizens' rights cannot be protected effectively. […] One of the reasons for the disappointing results of the revised CPL is the lack of public participation (Hu 2012).

In the context of exerting an influence in the future, this debate has resulted in positive experiences for Chinese society. The cooperation between experts and the media made a huge impact by increasing public pressure, with which the authorities have been forced to deal with. The experiences accumulated by all sides will influence future public participation in legislative change. On March 21, in the People's Daily, an article under the heading of "From Progress in Legislation to Challenges to Law Enforcement" pointed out that

> the draft CPL had been revised several times in the past 200 days, and had been drawing the attention of society as a whole. Some clauses even triggered fierce arguments. The debates and expression of diverse opinions proves that the Chinese society is constantly advancing, that citizens are becoming more aware of the laws and their rights and that there is increasing democracy, transparency and science in the legislative processes (Su 2012).

Certainly, allowing people to voice their opinions is a sign of progress. However, the legislative process will not be truly democratic, transparent and scientific until citizens' participation has been institutionalized in order to ensure that their opinions can be responded to and absorbed into the legislative process.

Unlike the simple and happy end of the Disney fairy tale or the desperate tragedy in the Hollywood movie "Who's afraid of Virginia Woolf", the debate on the CPL amendment has an open end, just like many phenomena in the transformation period of China.

References

Chen Baocheng 陈宝成 (2011) "'Bude qiangpo zizheng qizui' youwang xiejin xingsufa" "不得强迫自证其罪"有望写进刑诉法 [The principles of avoiding the unwilling self-incrimination might be written in the CPL], in *Nanfang dushibao* 南方都市报 [Southern Metropolis Daily], 17.8.2011.

Ding Jinkun 丁金坤 (2011) "Xingsufa xiugai shi 'bimao jinbu, buzu yidao'" 刑诉法修改是"皮毛进步，不足以道" [The progresses in the CPL amendment are too superficial to be worth mentioning], <http://blog.caijing.com.cn/expert_article-151570-23915.shtml>, accessed 20 May 2012.

Hu Yong 胡泳 (2012) "Xingsufa de miaotang yu jianghu" 刑诉法的庙堂与江湖 [CPL in the temple and in the society], <http://huyong.blog.sohu.com/211470978.html>, accessed 14 May 2012.

People.com.cn (2012) "Xingshi sugongfa xiuzheng'an yinfa gefang guanzhu" 刑事诉讼法修正案引发各方关注 [Amendments to the Criminal Procedure Law attract broad attention], 13.3.2013, <http://yuqing.people.com.cn/GB/17369612.html>, uploaded 13 March 2012, accessed 15 May 2012.

Su Ning 苏宁 (2012) "Cong lifa jinbu dao zhifa tiaozhan" 从立法进步到执法挑战 [From progress in legislation to challenges to law enforcement], in *Renmin Ribao* 人民日报 [People's Daily], 21.3.2012.

Wang Hanbin 王汉斌 (2011) "1982 nian xianfa de qicao guocheng" 1982 年宪法的起草过程 [The drafting process of the 1982 Constitution], in *Fazhi ribao* 法制日报 [Legal Daily], 23 May 2011.

Yao Dongqin 姚冬琴 (2012) "Lifazhe he zhifazhe de shinian jiaoliang" 立法者和执法者的十年较量 [A ten-year battle: legislator vs. enforcer], in *Zhongguo jingji zhoukan* 中国经济周刊 [China Economic Weekly] 12.

Katja Levy*

Laojiao Abolished, Arbitrariness Retained – Stability Maintenance in an Academic Debate in the PRC

On January 7th 2013, Meng Jianzhu, a Politburo member and the Secretary of the Central Commission for Political and Legal Affairs[1] under the Central Committee of the Communist Party of China, announced that the "Central Committee of the Communist Party of China (CPCCC) has already done research and will, after the related departments have asked the Standing Committee of the National Peoples' Congress (NPCSC) for approval, stop the use of Re-education through Labour within this year."[2] At the time, the full implications of this announcement were not clear: did the reference to abolishing the system of Re-education through Labour (*laodong jiaoyang* 劳动教养 or, abbreviated, *laojiao* 劳教, hereafter: *laojiao*) mean that it would be taken up again later or that it would be stopped forever? One commentator remarked that the Commission was absolutely right not to declare the abolition of the *laojiao* system and, instead, to ask the Standing Committee of the National People's Congress for approval, because in this way the various legislative powers would be properly respected. He continued: "The next step must then be that the State Council revokes its 'Preliminary Method' [still the basic legal document for the *laojiao* system – author's note] from 1957 and that the NPC regains its legislative power and agrees with the decision of the State Council" (Chen 2013: 64). This has still not happened, although most of the Re-education through Labour Camps have been shut down throughout the country. After almost 60 years, the Chinese leadership seems to be ready to abolish one of the most unfair, unconstitutional and non-rule of law sanctioning systems. However, many voices have been warning that other kinds of similar camps are ready to fill the gap that the abolition of the *laojiao* system would create, because one of the core functions of the *laojiao* system is stability maintenance, an issue that is still a matter of serious concern for the new leadership in the People's Republic of China (PRC).

The question addressed in this paper is how stability maintenance is conceptualized by the scholars debating the abolition of the *laojiao* system and if and how this conceptualization

---

*   I would like to thank Agnes Schick-Chen for her very helpful commentary on the Annual Conference of the Association of Social Science Research on China in Vienna in 2013. I am also grateful for the constructive comments of the participants in the ASC 2013 and in the Annual Conference of the European China Law Studies Association in Oxford 2013, as well as for the very useful comments and criticisms by the two reviewers of this journal. Last, but not least, many thanks to Sören Vogler for his assistance in collecting the material for this project.

1   In this position, Meng is the successor to Zhou Yongkang. Willy Lam observes that the Commission for Political and Legal Affairs has been strengthened during the era of Hu Jintao and Wen Jiabao and that this – together with other developments – is to be interpreted as a general trend towards the politicisation of law in recent years (Lam 2009: 42 f.).

2   This was not the first time that the end of *laojiao* was announced. The last similar announcement was made in 2012, but without any consequences (Feng 2013: 33). The end of the *laojiao* system was once more declared in point 34 of the "The Decision on Major Issues Concerning Comprehensively Deepening Reforms in Brief", the 60-point resolution of the third Plenum of the 18th Party Congress in November 2013 (Central Committee 2013).

differs from Western theoretical approaches on social and political stability. As Cheng Li (2009) has shown in his analysis of the political influence of think tanks and the public intellectuals involved, debates among Chinese intellectuals have started to exert a growing influence on policy making in China. It is therefore likely that the social stability maintenance concept analysed here has drawn the attention of the political elite of the PRC and, therefore, also of Chinese decision-makers. That this concept of stability is very much in line with the general concept of stability maintenance in the PRC will be shown in my analysis of the PRC legal system, which is severely weakened by parallel extra-legal mechanisms and can therefore not fully implement its ordering function. I argue that the main elements of the conceptualization in the debate are arbitrariness, threat, (legal) uncertainty and unpredictability, elements which are put into practice by systems like the *laojiao* system and which differ substantially from Western conceptions of stability maintenance. Western and Chinese thinkers have contradictory ideas about what is needed to maintain stability in a society and in a state. In Western theory[3], the key factors for maintaining stability are legitimacy, the relevance of individual attitudes, the provision of mechanisms with a "safety valve-function" and the legal system with its regulating and ordering functions. However, these factors seem to be ignored by Chinese thinkers, while other factors that create a situation of arbitrariness in which the individual feels insecure and threatened and therefore abides by the rules, are much more valued.[4] By comparing and contrasting these Western and Chinese lines of thought on maintaining stability, I also aim to contribute to the general discussion in the social sciences on effective means of maintaining social and political stability.[5] Given the fact that Western theory often claims to be universally deployable, it is remarkable that China has been able to maintain stability up to now without considering the core factors of Western theory.

Social stability, as referred to here, encompasses the ideas and theories that are concerned with keeping social conflict low or resolving it, and with maintaining peaceful conditions in Chinese society. Political stability refers to such conditions of a political system that

---

[3]   Western theory, in the sense referred to here, is limited to liberal democratic social science and legal thinking in Europe and the USA. A generalizing perspective which neglects individual national differences is used in this paper to carve out a more pronounced argument.

[4]   Feng also points to this particular Chinese view on stability maintenance, although without specifically mentioning the difference between Western and Eastern thinking: "Obviously, the Chinese communist regime is seeking a special kind of stability in which the priority is the regime stability of the one-party autocracy, rather than the normal social stability that is preserved on the foundation of justice, the rule of law, the protection of civil liberties and human rights, and prevails in the contemporary world" (Feng 2013: 33).

[5]   This study is part of a larger research project that analyses political and social stability concepts as well as social realities constructed and realized by Chinese leaders, academics and media with the goal of enhancing understanding of the motives of Chinese political decision-makers and enabling meaningful prognoses for future moves related to stability maintenance in the PRC. Within this project, several perspectives on stability are examined which have so far been neglected in research on stability. While the focus has usually been on legitimacy questions (most recently, by Sandby-Thomas 2011) or on various factors that are more or less likely to cause instability in the PRC (for example, Shambaugh 2000), the current project focuses on several subsystems (in the sense of Luhmann's social subsystems) of Chinese society, such as the legal system, the media, and the third sector, where institutions for stability – according to Western theories – are either likely to be provided or other factors (such as social capital) are produced that might have a stabilizing effect on Chinese society.

can include developments and minor changes and adaptations of this system, but do not lead to government change in a fundamental, revolutionary sense. Social and political stability can be considered as valuable assets of social and political systems because they provide a favourable environment for the individual citizen's personal security, daily life, economy and development. The study of the conceptualization of stability maintenance, as an issue of policy-analysis in the sense of the analysis *of* policy, can help to identify the ideas that influence political decision-making concerning stability maintenance in a political system and, as an issue of policy analysis in the sense of analysis *for* policy and political decision-makers, can also help to predict how political decision-makers will probably arrive at decisions concerning stability maintenance in the future.

Stability has been a crucial political slogan and policy goal in Chinese politics since the beginning of reform and opening. Qian Gang has conducted media analysis on the use of the political term (*tifa* 提法) "stability preservation" (*weihu wending* 维护稳定; abbreviated to *weiwen* 维稳) and has described the use of this and similar terms as being used to mark the opposite of social disorder, which had to be avoided at all costs during all the historical phases of the PRC. While Mao Zedong would seem to have preferred the terms "tranquility and unity" (*anding* 安定, *tuanjie* 团结), Deng Xiaoping first used the word "tranquility", and then later, began to refer to "stability" (*wending* 稳定). On the occasion of the crack-down on the democracy movement in 1989 and its aftermath, Deng Xiaoping coined the phrase "stability is of overriding importance" (*wending yadao yiqie* 稳定压倒一切). This was not used prominently while Jiang Zemin held office and, although the phrase reappeared in the political report to the 16th National Congress in 2002, when Hu Jintao came to power, it was dropped once again in the political report five years later. According to Qian, the abbreviated phrase for "stability preservation", *weiwen*, was used for the first time in the People's Daily in 2001, was used very frequently in 2008 and 2009, and has maintained a high rate of usage in China's media since then (Qian 2012: 17 ff.).

Around the year 2010, when the annual numbers of peasant uprisings and other forms of protest were estimated to have reached 180.000 or even more (Sun 2011) there was a shift to harsher measures concerning stability. A tight network of the so-called '*weiwen* offices' (*weiwen ju* 维稳局) or Stability Maintenance Offices that had (and still have) the broad task of watching, studying, preventing and predicting mass incidents was established all over the PRC at all administrative levels[6]. This trend towards increasing supervision and control was then, in a next step, intensified with the system of social management[7], which shifted the stability maintenance work into society by trying to integrate civil society organizations into the process of stability maintenance. Feng Chongyi points out that "[p]aradoxically, these increased efforts at stability preservation have not resulted in a more stable society but have sown more seeds for social instability, known in China as the vicious cycle of 'stability preservation leading to more instability' (*yue weiwen yue bu wen* 越维稳越不稳)" (Feng 2013). While Trevaskes noted that, as a result of the 18th Party Congress, the "'rigid' stability preservation approach is now out of political fashion", both she and Xie observed that the budget for domestic public security had increased and even surpassed the national defence budget (Trevaskes 2013: 71 f.; Xie 2013: 80).

---

[6] For details of *weiwen* offices, see also the report on the working conditions in *weiwen* offices; Xu and Li 2011.

[7] For information on Social Management, see amongst others: Pieke 2012; Fewsmith 2012.

In the following I will first analyse the concept of stability underlying the academic debate that emerged following the announcement that the *laojiao* system was to be abolished in 2013.[8] This academic debate was selected as a case study, because the *laojiao* system, a system of detention without recourse to judicial decisions and/or National People's Congress' laws as legal bases, is typical for the stability concept that is within the focus of this study, i.e. an arbitrary mechanism that employs feelings of threat and unpredictability to make individuals abide by certain rules.[9] Secondly, I will, by analysing the phenomenon of the circumvention of the legal system by the Chinese Communist Party (CCP) and state organs of the PRC show that this idea of stability maintenance by arbitrariness is not limited to the selected scholarly debate, but rather in line with common practice in the PRC. Thirdly, a corpus of Western theories on social and political stability will then be introduced and contrasted with the stability concept identified in the preceding two chapters. The paper will conclude with a discussion of my findings.

The *laojiao* system as an important instrument for stability maintenance

The *laojiao* system stands for a certain kind of stability maintenance which is based on legal uncertainty. There were practically no legal barriers to prevent the police from putting citizens into *laojiao* camps. The *laojiao* system is based on Mao's idea that man can be reformed and that this reform can be carried out by means of political and ideological instruction (Mühlhahn 2009: 204). It was established in 1955 by the Communist Party[10] and then officially endorsed by the State Council in 1957[11]. At first, *laojiao* was employed as an instrument to protect the newly installed leadership of the Communist Party. The number of inmates in *laojiao* camps grew rapidly during the anti-rightist campaign that started in 1958. The situation of the *laojiao* in the late 1950s was not only extremely bad because of the huge numbers of inmates in the camps but also because the disastrous economic experiment of the Great Leap Forward was followed by three bitter years of bad harvests and

---

[8]   I selected 26 of the articles on *laojiao*, published in 2013, in the China Knowledge Resource Integrated Database (CNKI) China Academic Journals Full Text-Database which were contributing in an academic manner to the debate on the abolition of *laojiao*, and conducted a qualitative-quantitative content analysis of those articles. The complete list of articles (primary sources) can be found at the end of this paper. The main selection criteria for these articles were as follows: abolition of *laojiao* is the main subject of the article; article is published in a Chinese academic journal (with a focus on social science or legal issues) or a magazine with either a social science or a legal focus; it is not just a piece of news but an article. The longest articles with the most detailed lines of argumentation were selected. The authors' professions include legal and social science professionals and academics (lawyers, procurators, law professors, social science experts, lecturers, journalists, graduate students); their professional affiliations include universities, party schools, police academies, the Chinese Academy of Social Sciences, procuratorates and the Communist Party Secretariat of a *laojiao* camp.

[9]   There are many more aspects of this debate which could be taken into consideration, most prominently, the discussions among Chinese academics conducting research on social stability (for example, Sun 2009; Hu 2010), and the official documents and speeches reflecting perspectives on the stability of the Chinese leadership itself. These aspects are beyond the scope of this article, which is focused on a specific academic debate (as well as its probable influence on political decisions), but should certainly be considered for study within the framework of future research.

[10] "Directives regarding the thorough elimination of covert counter-revolutionary elements" (25.8.1955).

[11] "The Resolution Regarding the Re-education Through Labour Issue".

widespread famines. The *laojiao* system was officially suspended during the Cultural Revolution, although some commentators say that the camps continued to exist in the form of so-called *cowsheds* where intellectuals were detained and tortured during that time (Cui 2013: 54).[12] After the Cultural Revolution, the *laojiao* system was reinstalled in 1979[13].

Yu Jianrong and others have pointed out that the function of *laojiao* changed, from being an instrument for political struggle until the cultural revolution to being an instrument for social governance or control after 1979 (Yu 2010: 67) to being an instrument of sanction in 2013 (Guo 2013). *Laojiao* and its antecedents mainly targeted prostitutes and drug addicts before the 1950s. The target groups and the duration of detention in the *laojiao* system have changed during the years of its existence as well. After the founding of the People's Republic, it was generally used to fight against counter-revolutionaries and other "bad elements" who were considered to have the ability to topple the newly established party-government of the PRC. There was also no time limit for the re-education process and we know of many people who have spent ten or even 20 years of their lives in *laojiao* camps. Nowadays, the targets include prostitutes and drug addicts as well as "troublemaking" petitioners and netizens among others, and their time in the re-education camps is limited to between one to four years.[14]

The *laojiao* system, until recently, was an extra-judicial instrument of control: the public security organs could decide on their own, without being subject to any control by the courts or the procuratorates, whether somebody should be sent to a *laojiao* camp and for how long. The *laojiao* system could therefore be described as a system of punishment and also of prevention beyond the legal system for dealing with petty criminals and social "trouble makers". Due to the lack of a legal basis in the individual cases, the system was arbitrary and unpredictable as well as a source of threat to the individual and it was adapted over time to the current situation and needs of the Chinese society.

The question of whether the *laojiao* system should be abolished or reformed has been debated since its revival in the early 1980s.[15] The developments in 2013 can be summarized

---

[12] Nevertheless, Yu Jianrong writes that during the Cultural Revolution "[a]ccording to statistics, in 1969, only 1000 people were held in RTL camps throughout the country, and RTL facilities were effectively closed down" (Yu 2010: 68).

[13] In 1979, with the "Supplementary Regulations Regarding Re-education through Labour" (by the State Council, 5.12.1979) "[…] *laojiao* was revived, strengthened, and assigned even greater importance, with assurances being given to the police that they would continue to have an alternative to the newly-regularized criminal process" [The PRC's first formal codes of criminal law and procedure on July 1, 1979] (Cohen and Lewis 2009: 4) which restored the Resolution from 1957 (Yu 2010: 66 ff.). "At that time [after June 4, 1989], 'shelter and investigation' played a more important role than *laojiao*. Statistics for 1989 show that more than 1.5 million people were detained under that regulation, perhaps six times as many as under *laojiao*" (Cohen and Lewis 2009: 5).

[14] For a comprehensive description of the *laojiao* system, see Biddulph 2007.

[15] A prominent example is the open letter, dated 2007, entitled "A citizens' proposal on beginning the procedure of constitutional review, the abolition of the system of reeducation through labor" which was written and signed by the well-known lawyers, Mao Yushi and He Weifang, as well as altogether 69 other scholars and law practitioners, and sent to the Legal Working Commission of the NPCSC and the Legal Office of the State Council. The letter gives a good overview of the main reasons that were put forward for the case to reform *laojiao*: it violates the individual right of liberty in the Chinese constitution, it is in conflict with several superior laws (Lawmaking Law, Law on administrative

as follows: Meng Jianzhu announced the abolition in January; in March, the Premier, Li Keqiang, announced that details of the "reform" to the system would be made known before the end of 2013. According to Chinese media reports, several provinces, for example, Guangdong, Shandong, and Yunnan, had stopped approving new cases for *laojiao* in the first months after the announcement in January and many centres built for that purpose had been turned into drug treatment centres. But the future of the system in general remains unclear. On October 23, it was reported that Zhou Qiang, the President of the Chinese Supreme Court, had announced that courts should speed up the handling of minor offences and "co-operate in the reform of *laojiao*". And finally in November 2013, the abolition was reconfirmed in the resolution of the third plenum of the 18th CCP congress. But, according to Chinese experts, the future of the *laojiao* camps is still uncertain; although many of them have been closed and the inmates released, it is still possible that the *laojiao* camps are either substituted by very similar means of detention and "re-education" or that they are re-opened for similar uses under different names (Yu 2013).

Using a combination of qualitative and quantitative content analysis, I will examine the debate that emerged in academic journals and magazines following Meng Jianzhu's announcement in January 2013, to show that the majority of the Chinese experts contributing to the debate see a connection between the *laojiao* system – or similar instruments – and the maintenance of stability in China's society, albeit to a different degree. The following different statements can be identified in the debate: a) *laojiao* has played a role in stability maintenance throughout or at different points in the history of the PRC; b) the authors characterize the relationship between the *laojiao* system and stability in different ways; c) the majority of the authors want to see *laojiao* abolished or reformed and d) rule of law arguments are the preferred line of reasoning in the discussion on the abolition of *laojiao*.

a) Laojiao has played a role in stability maintenance throughout or at different points in the history of the PRC

The majority of the authors (68%) maintain that the *laojiao* system has, at one point or another, played a role in China's stability maintenance: either in the early years of the PRC, when *laojiao* was directed against the enemies of the new communist leadership; at the beginning of the 1990s, when the targets of *laojiao* were mainly prostitutes and drug addicts; or during the entire period from the beginning of the PRC until the present day. None of the authors expressed explicitly the opinion that *laojiao* did not play any role at all in maintaining stability. However, eight authors did not mention a time period in China's recent history when *laojiao* played a specific role in maintaining stability (see Table 1). The authors identified different periods as the time when the *laojiao* was used as

---

sanctions); it is in conflict with international pacts and agreements; it damages the authority of criminal law; it violates the principle of appropriateness of a criminal punishment; it violates the principle of equality of sanctions for similar deeds. At the end of the letter, the scholars ask the NPCSC to examine the constitutionality of the *laojiao* system. The letter caused a new high tide in the debate on *laojiao*, but did not produce any other results (Song and Cao 213: 248), apart from further tides of debate and public letters. Recently, cases of persons released from *laojiao* who have begun to seek compensation for being detained have caused the debate to flare up again. And at the beginning of 2013, there was the statement made by Meng Jianzhu, announcing that *laojiao* would be suspended within the year.

an instrument for maintaining social stability, for example, Guo Zhiyuan noted that this started in 1979 and Tong Zhiwei pointed to the 1980s, when new target groups were added to the system[16]; Lu Ning observed that due to economic development, crime rates went up in the 1990s and that that was the time when *laojiao* changed into a sanctions system for petty criminals. Finally, another group of authors (Cui Min, Zhang Yiduo, Lu Ning, Zhang Xinghua) expressed the opinion that, in 2009, the system became an instrument for maintaining stability, particularly in the hands of the local governments against "annoying" petitioners, such as Tang Hui.[17]

All in all, among the experts discussing the abolition of the *laojiao* system, I found that a broad majority were of the opinion that this system has played a role in maintaining stability in Chinese society, at least temporarily.

Table 1: When did the laojiao system play a role in stability maintenance in the PRC?

Time when *laojiao* played a role for stability maintenance	Number of statements	Percentage
At some point during the history of the PRC:	18	68%
• Only in the 1950s	4	15%
• Only from the 1990s onwards	4	15%
• In the 1950s and then again since the 1990s	5	19%
• All the time	5	19%
Not specified	8	30%

Author's compilation (percentages do not add up to 100 because of rounding up/down).

While the above table only sheds light on the fact that most of the authors see a connection between stability maintenance and the *laojiao* system at some point in Chinese history, the next section shows that the authors characterize the relationship between stability maintenance and the *laojiao* system in different ways.

b) The authors characterize the relationship between the laojiao system and stability in different ways

In this section of the study, the source articles were scrutinized for statements on the character of the relations between the *laojiao* system and maintaining stability.[18] While

---

[16] In 1979, the detainees in investigative detention (*shourong shencha* 收容审查) were added to the *laojiao* system. The system was also extended to people from the countryside. In 1982, the number of target groups was extended officially from 2 to 6 and then extended again later, several times. Nowadays, it has become a "basket" mechanism for dealing with all kinds of deeds.

[17] Tang Hui is the mother of a teenage girl who had been raped and forced into prostitution. When the culprits who were responsible for this crime were sentenced to rather mild punishments, Tang Hui submitted petitions and the media reported extensively on the case. Since she refused to give up the struggle, she was sent to a *laojiao* camp but had to be released again, after a very short time, due to nationwide protests in the Chinese media and social media networks (Moore 2013).

[18] Only 15 of the 26 articles examined contained more elaborate statements on the quality of the relationship between stability maintenance and *laojiao*. This is due to the fact that some of the articles were concerned with very detailed questions related to the legal functions and position of *laojiao* and less concerned with more general questions related to Chinese society and politics.

not all authors who dealt with more general questions of the function of the *laojiao* system in society viewed *laojiao* as an instrument for stability maintenance, most of them saw different kinds of relationships between *laojiao* and stability maintenance. Four categories of statements on these relationships were identified in the debate: (1) *laojiao* is a source of stability, (2) the abolition of *laojiao* will have an impact on stability, (3) stability is used as an excuse to send people to *laojiao* camps, and finally (4) *laojiao* itself is the source of instability (see Table 2)[19]. The first two categories directly support the argument that *laojiao* is considered to play a role in stability maintenance, because they explain the system's function towards this goal in different ways. The third category, stability as an excuse for sending people to *laojiao* camps, can be considered as supporting, albeit indirectly, the argument: in these kinds of statements, cases are described in which public security organs send individuals – usually "troublesome" petitioners who would not give up accusing the local authorities or the public security organs – to *laojiao* camps because they want to silence these persons. Since the public security organs and local authorities provide "maintaining stability" as a reason, we can deduce that they assume it to be generally accepted that *laojiao* camps are used to maintain stability, otherwise they would provide other reasons (excuses) for the detention of these individuals instead, for instance, the need for re-education. Finally, the fourth category of statements, that *laojiao* is leading to instability, can also be read as supporting the claim that there is a relation (albeit a negative relation) between *laojiao* and stability: even in the articles in which *laojiao* is described as a source of instability rather than as a cure, the authors still refer to the general discourse on the stabilizing function of the *laojiao* system. This necessarily leads to the assumption that the authors of the articles usually view the *laojiao* system as playing a role in stability maintenance.

Table 2: Relationships between the laojiao system and stability

Argument	Authors
(1) *Laojiao* as a source of stability	
• *Laojiao* helps crime prevention. Crime prevention helps stability.	Tang Guilan
• *Laojiao* was established to ensure the maintenance of public security, i.e. stability; this was based on the 1954 Constitution, Art. 100.[20]	Tong Zhiwei
• The inmates of *laojiao* camps would destabilize society, if they were released.	Xiao Huibin
• *Laojiao* is still useful for stability maintenance, but must be adjusted to conform to rule of law principles.	Yue Liling
• Stability maintenance is only a short term goal for *laojiao*; China is pursuing the protection of human rights.	Chen Youxi
• *Laojiao* is used for social control.	Gao Changjian
• The stabilizing function was the political function of *laojiao* from the very beginning	Zhang Yiduo

---

[19] Table 2 shows statements from source articles which I have translated, summarized and partly rephrased in order to categorize them.

[20] Article 100: Citizens of the People's Republic of China must abide by the Constitution and the law, observe labour discipline, observe public order and respect public morality. 第一百条　中华人民共和国公民必须遵守宪法和法律，遵守劳动纪律，遵守公共秩序，尊重社会公德 (Chinese Constitution 1954, Art. 100).

(2) The abolition of *laojiao* and its impact on stability	
• When the *laojiao* system is abolished, stability will not suffer, because the stabilizing functions of the *laojiao* system will be transferred to existing laws.	Chu Chen'ge
• When the "Investigation and Repatriation Regulation" was abolished in 2003[21], no instability ensued. Therefore it is also unlikely that the abolition of *laojiao* would lead to instability.	Cui Min
• In 2010, *laojiao* was almost abolished and replaced by the "Minor offenses rehabilitation" (*weifa xingwei jiaozhi* 违法行为矫治), but due to fears of instability, the replacement was cancelled and *laojiao* continued.	Liu Wei
• Some scholars expect too much instability, if *laojiao* is abolished or abolished too quickly.	Ma Huaide (cit. by Zhang Yiduo); Qiao Xinsheng (cit. by Song Liwen and Cao Keliang); Yu Jianrong
(3) Stability as an excuse	
• Stability is used as an excuse to use *laojiao*, while the real reason often is nothing but an act of revenge on the part of local governments against pestering petitioners.	Hong Liu
(4) *Laojiao* as a source of instability	
• The *laojiao* system, as it stands today, is a source of instability and therefore has to be reformed.	Chen Youxi, Tang Guilan
• If China concentrates too much on stability maintenance and does not reform the *laojiao* system, China's image will suffer.	Chi Yan
• The growing dissatisfaction with *laojiao* is itself a source of instability.	Lu Guancheng

Author's compilation.

Taking into account the different characterizations of the relation between the *laojiao* system and stability maintenance mentioned by the various contributors to the debate, we can conclude that these scholars consider *laojiao* to play a role in stability maintenance.

---

[21] This argument refers to the famous Sun Zhigang Incident, in the course of which the Chinese citizen, Sun, was detained because he was not able to produce his ID card for Public Security officers. The detention was based on the "Investigation and Repatriation Regulation", an administrative regulation. When Sun died in custody, a group of lawyers demanded that the administrative regulation be abolished, stating several legal reasons, including Art. 37 in the Chinese Constitution, which prohibits the detention of Chinese citizens without the permission of the Procuratorate or a court's decision, and Art. 8 and Art. 9 in the Legislation Law of the PRC that prohibits the detention of an individual if this is not based on a proper law (for details of this case, see Hand 2006). Here, the author, Cui Min, refers to the concerns at that time that, after the abolition of the "Investigation and Repatriation Regulation", the state would not be able to control the movements of migrants in the cities and that this would lead to uncontrollable chaos. However, the State Council revoked the administrative regulation without the anticipated instability ensuing.

c) The majority of the authors want to see laojiao abolished or reformed

The analysis of the arguments concerning the function of *laojiao* as an instrument for stability maintenance shows that, in a sense, *laojiao* is to be understood as means of threat and prevention against all those who plan to destabilize society. This leads to the concern of some authors that should *laojiao* ever really be abolished, chaos might be the natural outcome. Even some outspoken reformers, such as Ma Huaide, hesitate to demand the abolition of this system in one step (Zhang 2013: 159). Nevertheless, the overwhelming majority of authors want the *laojiao* system to be changed, either by abolishing the system altogether or by reforming it in different ways; only one of the authors wanted to retain the system and two others did not express an opinion on the question of whether the system should be abolished or not (see Table 3).

Table 3: Abolish, reform or retain the laojiao system?

Suggestion for the future of *laojiao*	Number of statements	Percentage
Abolish *laojiao*	11	42%
Reform *laojiao*	12	46%
Retain *laojiao*	1	4%
Not specified	2	8%

Author's compilation.

d) Rule of law arguments are the preferred line of reasoning in the discussion on the abolition of laojiao

The arguments used in the articles can be divided into three categories:

(1) Arguments in the broader context of the legal system: on the one hand, arguments concerning the field of law to which the *laojiao* system belongs: should it be seen as an administrative measure, as administrative punishment or as criminal punishment? On the other hand, arguments concerning the kind of law or legal construction that should replace the *laojiao* system, for example, "Minor offences rehabilitation" or "Security Defence Punishments" (*bao'an chufen* 保安处分)[22] and also other arguments over whether the *laojiao* system should be dissolved and its remains distributed around the existing system of administrative punishment and/or criminal law. (2) Political arguments: these concern the role played by *laojiao* in maintaining social and political stability; the role played by public security organs in obstructing *laojiao* reforms etc. (3) Rule of law and human rights arguments: these deal with matters concerning the predictability of the law and legal outcomes, constitutionality, the legal basis of *laojiao*, checks and balances, constraints on the individual's right to liberty, etc.

In the Chinese academic debate on the abolition of the *laojiao* system, we can identify a clear focus in the various kinds of arguments: the majority of all 43 kinds of arguments are legal system arguments, political arguments follow next, and rule of law and human rights arguments take a backseat (see Table 4).

---

[22] There is a similar kind of legal norm in German law, "Maßregeln der Besserung und Sicherung". These measures are mainly concerned with maintaining safety/security in society and less with the punishment of any culprit.

Table 4: Subject areas of the arguments employed in the debate

Type of argument	Number of arguments
1 Law system	24
2 Political arguments	10
3 Rule of law	9
Sum	43

Author's compilation.

However, the number of different arguments alone does not disclose information about the specific arguments that were most frequently employed by the specific opinion-holders in the debate on the future of *laojiao*. The analysis of the individual sets of arguments that were used in each article revealed that rule of law arguments were by far the most frequently used arguments by authors who are in favour of abolishing the *laojiao* system, while the arguments of authors in favour of reform were divided equally between the categories of law system arguments and rule of law arguments. In other words, the authors who want to abolish or reform the *laojiao* system seem to prefer to use arguments related the rule of law or the system of laws rather than those in the political or mixed categories (see Table 5).

Table 5: Kinds of arguments used by the various authors

Opinion concerning future of *laojiao* Kind of argument	Neutral	Abolish	Reform	Maintain
• Mainly* law system arguments	0	1	5	0
• Mainly political arguments	1	1	0	0
• Mainly rule of law arguments	1	6	5	1
• Rather** political and rule of law arguments	0	1	2	0
• Rather legal system and political arguments	0	2	0	0
• Rather rule of law and legal system arguments	0	0	0	0
	2	11	12	1

Author's compilation.

* "Mainly" indicates that most of the arguments clearly belonged to one of these categories.

** "Rather" indicates that the majority of arguments was divided evenly among more than one category.

To sum up, the majority of the authors examined for this research think that *laojiao* has played a role in stability maintenance at some point in Chinese history (Table 1) and find it most useful to use rule of law and human rights arguments to convince their readers of the necessity to change the *laojiao* system (Table 3). We have also seen that although the authors characterize the relationship between *laojiao* and stability in different ways, they still see a relationship between the two (Table 2). With reference to the main question in this paper, that is, the concept of stability in the academic debate on *laojiao* reform, we can therefore conclude, at this point, that even those participants in the debate on *laojiao* who consider rule of law arguments to be most appropriate for their contributions to the discussion, also view *laojiao* or similar mechanisms as suitable instruments for stability maintenance. Even when these authors plead for the abolition of the *laojiao* system, they still express concern about the potential consequences of the abolition on the future of stability maintenance in the PRC. The debate is still dominated by the idea that an arbitrary mechanism based on threats and unpredictability that conveys a feeling of (legal) uncertainty (as the *laojiao* system did) is appropriate for maintaining social stability.

In the next section, I will describe some other forms of extra-legal measures in Chinese society and in the political system to show that in the PRC the legal system is weakened by several parallel systems with similar functions and therefore seems, on its own, not to be considered up to the task of guaranteeing social order in the PRC. This general view on the function of the legal system is in line with the minor or non-existent role of the legal system in the stability maintenance concept in the debate described above.

The weakened legal system of the PRC

A legal system can only fulfil its ordering function properly, if there is legal certainty, i.e. if the individual can be certain that the law will be applied under all circumstances. Gustav Radbruch explained this point by describing the relation between justice and legal certainty:

> The conflict between justice and legal certainty should be resolved in that the positive law, established by enactment and by power, has primacy even when its content is unjust and inappropriate, except the contradiction between positive law and injustice reaches a level that is so intolerable that the law must give way to justice as an 'incorrect law'. It is impossible to draw a sharper line between the cases of legalized injustice and laws which remain valid despite their incorrect content. However, another boundary can be drawn with the utmost precision: where justice is not even aimed at, where equality, being the core of justice, is deliberately neglected in the enactment of a positive law, then this law is not simply 'incorrect law', it cannot claim legal status whatsoever (Radbruch 1932, §9).[23]

In other words, according to this so-called Radbruch formula, there cannot be another judging system in addition to the legal system – not even justice itself. The only exception to this rule would be in the case that a legal rule is so unjust that it can no longer be considered to belong to the legal system.

In the PRC, in contrast to this general rule in Western legal thought, the legal system is not the only system that deals with legal issues. I therefore argue that in China the legal system is weakened considerably,[24] because there are parallel systems in addition to the legal system that fulfil similar functions – one of these functions being stability

---

[23] Author's translation.

[24] Carl F. Minzner (2011) describes this process of de-emphasizing the role of formal law and court adjudication in the PRC as a more recent phenomenon.

maintenance. To illustrate this point, I will describe some examples concerning the circumvention of the legal system in the PRC, as these are practiced today.

In the PRC, there are several mechanisms that fulfil functions similar and parallel to the legal system, but they are deliberately situated outside this system. Within the Party for instance, there are two parallel systems to deal with corruption and crime: the Disciplinary Commission, which takes care of inner-party corruption cases, and the so-called 'shuanggui' (双轨)-System according to which the Party possesses the power to detain CCP members suspected of corruption or other breaches of discipline[25] (Backer and Wang 2013: 105). Another form of what I call the circumvention of China's legal system is the habit of resolving certain problems by implementing administrative measures instead of allowing the courts to play a role in the decision-making process, for example, in the case of the Wukan uprising in 2012. In Wukan, a conflict over land ownership had led to public mass protest and was not resolved by clarifying the land owner's rights as a result of a proper court decision but silenced by employing the negotiation skills of an "administrative working group" (Lubman 2012). Intellectual Property Rights infringements are also partly dealt with through administrative procedures, which hamper the finding of a solution to the still pervasive problem of violations of intellectual property rights (Levy 2007). Political campaigns are another form of solution for some kinds of social and/or legal problems, e.g. mass campaigns against crime, against corruption, against the infringement of intellectual property rights and so on.[26]

The legal system is also often circumvented when decisions on constitutional cases have to be made. One of the most prominent cases of this type was the case of Sun Zhigang in 2003. What is important here is that the administrative regulation, the "Measures on Custody and Repatriation of Vagrants and Beggars" of 1982, which was obviously against the Chinese Constitution, was not revoked by the Standing Committee of the National People's Congress in accordance with Art. 90, Lawmaking Law of the PRC, but was quietly withdrawn by its creator, the State Council, which also replaced it with a new regulation, instead of letting the Standing Committee of the NPC make a decision in this case and with this creating a precedent for future reference.[27] Dispute resolution is another large and very prominent area where the application of the law in the narrow sense is avoided and replaced with arbitration and mediation processes (cf. Hand 2012: 132 ff.). As a final example of this tendency to avoid recourse to the law, there is Benjamin Liebman's observation on the Chinese legal system's re-emphasis on populism that also fits into this broader context:

> Populism in the Chinese legal system refers to a range of forms of public expression, from public opinion created by the state-run media, to opinion in Internet forums, to collective action and individual protest by persons seeking redress of grievances. Populism also refers to efforts by legal institutions to seek public support by aligning outcomes with perceived dominant social norms or conceptions of popular morality or by making legal institutions more accessible. Many of these contemporary manifestations of populist legality have historical antecedents (Liebman 2011: 166).

---

[25] For further details, see among others, Catá Backer and Wang 2013, Sapio 2008.

[26] Elizabeth J. Perry (2011) has analysed the ongoing use of political campaigns and compared them to their predecessors in Mao's times.

[27] For a full discussion of the Sun Zhigang case, see for example, Hand 2012: 114 ff.

Again, the legal system is not considered up to the task of bringing order to society; the efficacy of the legal system is watered down by measures outside the legal system.

To summarize: similar to the stability maintenance concept in the debate on *laojiao* above, the avoidance strategies described here show clearly that the legal system is not considered a vital factor in the stability maintenance in the PRC. According to Western thinking, in contrast, as will be shown in the next section, legal systems, among other mechanisms, have the function of stabilizing societies by offering institutionalized, predictable and transparent ways of resolving conflicts among citizens as well as between citizens and the state.

Stability concepts in Western social sciences and legal theory

The following overview of the key Western theoretical approaches to political and social stability will show how these differ from the concepts of stability maintenance underlying the debate of Chinese scholars and the basic idea of the PRC legal system as described in the previous sections. I will examine aspects of political stability, usually with strict reference to regime stability alone, and social stability, which is understood here as social peacefulness, considering political and social stability as points on a continuum that begins at one end with political instability, passes first to social instability, then to social stability and proceeds, finally, to political stability at the other end of the continuum. It is necessary to look at the idea of stability as a whole, including the political, social and legal aspects. In Western thought, as far as the *political* system is concerned, acceptance by the people (legitimacy) is considered essential for stability. As for *social* stability, it will be shown that the relevance of individual attitudes and the provision of "safety valves" pervade most approaches undertaken by Western authors. In Western *legal thought*, the ordering function of the legal system is the most important factor with regard to maintaining stability.

There is, of course, a wide range of Western theories on *political* stability. Hurwitz (1973) categorized the elements of a stable political system (and the authors who employed these elements in their analyses) as the absence of violence[28], duration of government[29], a legitimate and constitutional government[30], and the absence of change[31]; he also described political stability as characterized by the existence and absence of certain factors[32].

---

[28] Ted Gurr and Charles Ruttenberg (1967) analysed all the collective and non-state attacks on persons and property with the intention to destroy, within a political unit. Bruce M. Russet et al. (1964) counted fatalities in conflicts between social groups as indicators of political instability. Ivo K. and Rosalind Feierabend (1967) measured the degree of aggression in individuals and groups towards other groups or officeholders. Rummel (1963) researched the relation between non-state violence and international violence in the years, 1955-1957.

[29] Arthur S. Goldberg (1968) measured political stability by the probability that the current political system will be replaced by another one, and that the length of time that it remains in power again depends on the strength of interest in regime change. Arthur S. Banks and Robert B. Textor (1963) ranked 115 countries with reference to regime and cabinet changes.

[30] For Needler (1968), political stability was tantamount to legitimacy, which he measured in years of governance according to the constitution of a country. Seymour Martin Lipset (1959) considered a state legitimate and politically stable if there had been no political movement that would operate against democratic rules in the last 25 years.

Other approaches have been employed to examine the underlying causes of stability in political systems: Eckstein (1966) found that congruence between the social norms of the polity and the country's public governmental authority patterns is one of the causes of stability; Jack A. Goldstone et al. (2010) identified two causal factors in political stability: the completeness of the development of a system (be it democratic or authoritarian) and the degree of democratic development. And Samuel P. Huntington (1968) defined political stability as dependent on the degree of adaptability, complexity, autonomy and coherence in its organizations and processes. Almond and Verba (1963), as well as Harry Eckstein (1969), found that the degree of congruence between the values of the citizens of a country and the values of their government is decisive for a country's political stability (Cultural Congruence Hypothesis Approach). Sheafer and Shenhav (2013) have recently developed this approach further by emphasizing the importance of the fact that not only do the values of the people have to be congruent with the values of government, but also that the direction of this congruence is of vital importance: if people demand less freedom, for example, than the government is ready to provide, political stability is more likely than in cases where people demand more freedom than is offered.

The results of these studies all point in one direction: that the key causal factor in maintaining political stability can be summed up as the acceptance of the government by the governed, in one word, as legitimacy.

Social stability has an equally broad theoretical background in Western thought. These theories can be categorized as those that concern the role played by the attitudes and feelings of the individual in maintaining social order and as those that consider "safety valves", i.e. the mechanisms in a society that allow its members to release their anger and/or express their grievances in a way that does not lead to the permanent destruction of social stability.

First of all, there are the theories of mass psychology which state that individuals' behaviour loses its rationality in large groups (Le Bon 1903) and that masses of people suffering from feelings of frustration become an uncontrollable force, and can threaten social stability (Tarde 1890).[33] Another theory belonging to this group is the so-called Tocqueville-

---

[31] For Claude Ake (1967), a political system was stable if neither internal nor external influences caused its structures to change. G. Lowell Field (1967) similarly underscored the relation between stability and the absence of structural change.

[32] Lijphart, for example, suggested that a political system is stable if factors such as, governmental longevity, constitutional continuity, effective decision-making, and positive systemic acceptance and support are present and factors such as, revolution, violence and political movements opposed to the existing system are absent (Lijphart 1968).

[33] In the 1970s, the phenomenon of social movements inspired new insights into the theories on mass psychology that have been mentioned above. McCarthy and Zald, two influential representatives of the resource mobilisation theory, argued that people organized into large groups did not act irrationally, but would rather weigh the costs of their behaviour against its benefits. The rational-choice scholar, James Samuel Coleman (1990), also criticized the ideas of mass psychology, arguing that the feeling of frustration would rarely be strong enough to cause instability. People act rationally, he argued, even in large groups or under conditions of social instability; what is far more likely to cause instability is the formation of closed systems within segregated societies, in which ideologies can spread easily, rebellion is more effective and group identification is very important.

effect, the phenomenon that revolutions tend not to break out in times of high social tensions but afterwards, when the risk for revolutionaries is less acute[34]. Crane Brinton explains this phenomenon in terms of the gap between an individual's expectations and reality, when the pace of the growth of the individual's expectations overtakes the pace of the improvement in the situation of the individual in reality. Another explanation has become even more influential in Western thinking on stability: Runciman (1966) and Gurr (1970) conducted research on the phenomenon of "relative deprivation", as experienced by those individuals who lag behind in economic development in comparison with their fellow citizens and, as a result of which, they become resentful and are likely to rebel. All of these approaches consider the individual attitude as having an impact on social stability.

The second group of theories is concerned with 'safety valve' mechanisms, for example, Kornhauser's theory on middle-class organisation (1959). Kornhauser claimed that societies with a developed and organized middle-class are less likely to break apart (or at least, less likely to become unstable) because what he called the middle-class organisation is the place where advocacy groups and dialogue-mechanisms are formed and these can help to channel social grievances. Lewis Coser's theory on the functions of social conflict (1956) which referred to Georg Simmel's discussion on struggle, "Streit" (1908), has, in the same vein, heavily influenced Western views on social stability. Coser described social conflict as a safety valve; although conflict can have a corrosive effect on society, it nevertheless plays a very important role in the development of groups and entire societies. Ulrich Beck (1986) argued that the main characteristic of today's societies is that they face uncontrollable risks and that this leads to the loss of meaning for hitherto central sociological and political categories, such as family, class and nation. These developments, according to Beck, also heighten the risk of social instability.

Social stability – viewed against the backdrop of these Western theoretical approaches – is achieved and guaranteed mainly by taking the individual attitudes of the citizens into account and by providing 'safety valve' mechanisms.

In addition to this corpus of theories of political science and sociology, two further concepts are rooted in Western *legal* thought: firstly, there are the social contract theories concerned with individual freedom and state power. Social contract theories consider the reasons for which people choose to give up the freedom that they could enjoy in their supposed natural state and choose instead to live in a society in which a few exert power over the many and freedom is rather limited.[35] One common feature of all social contract theories is that they introduce the state with its institutions and laws as the source of order and security for the people. Secondly, in Western legal thinking, the laws and legal institutions usually have four basic functions[36] – conflict prevention, conflict resolution, power restriction and, last but not least, the regulatory and ordering function. Based on the

---

[34] Recently, this effect has become a topic of lively discussion in China (Siemons 2013).

[35] This idea of a social contract has been elaborated on by several important legal and political thinkers, including, prominently, Thomas Hobbes, John Locke and Jean-Jacques Rousseau. In all cases, the social contract and the 'the state of nature' are heuristic constructs to visualize the idea of the origins of society. Every social contract theory is based on a different view of the human character and of the nature and limitations of the power of the sovereign.

[36] Cf. Raiser 2009: 184 f. and Baer 2011: 104 ff.

social contract, the state has the monopoly on the legitimate use of force. It is able to create laws and institutions to avoid conflict arising among the people, for example, through prohibitive rules. The provision of certain institutions can help to channel protests and conflicts. The function of conflict resolution is put into practice by means of laws and statutes and procedures through which conflicts can be resolved peacefully and transparently. In Western thinking, laws also constrain the power of the state by upholding human rights and fundamental rights which serve as barriers to the state's exercise of power. The regulatory and ordering function entails three aspects: the reduction of complexity (Luhmann 1993), the rationalisation of procedures (Weber 1967) and the instrumentalisation of law for the enforcement of certain policies and ideologies, for example, in Marxist legal theory. All four functions of law in Western legal thought are closely connected with the maintenance of social and political stability.

In conclusion, in Western social sciences and legal thought, the stability of a political system and a society is heavily influenced by legitimacy, the relevance of individual attitudes, the provision of 'safety valve' mechanisms[37] for channelling conflicts and the right of articulation as well as the legal system with its regulating and ordering functions. In contrast, the concepts of stability maintenance in the academic debate on *laojiao* and underlying the role of the legal system in the PRC rather emphasize different aspects, namely using arbitrary mechanisms to create an atmosphere mainly characterized by threat and legal uncertainty. By comparing these two conceptualizations of stability maintenance, we can see that they are two entirely different, even contradicting concepts.

Two arguments could be brought forward to weaken the argument that these Western and Chinese concepts on stability maintenance contradict each other. On the one hand, it could be argued that since the *laojiao* system is now in the process of being completely abolished, the above analysis of the Chinese stability concept can be refuted, because one of its main mechanisms – the *laojiao* system – is being removed. Several factors speak against such a line of argumentation. First of all, the abolition of the re-education through labour system does not mean that unpredictable, non-transparent and threatening measures have ceased to be applied. It has been reported that the former *laojiao* camps have come back into use again as "Compulsory Drug Rehabilitation (*qiangzhi jiedu* 强制戒毒) Centres" (Ford 2013) or as "Custody and Education (*shourong jiaoyu* 收容教育) Centres" for the "re-education" of prostitutes (Asia Catalyst 2013), to name just two examples. Secondly, the above-mentioned various other forms of circumvention of the legal system are also still firmly in place and this does not show any sign of changing in the near future.

On the other hand, it could be argued that the frequently discussed adaptability of Chinese institutions (first and foremost: Nathan 2003) has been neglected in this discussion. Did the Chinese political system not adapt to Chinese economic and international developments in such a way as to guarantee the survival of the regime and the Party? Take the very thorough adaptation of the Chinese economic system to the demands of the World

---

[37] It should be mentioned that some authors have identified Chinese 'safety valve' mechanisms in the dealings of Chinese authorities with recent protests. Günter Schucher, for example, finds that the Chinese leadership is channelling social protests by selectively tolerating these protests and thus legalizing them (Schucher 2009). The articles which were analyzed for this paper do not refer to this or any similar mechanisms.

Trade Organisation after China's accession to this international organisation in 2001 as an example, or take the other systemic adaptations, for example, the introduction of village elections to conform to grassroots political needs and international pressure, and the smooth leadership transitions since 2002 as providing further evidence. These adaptations have surely consolidated the political system under the leadership of the Chinese Communist Party. Are these developments not also part of an overall Chinese "stability maintenance concept" that have to be considered here? While agreeing that the adaptive ability of the political system is definitely one, if not the most important, factor in regime survival and Party resilience in the PRC, I would counter this by arguing that the basic feature of the PRC legal system, i.e. that it can be avoided and/or substituted by other systems, which leads to the above mentioned atmosphere of fear and uncertainty has not been adapted so far and legal certainty has not yet been achieved. I would go even further and argue that the atmosphere of uncertainty in the system is currently being enhanced by the anti-corruption campaign which was launched when the new government under Xi Jinping took office in 2013. The mechanism of maintaining stability through arbitrariness and uncertainty is now encompassing the political elite which has been exempted from these mechanisms so far.

Conclusion
Currently we have at least two very different concepts on stability maintenance co-existing in different political systems: while most Western approaches rely on legitimacy, attention on individual attitudes, provision of 'safety valve' mechanisms and the ordering function of the legal system, in the Chinese academic debate on *laojiao,* we find a very different definition of the factors that help to maintain stability in which these ideas are not taken into consideration. The fact is that, today (beginning of 2015), although the *laojiao* system really has been abolished or, in some areas, is in the process of being abolished, very similar mechanisms of detention and re-education nevertheless continue to be used and several extra-legal measures are considered necessary for stability maintenance by the leadership in the PRC. It has been shown that although the participants of the debate on *laojiao* mainly use rule of law arguments and find mostly that the *laojiao* system has to be changed somehow, in other words, are in line with some aspects of Western thinking on stability maintenance, they all in all are still convinced that stability can only be obtained and maintained by arbitrary mechanisms similar to the *laojiao* system. If it is true that academic debates influence political decision-makers in the PRC we cannot expect changes in this attitude in the PRC towards stability maintenance in the near future. This supports the claim that the PRC, with regard to policies for stability maintenance, is again intent on going its own way "with special Chinese characteristics" as it has done in the past, in so many other policy areas.

References
Almond, Gabriel A. and Sidney Verba (1963) *The Civic Culture*, Princeton, N.J.: Princeton University Press.
Asia Catalyst (ed.) 2013 "Custody and Education" Arbitrary Detention for Female Sex Workers in China, <http://asiacatalyst.org/blog/AsiaCatalyst_CustodyEducation2013-12-EN.pdf>, accessed 9 November 2013.

Catá Backer, Larry and Wang Keren (2013) State and Party in the Scientific Development of a Legitimate Rule of Law Constitutional System in China: The Example of Laojiao and Shuanggui, Paper prepared for the Conference: Rule of Law with Chinese Characteristics, Vol. 2013, pp. 101-169, <http://ssrn.com/abstract=2273044>, accessed 9 November 2013.

Baer, Susanne (2011) *Rechtssoziologie. Eine Einführung in die interdisziplinäre Rechtsforschung*, Baden-Baden: Nomos.

Beck, Ulrich (1986) *Risikogesellschaft. Auf dem Weg in eine andere Moderne*, Frankfurt am Main: Suhrkamp.

Biddulph, Sarah (2007) *Legal reform and administrative detention powers in China*, Cambridge: Cambridge University Press.

Brinton, Crane (1958) *The anatomy of revolution*, New York: Vintage Books.

Central Committee of the CCP 中共中央 (2013) Authorized release: the Decision on Major Issues Concerning Comprehensively Deepening Reforms 授权发布:中共中央关于全面深化改革若干重大问题的决定, <http://news.xinhuanet.com/politics/2013-11/15/c_118164235.htm>, English translation: <http://www.china.org.cn/china/third_plenary_session/201311/16/content_30620736.htm>, accessed 14 December 2013.

Cheng Li (2009) "China's New Think Tanks: Where Officials, Entrepreneurs, and Scholars interact", *China Leadership Monitor* 29, <http://www.hoover.org/research/chinas-new-think-tanks-where-officials-entrepreneurs-and-scholars-interact>, accessed 1 November 2014

Cohen, Jerome A. and Margaret K. Lewis (2009) The enduring importance of police repression: "laojiao," the rule of law and Taiwan's alternative evolution. Paper Prepared for The impact of the 1989 pro-democracy movement and its repression on the evolution of the politics, economy, and international relations of the PRC, City University, Hong Kong, June 1-3, 2009, <http://ssrn.com/abstract=1423942>, accessed 9 November 2013.

Coleman, James S. (1990) *The Foundations of Social Theory*, Cambridge: Harvard University Press.

Coser, Lewis (1956) *The Functions of Social Conflict*, Glencoe, I.L.: Free Press.

De Tocqueville, Alexis (2013) *Der alte Staat und die Revolution*, Warendorf: J. Hoof-Verlag (original: L'ancien régime et la révolution. Paris 1856).

Deng Xiaoping (1987) Woguo fangzhen zhengce de liang ge jiben dian (4.7.1987) 我国方针政策的两个基本点 [Two basic points concerning Chinese policies], <http://www.people.com.cn/ GB/channel1/10/20000529/80789.html>, accessed 9 November 2013.

Eckstein, Harry (1966) *Division and Cohesion in Democracy: A Study of Norway*, Princeton, N.J.: Princeton University Press.

Eckstein, Harry (1969) "Authority Relations and Government Performance: A Theoretical Framework", in *Comparative Political Studies* 2, pp. 269-325.

Feng, Chongyi (2013) "Preserving Stability and Rights Protection: Conflict or Coherence?", in *Journal of Current Chinese Affairs* 42:2, pp. 21-50.

Fewsmith, Joseph (2012) "'Social Management' as a Way of Coping With Heightened Social Tensions", in *China Leadership Monitor* 36, <http://www.hoover.org/publications/ china-leadership-monitor/8701>, accessed 9 November 2013.

Ford, Peter (2013) "China votes to abolish notorious re-education camps", in *The Christian Science Monitor*, 30.10.2013, <http://www.csmonitor.com/World/Asia-Pacific/2013/ 1230/China-votes-to-abolish-notorious-re-education-camps>, accessed 9 November 2013.

Goldstone, Jack A., Robert H. Bates, David L. Epstein, Ted R. Gurr, Michael B. Lustik, Monty G. Marshall, Jay Ulfelder, and Mark Woodward (2010) "A Global Model for Forecasting Political Instability", in *American Journal of Political* Science 54:1, pp. 190-208.

Gurr, Ted Robert (1970) *Why Men Rebel*, Princeton: Princeton University Press.

Hand, Keith (2006) "Using Law for a Righteous Purpose: The Sun Zhigang Incident and Evolving forms of Citizen Action in the People's Republic of China", in *Columbia Journal of Transnational Law* 45, pp. 114-195.

Hand, Keith (2012) "Resolving Constitutional Disputes in Contemporay China", in *University of Pennsilvania East Asia Law Review* 7, pp. 51-159.

Hu Angang 胡鞍钢 (2010) *Zhuanxing yu wending. Zhongguo ruhe changzhijiu'an* 转型与稳定. 中国如何长治久安 [Transition and Stability. How China Can Live Long and Peacefully] Beijing: Renmin chubanshe.

Huntington, Samuel P. (1968) *Political Order in Changing Societies*, New Haven and London: Yale University Press.

Hurwitz, Leon (1973) "Contemporary approach to political stability: a review essay", in *Comparative Politics* 5, pp. 449-463.

Jiang Zemin 江泽民 (1997) Gaoju Deng Xiaoping lilun weida qizhi, ba jianshe you zhongguo tese shehui zhuyi shiye quanmian tui xiang ershiyi shiji – Jiang Zemin zai zhongguo gongchandang di shiwu ci quanguo daibiao dahui shang de baogao (12.9.1997) 高举邓小平理论伟大旗帜,把建设有中国特色社会主义事业全面推向二十一世纪——江泽民在中国共产党第十五次全国代表大会上的报告（1997年9月12日）[Hold high the banner of Deng Xiaoping Thought, push the cause of building a socialism with Chinese Characteristics to the 21st century – Jiang Zemin's Report to the 15th National Congress of the CPC (12.9.1997)], <http://news.xinhuanet.com/ziliao/2003-01/20/content_697189.htm>, accessed 9 November 2013.

Kornhauser, William (1959) *The Politics of Mass Society*, Glencoe: The Free Press.

Lam, Willy (2009) "The politicisation of China's law-enforcement and judicial apparatus", in *China Perspectives* 2, pp. 42-51.

Le Bon, Gustave (2011) *Psychologie der Massen*, Köln: Anaconda (original: Psychologie des foules, 1895).

Lee, Felix (2013) "Willkürjustiz: Chinas Führung diskutiert Aus für Arbeitslager", in *ZEIT Online*, 9.11.2013, <http://www.zeit.de/politik/ausland/2013-01/china-arbeitslager-justizreform>, accessed 9 November 2013.

Levy, Katja (2007) "Der Schutz des geistigen Eigentums in der VR China – Status quo und Grenzen / Protection of intellectual property rights in the People's Republic of China – Status quo and limitations", in *China aktuell* 3, pp. 29-60.

Liang Bin and Corinice Wilson (2008) "A critical review of past studies on China's corrections and recidivism", in *Crime Law and Social Change* 50, pp. 245-262.

Liebman, Benjamin I. (2011) "A return to populist legality? Historical legacies and legal reform", in Heilmann, Sebastian and Elizabeth J. Perry (eds.) *Mao's Invisible Hand. The Political Foundations of Adaptive Governance in China*, Cambridge, Mass.: Harvard University Press, pp. 165-200.

Lijphart, Arend (1968) *The Politics of Accommodation: Pluralism and Democracy in the Netherlands*, Berkeley and Los Angeles: University of California Press.

Lubman, Stanley (2012) "The Wukan protests and the rule of law", in *The Wallstreet Journal*, 7.12.2012, <http://blogs.wsj.com/chinarealtime/2012/01/07/the-wukan-protests-and-the-rule-of-law/>, accessed 9 November 2013.

Luhmann, Niklas (1993) *Das Recht der Gesellschaft*, Frankfurt am Main: Suhrkamp.

McCarthy, John D. and Mayer N. Zald (1977) "Resource mobilization and social movements: a partial theory", in *American Journal of Sociology* 82:6, pp. 1212-1241.

Minzner, Carl F. (2011) "China's turn against law", in *The American Journal of Comparative Law* 59, pp. 935-984.

Moore, Malcolm (2013) "Chinese Mother Sent to a Labour Camp for Complaining of Daughter's Rape Utterly Broken by the System", in *The Telegraph*, 16.7.2013, <http://www.telegraph.co.uk/news/ worldnews/asia/china/10182631/Chinese-mother-sent-to-a-labour-camp-for-complaining-of-daughters-rape-utterly-broken-by-the-system.html>, accessed 1 November 2013.

Mühlhahn, Klaus (2009) *Criminal Justice in China. A History*, Cambridge et al.: Harvard University Press.

Nathan, Andrew J. (2003) "Authoritarian resiliance", in *Journal of Democracy* 14:1, pp. 6-17.

Perry, Elizabeth J. (2011) "From mass campaigns to managed campaigns: 'constructing a New Socialist Countryside'", in Heilmann, Sebastian and Elizabeth J. Perry Elizabeth (eds.) *Mao's Invisible Hand. The Political Foundations of Adaptive Governance in China*, Cambridge Mass.: Harvard University Press, pp. 30-61.

Pieke, Frank N. (2012) "The Communist Party and social management in China", in *China Information* 26:2, pp. 149-165.

Qian Gang (2012) Watchwords. Reading China through its political vocabulary. JMSC Working Papers. The University of Hong Kong, Journalism and Media Studies Centre.

Radbruch, Gustav (1932) „Gesetzliches Unrecht und übergesetzliches Recht", in Dreier, Ralf and Stanley L. Paulson (eds.). *Gustav Radbruch – Rechtsphilosophie*, study edition, 2. rev. edition, Heidelberg: Müller, pp. 211-219.

Raiser, Thomas (2009) *Grundlagen der Rechtssoziologie*, 5th edition, Stuttgart: UTB.

Runciman, Walter G. (1966) *Relative Deprivation and Social Justice: a Study of Attitudes to Social Inequality in Twentieth-Century Britain*, London: Routledge and Kegan Paul.

Russet, Bruce M. et al. (1964) *World Handbook of Political and Social Indicators*, New Haven: Yale University Press.

Sandby-Thomas, Peter (2011) *Legitimating the Chinese Communist Party since Tiananmen. A critical analysis of the stability discourse*, London and New York: Routledge.

Sapio, Flora (2013) "Shuanggui and Extralegal Detention in China", in *China Information* 22:1, pp. 7-37.

Shambaugh, David (ed.) (2000) *Is China Unstable? Assessing the Factors*, Armonk and London: M.E. Sharpe.

Sheafer, Tamir and Shaul Shenhav (2013) "Political culture congruence and political stability: revisiting the congruence hypothesis with prospect theory", in *Journal of Conflict Resolution* 57:2, pp. 232-257.

Siemons, Mark (2012) "Umerziehung durch Arbeit. Die maoistische DNA des modernen China", in *Frankfurter Allgemeine Zeitung*, 16.10.2012, <www.faz.net/aktuell/feuilleton/ umerziehung-durch-arbeit-die-maoistische-dna-des-modernen-china-11926916.html>, accessed 9 November 2013.

Siemons, Mark (2013) "Steht China vor einer Revolution? Das Politbüro liest Tocqueville", in *Frankfurter Allgemeine Zeitung*, 12.2.2013, <www.faz.net/aktuell/ feuilleton/das-politbuero-liest-tocqueville-steht-china-vor-einer-revolution-12058139.html>, accessed 9 November 2013.

Simmel, Georg (1908) "Der Streit", in ibid. (1992[1908]) *Soziologie. Untersuchungen über die Formen der Vergesellschaftung*, Vol. 11, ed. by Otthein Rammstedt. Frankfurt am Main: Suhrkamp, pp. 186-255.

Smith, Aminda (2012) "Remoulding minds in postsocialist China: Maoist reeducation and twenty-first-century subjects", in *Postcolonial Studies* 15:4, pp. 453-466.

Strittmatter, Kai (2013) "China plant Reform der Umerziehungslager", *Süddeutsche Zeitung*, 7.1.2013, <www.sueddeutsche.de/politik/2.220/umstrittene-zwangsarbeit-china-plant-reform-der-umerziehungslager-1.1566500>, accessed 9 November 2013.

Sun, Liping (2009) "Zhongguo de zui da weixian bu shi shehui dondang er shi shehui kuibai" 中国的最大危险不是社会动荡而是社会溃败 [Biggest Threat to China is not Social Turmoil but Social Decay], in *Zhongguo shuzi shidai* 中国数字时代 [China Digital Times], <http://chinadigitaltimes.net/2009/03/sun-liping-%E5%AD%99%E7%AB%8B%E5%B9%B3-the-biggest-threat-to-china-is-not-social-turmoil-but-social-decay>, accessed 9 November 2013.

Sun Liping 孙立平 (2011) *Shehui shixu shi dangxia de yanjun tiaozhan* 社会失序是当下的严峻挑战 [Social Disorder is a Severe Challenge Today], in *Jingji guancha bao* 经济观察报 [The Economic Observer], <http://opinion.hexun.com/2011-02-25/127571301.htm>, accessed 9 November 2013.

Tarde, Gabriel (2009) *Die Gesetze der Nachahmung*, Frankfurt: Suhrkamp (original: Les lois de l'imitation, 1890).

Trevaskes, Susan (2013) "Rationalising stability preservation through Mao's not so invisible hand", in *Journal of Current Chinese Affairs* 42:2, pp. 51-77.

Weber, Max (1967) *Rechtssoziologie*, Neuwied: Luchterhand.

Xie Yue (2013) "Rising central spending on public security and the dilemma facing grassroots officials in China", in *Journal of Current Chinese Affairs* 42:2, pp. 79-109.

Xu Kai 徐凯 and Li Wei'ao 李微敖 (2011) "The machinery of stability preservation", Caijing Magazine, translated from Chinese in *Duihua Human Rights Journal*, 28.6.2011, <http://www.duihuahrjournal.org/2011/06/translation-machinery-of-stability.html>, accessed 9 November 2013.

Yu Jianrong 于建嵘 (2009) "Gangxing wending: Zhongguo shehui xingshi de yige jieshi kuangjia" 刚性稳定: 中国社会形势的一个解释框架 [Rigid Stability: An Explanatory Framework for China's Social Situation], <http://view.news.qq.com/a/20090515/000033.htm>, accessed 9 November 2013.

Yu Jianrong 于建嵘 (2010) "From tool of political struggle to means of social governance. The two stages of the re-education through labour system", in *China Perspectives* 2, pp. 66-72.

Yu, Verna (2013) "Labour camps may become a thing of a past, but what will replace them?", *South China Morning Post*, 5.11.2013, accessed 9 November 2013.

Zhaoyang News (2006) "Weiwenban ge xiang gongzuo qingkuang huibao" 维稳办各项工作情况汇报 [Report on the working conditions of Weiwen-Offices], in *Zhaoyang xinxi wang* 昭阳信息网 [Zhaoyang News], 12.12.2006, <http://www.zynews.com.cn/fh/dangzhengshiwu/ShowArticle.asp?ArticleID=55>, accessed 9 November 2013 [meanwhile, the website has been deleted or moved; copy with the author].

Appendix
Primary Sources
Chen Youxi 陈有西 (2013) "Feichu laodong jiaoyang zhidu shi zhongguo renquan jinbu de biran yaoqiu" 废除劳动教养制度是中国人权进步的必然要求 [The abolition of the re-education through labour system is a necessity for the progress of human rights in China], in 21 *Shiji* 21 世纪 [21st Century] 1/2, pp. 59-64.

Chi Yan 赤艳 (2013) "Laodong jiaoyang zhidu gaige zouxiang yanjiu" 劳动教养制度改革走向研究 [On trends in the reform of the re-education through labour system], in *Fazhi yu shehui* 法治与社会 [Rule of Law and Society] 2, pp. 40-41.

Chu Chen'ge 褚宸舸 (2013) "Tingzhi shiyong laojiao zhidu jiqi 'hudie xiaoying'"停止使用劳教制度及其"蝴蝶效应" [The abolition of the re-education through labour system and its "butterfly effect"] in *Lilun shiye* 理论视野 [Theoretical Horizon] 3, pp. 33-35.

Cui Min 崔敏 (2013) 劳教: 存活 57 年的"法制怪胎" [Re-education through labour: the "legal freak" that survived 57 years], in *Zhongguo xinwen zhoukan* 中国新闻周刊 [I-Newsweek], 14.1.2013, pp. 52-54.

Du Xuejing 杜雪晶 (2013) "Lun laodong jiaoyang zai zhongguo de falü – yi shehui weihaixing yu renshen weixianxing wei jichu de falü fenxi" 论劳动教养在中国的法律归宿——以社会危害性与人身危险性为基础的法律分析 [On the final legal settling place of re-education through labour in China – a legal analysis on the basis of social and personal dangerousness], in *Xi'nan zhengfa daxue xuebao* 西南政法大学学报 [Journal of Southwest University of Political Science and Law] 15:2, pp. 91-95

Faxue 法学 (2013)劳动教养制度: 停用之后何处去[The re-education through labour system: where to go after its abolishment?], in *Faxue* 法学 [Legal Studies] 2, pp. 3-4.

Gao Changjian 高长见 (2013) "Laodong jiaoyang zhidu de fali fenxi" 劳动教养制度的法理分析 [Jurisprudential analysis of the re-education through labour system], in *Zhongguo dang zheng ganbu luntan* 中国党政干部论坛 [Chinese Cadres Tribune] 1, pp. 51-54.

Guo Zhiyuan 郭志远 (2013) "Laodong jiaoyang zhidu: fazhi wenming de 'banjiaoshi'" 劳动教养制度: 法治文明的"绊脚石" [The system of re-education through labour: the stumbling-block of the rule of law civilization], in *Lilun shiye* 理论视野 [Theoretical Horizon] 3, pp. 29-32.

Han Xiaoyan 韩晓燕 (2013) "Laodong jiaoyang zhidu xingzhi bianxi" 劳动教养制度性质辨析 [On the nature of the system of re-education through labour], in *Tiedao jingguan gaodeng zhuanke xuexio xuebao* 铁道警官高等专科学校学报 [Journal of Railway Police College] 1, pp. 79-82.

Han Yong 韩永 (2013) "Minjian jieli fei laojiao. Zai zhongyang jueding dui laojiao zhidu jinxing zhongda gaige zhiqian, minjian huding feichu laojiao de jieli xingdong chixu liao jin 20 nian" 民间接力废劳教. 在中央决定对劳教制度进行重大改革之前, 民间呼叮废除劳教的接力行动持续了近 20 年 [Relay within the people to abolish *laojiao*. Before the Central Committee decided to implement great reforms on the re-education through labour system, the peoples' relay appeal to abolish *laojiao* lasted almost 20 years], in *Zhongguo xinwen zhoukan* 中国新闻周刊 [I-Newsweek], 14.1.2013, pp. 50-51.

Hong Liu 洪流 (2013) "Laojiao zhidu tingyong zhi hou" 劳教制度停用之后 [After the abolition of re-education through labour], in *Xinmin zhoukan* 新民周刊 [Xinmin Weekly] 3, p. 86.

Li Xiaofu 李晓郛 and Yang Xiaoyu 杨晓瑜 (2013) "Laodong jiaoyang zhidu de falü wenti" 劳动教养制度的法律问题 [Legal issues of the re-education through labour system], in *Tangshan xueyuan xuebao* 唐山学院学报 [Journal of Tangshan College] 26:2, pp. 69-72, 86.

Liu Wei 刘炜 (2013) "Feichu laojiao de lishi husheng" 废除劳教的历史呼声 [History's call for the abolition of re-education through labour], in *Fazhi yu shehui* 法治与社会 [Rule of Law and Society] 5, pp. 56-57.

Liu Wenbin 刘文斌 (2013) "Woguo laodong jiaoyang zhidu de chengxu jiazhi que wei" 我国劳动教养制度的程序价值缺位 [On the absence of procedural value in China's re-education through labour system], in *Jinri zhongguo luntan* 今日中国论坛 [China-Today Forum] 1, pp. 14-15.

Lu Guancheng (2013) "Feichu laogong jiaoyang zhidu shi zai bi xing" 废除劳动教养制度势在必行 [The abolition of re-education through labour is imperative], in *Fazhi yu shehui* 法治与社会 [Rule of Law and Society] 2, pp. 40-41.

Lu Ning 鲁宁 (2013) "'Weifa jiaozhi' qudai laojiao chuangkouqi" "违法矫治" 取代劳教窗口期 [The time slot in which "the treatment of illegalities" replaces re-education through labour], in *Shehui guancha* 社会观察 [Observer] 3, pp. 50-52.

Mo Hongxian 莫洪宪 and Wang Denghui 王登辉 (2013) "Cong laodong jiaoyang shiyou de leixinghua kan zhidu chonggou" 从劳动教养事由的类型化看制度重构 [From the typology of the matter of *laojiao* looking at the reconstruction of the system], in *Zhongguo jianchaguan* 中国检察官 [The Chinese Procurators] 171:5, pp. 75.

Song Liwen 宋莉文 and Cao Keliang 曹克亮 (2013) "Lun woguo laodong jiaoyang zhidu" 论我国劳动教养制度 [On China's system of re-education through labour], in *Chenggong (Jiaoyuban)* 成功(教育版）[Success (Education Edition)] 5, pp. 248-249.

Tang Guilan 唐桂兰 (2013) "Laodong jiaoyang zhidu cunzai yu feichu yanjiu" 劳动教养制度存在与废黜研究 [Study on the existence and disposal of the re-education through labour system], in *Yunnan jingguan xueyuan xuebao* 云南警官学院学报 [Journal of Yunnan Police Officer Academy] 2, pp. 45-49.

Tong Zhiwei 童之伟 (2013) "Bingqi laojiao shi shishi xianfa zhongyao buzhou" 摒弃劳教制度是实施宪法重要步骤 [The abolition of re-education through labour as an important step for the implementation of the constitution], in 21 *Shiji* 21 世纪 [21st Century] 1/2, pp. 65-69.

Xiao Huibin 肖惠斌 (2013) "Shuli fazhi siwei, zhua hao fazhi jiaoyu" 树立法治思维, 抓好法制教育 [Introduce rule of law thinking, do a great job in legal education], in *Xuexi yuekan* 学习月刊 [Xuexi Yuekan] 522, pp. 102-103.

Yang Yang 杨阳 (2013) "Tuijin woguo laojiao zhidu gaige de sikao" 推进我国劳教制度改革的思考 [Pushing forward the reflexion on China's reform of the re-education through labour system], in *Shenzhou* 神州 [Shenzhou] 10, p. 184.

Yu Jianrong 于建嵘 (2013) "Laodong jiaoyang zhidu de fazhan yanbian ji cun fei zhi zheng" 劳动教养制度的发展演变及存废之争 [The development and evolution of the re-education through labour system and the struggle over its existence or abolition], in *Zhongguo dang zheng ganbu luntan* 中国党政干部论坛 [Chinese Cadres Tribune] 1, pp. 59-61.

Yue Liling 岳礼玲 (2013) "Cong guifan xingzhi kan laodong jiaoyang zhidu de feichu" 从规范性质看劳动教养制度的废除 [Looking at the abolition of re-education through labour from a normative perspective], in *Faxue* 法学 [Legal Studies] 2, pp. 12-18

Zhang Xinghua 张兴华 (2013) "Fazhi shijiao xia de xianxing laodong jiaoyang zhidu" 法治视角下的现行劳动教养制度 [The current system of re-education through labour from the rule of law perspective], in *Fazhi yu shehui* 法制与社会 [Legal System and Society] 2013:5, pp. 49, 59.

Zhang Yiduo 张一多 (2013) "Cong laojiao zhidu kan sifa gaige" 从劳教制度看司法改革 [Look at judicial reform from the perspective of re-education], in *Fazhi yu shehui* 法制与社会 [Legal System and Society] 2, pp. 158-159.

Mechthild Leutner und Martin Leutner

Verfolgte Chinawissenschaftler 1933-1945: Die fehlende Generation – Eine längst überfällige Bestandsaufnahme

Die nationalsozialistische Diktatur der Jahre 1933 bis 1945 brachte für alle Teile der Gesellschaft in Europa schwerwiegende Beeinträchtigungen. Auch die wissenschaftliche Beschäftigung mit China in Deutschland und Europa war davon in großem Maße betroffen. Eine Reihe etablierter Sinologen und vor allem die überwiegende Mehrheit der jungen Nachwuchswissenschaftler mussten Deutschland verlassen, einige erlitten Berufsverbote, drei wurden ermordet und nur wenige Wissenschaftler, darunter meist Nationalsozialisten, behielten ihre Positionen bei.

Dass auch die Sinologie von der Verfolgung während des NS-Regimes betroffen war, dass zahlreiche Personen ins Exil gezwungen wurden, ist mehrfach angemerkt und erstmals von Martin Kern 1998 aufgelistet worden. Doch eine systematische Aufarbeitung des Ausmaßes der Verfolgung und deren Auswirkungen auf das Fach steht nach wie vor aus. Während in anderen Disziplinen ab den 1970er Jahren eine umfassende Aufarbeitung von Verfolgung und Exil eingesetzt hat, wird dieses Kapitel der Wissenschaftsgeschichte in der Sinologie bis heute kaum thematisiert. Nur wenige Aufsätze, die kaum rezipiert wurden, sind dazu bisher veröffentlicht worden;[1] eingehende Studien zu Einzelpersonen fehlen ebenso wie überhaupt eine Bestandsaufnahme, die über die von Martin Kern 1998 erstmals zusammengestellten Daten zu den Emigranten und Emigrantinnen hinaus geht, längst überfällig ist. Die Gründe dafür sind mehrere: Außer der allgemeinen Tabuisierung dieser Thematik in der frühen Bundesrepublik Deutschland sind hier speziell zwei zu nennen: Erstens das bis zur Gegenwart noch nachwirkende Verständnis von Sinologie als vorrangig philologisch-historische Wissenschaft, die sich mit China lediglich auf der Grundlage chinesischsprachiger Texte befasst, diese übersetzt und interpretiert. Eine Auseinandersetzung mit der Geschichte der eigenen Disziplin fand erst dann Berücksichtigung, nachdem sich stärker ein sozialwissenschaftliches, methodisch-theoretisch orientiertes Verständnis durchgesetzt hatte.[2] Zweitens fehlten, da sie zur Emigration gezwungen worden waren, genau die Personen, die eine Befassung mit dieser Thematik, eine Selbstreflexion hätten einfordern können, genau diejenigen, die hier auch ein breiteres Wissenschaftsverständnis hätten vertreten können, da sie alle ihre berufliche Tätigkeit außerhalb Deutschlands fortführten. Das noch junge Fach Sinologie, die China-Wissenschaften insgesamt, die erst ab den 1920er Jahren breiter an den Universitäten verankert worden waren, erlitt große Verluste: Einmal im Hinblick auf die institutionelle Verankerung des Faches an den Universitäten, welches rein zahlenmäßig erheblich reduziert und in qualitativer Hinsicht auf ein äußerst verengtes Fachverständnis zurückgeworfen wurde. Zum anderen bewirkten die Jahre der Verfolgung und des Exils, die prekären Lebensverhältnisse und die sehr eingeschränkten wissenschaftlichen

---

[1] Neben der Erwähnung einzelner Personen und Ereignisse in übergreifenden Zusammenhängen, zum Beispiel zur Situation der Sinologie allgemein, handelt es sich vor allem um die Beiträge von Kern 1998, Felber 1996, Führer 2001, Leutner 2001 und Walravens 1994, 1996, 1999a, 1999b, 2000, 2001.

[2] Bis in die 1980er Jahre galt aus diesem philologischen Verständnis heraus selbst die Beschäftigung mit der Geschichte der deutsch-chinesischen Beziehungen als ein nicht-sinologisches Thema.

Chinese History and Society/Berliner China-Hefte 45 (2015), pp. 115-139

Qualifizierungs- und Arbeitsmöglichkeiten in diesen Jahren (und teilweise auch darüber hinaus), sozusagen eine „verlorene Zeit", sowie eine verzögerte Weiterentwicklung des Faches, nicht nur, aber besonders in Deutschland. Um nur ein Beispiel zu geben: Das bereits von Otto Franke (1863-1946) in den frühen 1920er Jahren entwickelte moderne regionalwissenschaftliche Verständnis[3], von einer Spezialisierung und Differenzierung der Sinologie, wurde erst in den 1950er Jahren von seinem in die USA emigrierten Schüler Hellmut Wilhelm, als Professor am Far Eastern and Russian Institute der University of Washington, Seattle[4], wieder aufgegriffen und fand seinen Niederschlag im Konzept der Area Studies. Dieses wurde dann wiederum ab den 1960er Jahren allmählich auch in der BRD rezipiert. Dass die Area Studies in dieser Periode primär von politisch-strategischen Überlegungen der USA in der Periode des Kalten Krieges geprägt waren, wurde insbesondere in den 1970er und 1980er Jahren unter anderem von der Gruppe um das *Bulletin of Concerned Asian Scholars* kritisiert.

Wir versuchen mit unserem Beitrag – anknüpfend an die Ausstellung „Verfolgte China-Wissenschaftler"[5] – eine erste systematische Bestandsaufnahme von Verfolgung und Exil in den Jahren 1933 bis 1945 vorzunehmen. Aus den wenigen veröffentlichen Arbeiten, aus Nachrufen und Würdigungen einzelner Personen wurden vor allem biographische Kerndaten mit Schwerpunkt auf Art und Auswirkungen der Verfolgung und die auf China bezogenen Publikationen zusammengetragen. Dabei wurden nicht allein SinologInnen und „China-WissenschaftlerInnen" im engeren Sinne, nämlich die an Universitäten, Museen und Bibliotheken mit China Beschäftigten, berücksichtigt, sondern alle, die modernes oder klassisches Chinesisch studiert hatten oder sich in der Emigration aneignen sollten und die China zum Objekt ihrer wissenschaftlichen und beruflichen Laufbahn und Interessen machten. China war dabei häufig auch verbunden mit anderen Forschungs-gegenständen oder eingebettet in andere sogenannte orientalische Fächer.[6]

Im Folgenden skizzieren wir zunächst die Situation des Faches zu Anfang der 1930er Jahre, insbesondere hinsichtlich seiner Verankerung an den Universitäten, machen dann auf der Grundlage der biographischen Daten einige Aussagen zu den Verfolgten, suchen drittens die Umstände der Verfolgung aufzuzeigen, gehen viertens auf die gewählten Exilorte und den späteren beruflichen Werdegang der Emigranten ein, um fünftens die

---

[3] Die Anfänge der Regionalwissenschaften, auch der sogenannten „anwendungsbezogenen" wissen-schaftlichen Beschäftigung mit dem gegenwärtigen China, sind bereits mit der Gründung des Seminars für Orientalische Sprachen an der Universität Berlin 1887 verbunden. Hier erfolgte auch der Versuch, diese konzeptionell weiterzuentwickeln als sogenannte Kolonial- und später Auslands-wissenschaften.

[4] George E. Taylor, sein Kollege und Spezialist für Russland wies ausdrücklich auf die Bedeutung Wilhelms in diesem Kontext hin (Taylor 1992: 8 ff.).

[5] Eine im Juli 2013 im Institut für Sinologie der Freien Universität Berlin eröffnete Ausstellung über die nationalsozialistische Verfolgung von China-WissenschaftlerInnen und ihre Auswirkung auf das Fach brachte erstmals diese Thematik in eine universitäre Öffentlichkeit. Sie dokumentiert auf Einzelpostern zu den betroffenen Personen die Breite der Verfolgung. Die Zahl der von uns identifizierten Verfolgten stieg seitdem von 40 auf 49.

[6] So wurde auch der Maler und Kunstsammler, Alfred Oppenheim, der als Mitarbeiter eines Frankfurter Auktionshauses Kataloge zur ostasiatischen Kunst zusammenstellte und eine entsprechende Expertise über chinesische Kunst besaß, mit aufgenommen.

Situation Deutschlands nach dem Krieg zu benennen und im Fazit die Bedeutung des Fehlens dieser Generation für die Entwicklung des Faches Sinologie festzuhalten.

Situation des Faches in der Weimarer Republik und während der NS-Zeit

Die wissenschaftliche Beschäftigung mit China begann in der Weimarer Republik einen ersten Aufschwung zu nehmen. Neben der bereits zu Ende des Kaiserreiches existierenden Verankerung des Faches in Berlin, Leipzig und Hamburg wurde an vier weiteren deutschen Universitäten – Göttingen, Bonn, Frankfurt und Heidelberg – das Fach Sinologie eingerichtet oder fanden erste Anstrengungen zu seiner Institutionalisierung statt. Das Fach befand sich also institutionell wie auch von seiner fachlichen Differenzierung und Spezialisierung her – im Unterschied zu den großen etablierten Fächern wie z. B. Geschichte oder Germanistik – noch im Aufbau, wie dies für alle sogenannten Auslandsstudien, die heute mit dem Begriff Regionalstudien belegt werden, der Fall war.[7] Es war daher in den 1920er und Anfang der 1930er Jahre auch gerade die jüngere Generation, die das Wagnis des Studiums dieses doch nach wie vor exotischen Faches auf sich nahm und die in besonderer Weise von der nationalsozialistischen Diktatur betroffen war. Die Anzahl der an den Universitäten bereits Lehrenden und der in Museen und Bibliotheken Tätigen war insgesamt im Verhältnis zu anderen Disziplinen noch gering, so dass das Berufsverbot und die Emigration einzelner Personen ungleich größere Konsequenzen hatte.

Rufen wir uns kurz die Situation an den einzelnen Universitäten ins Gedächtnis: Berlin, Leipzig, Wien und Hamburg waren die ersten Universitäten, die bereits im 19. Jh. bzw. vor dem Ersten Weltkrieg sinologische Lehrstühle eingerichtet hatten. In Berlin hatte ab 1832 Wilhelm Schott (1802-1889) und in Leipzig ab 1878 Georg von der Gabelentz (1840-1893) Klassisches Chinesisch auf einer Professur gelehrt. Auch in Wien war 1843 mit August Pfizmaier (1808-1887), einem Dozenten für morgenländische Sprachen, Chinesisch als Lehrfach eingeführt worden. Im Jahr 1887 war am Berliner Seminar für Orientalische Sprachen (SOS) der erste und einzige Diplomstudiengang Modernes Chinesisch mit Carl Arendt (1838-1902) als Professor eingerichtet worden. In Hamburg war 1909 eine Professur für Sinologie eingerichtet und mit Otto Franke besetzt worden.

Auf diese erste Phase der Institutionalisierung des Faches im deutschsprachigen Raum folgte erst in der Weimarer Republik eine Fortsetzung, durch die Einrichtung, bzw. die versuchte Etablierung weiterer Professuren für Sinologie oder Teilprofessuren für Ostasien allgemein. Die Universitäten in Göttingen, Bonn, Frankfurt und Heidelberg, ebenso wie erneut in Wien, suchten hier im Kontext der allgemeinen Aufwertung von sog. auslandswissenschaftlichen Studien nachzuziehen und Professuren einzurichten, oder – mangels knapper finanzieller Ressourcen – wenigstens Lehraufträge oder außerplanmäßige Professuren für Sinologie, als Vorstufen späterer Ordinariate, anzubieten. Das Fach befand sich also in einer Situation des Aufbruchs und des Ausbaus. Dies wird auch

---

[7]   Bereits vor dem Ersten Weltkrieg hatte in Deutschland eine breitere Debatte über die Notwendigkeit der wissenschaftlichen Beschäftigung mit dem Ausland begonnen und waren unterschiedliche Modelle der Institutionalisierung diskutiert worden; von der teils favorisierten Idee der Schaffung einer eigenen Auslandshochschule bzw. der Entwicklung des SOS zu einer eigenständigen Auslandshochschule, waren die zuständigen Bildungspolitiker inzwischen abgekommen und favorisierten die Integration in bestehende Fakultäten.

sichtbar an der dünnen Personaldecke, gebildet durch die noch geringe Anzahl der in dieser Disziplin bereits habilitierten Personen, die mehrfach, auf der Suche nach Lehraufträgen und besser ausgestatteten und finanzierten Stellen, zwischen den Universitäten wechselten. Wie an den Universitäten wurden auch in Ethnologischen und Kunsthistorischen Museen entsprechende Stellen mit china- bzw. ostasienwissenschaftlicher Expertise eingerichtet. Auch die Gründung neuer Zeitschriften trug diesen Entwicklungen Rechnung. Zusätzlich zu der seit 1847 publizierten *Zeitschrift der Deutschen Morgenländischen Gesellschaft* und den seit 1898 verlegten *Mitteilungen des Seminars für Orientalische Sprachen*, die jeweils auch auf China bezogene Beiträge enthielten, kamen nun weitere Zeitschriften: ab 1912 in Berlin die *Ostasiatische Zeitschrift* (Mitbegründer William Cohn) als Fachzeitschrift für ostasiatische Kunst, ab 1920 die *Asia Major* in Leipzig (Bruno Schindler), die kulturwissenschaftlich orientierten Sinologen der jüngeren Generation ein Forum bot und deren englischsprachige Beiträge auch international besser rezipiert werden konnten. Die 1925 von Richard Wilhelm begründete, ebenfalls kulturwissenschaftlich ausgerichtete Zeitschrift *Sinica,* herausgegeben vom China-Institut in Frankfurt, später von Erwin Rousselle [8] fortgeführt, suchte auch erstmals chinesische Autoren in den wissenschaftlichen Diskurs außerhalb Chinas zu integrieren.

Anfang der 1930er Jahre konzentrierte sich die wissenschaftliche Auseinandersetzung mit China an der Berliner Universität, einmal im Sinologischen Seminar, welches zur Philosophischen Fakultät gehörte, und zum anderen am SOS, welches nach wie vor und bis 1945 die einzige Möglichkeit bot, systematisch, in einem zweijährigen Studiengang für modernes Chinesisch, das Diplom Chinesisch zu erwerben.[9] Seit 1923 hatte, nach dem Tod von Jan Jakob Maria de Groot (1854-1921), der aus Hamburg berufene Otto Franke den Lehrstuhl für Sinologie inne. Auf Grund seines breiten Verständnisses des Faches – sowohl die Erforschung des modernen China wie dessen Geschichte und nicht zuletzt eine methodisch-theoretische Fundierung gehörten zu seinem Credo – gelang es ihm, das Fach maßgeblich auszubauen und Berlin als in der Sinologie führend zu etablieren. Sowohl das Chinesisch-Studium am SOS als auch die Frankesche Ausprägung und dessen exzellenter Ruf zogen eine Reihe junger StudentInnen aus allen Teilen Deutschlands an. Darauf konnte der aus Leipzig, im Jahr 1932 nach Frankes Emeritierung, berufene Erich Haenisch (1880-1966) aufbauen. Doch eine Fortsetzung der Frankeschen Ausrichtung war damit nicht gegeben – im Gegenteil, Haenisch brachte ein engeres Wissenschaftsverständnis mit Betonung des Klassischen und der Philologie mit. Herausragende Schüler Frankes – Wolfram Eberhard und Hellmut Wilhelm, Stefan Balázs und Johannes/John Mish – suchten entsprechend ihre beruflichen Perspektiven außerhalb Berlins, und mussten sie dort ab 1933 auch suchen, sei es dass ihre jüdische Herkunft oder ihr jüdischer Ehepartner sie zum Verlassen Deutschlands zwangen oder dass ihre entschiedene Ablehnung des NS-Regimes sie dazu brachte, sich berufliche Möglichkeiten außerhalb des NS-Einflusses zu erschließen. Der nationalkonservative, aber anti-national-

---

[8] Ab 1897 hatte das SOS bereits alljährlich die *Mitteilungen des Seminars für Orientalische Sprachen*, herausgegeben, deren Abt. *Ostasien* von den Dozenten für Chinesisch und Japanisch redaktionell betreut wurde.

[9] Auch in den Sinologischen Seminaren der Universitäten in Leipzig und Hamburg wurde in den 1930er Jahren modernes Chinesisch neben dem klassischen Chinesisch angeboten, allerdings längst nicht systematisch (Franke 1995: 35 f.; Leibfried 2003: 126).

sozialistisch gesinnte Haenisch, der 1942 in einem Bericht des Chefs der Sicherheitspolizei und des SD für die Parteikanzlei, der an das Reichswissenschaftsministeriums weitergeleitet wurde, als „etwas reserviert" gegenüber dem Nationalsozialismus geschildert wird (Bericht 1942: 7), setzte sich als einziger der im akademischen Betrieb verbliebenen Sinologen für verfolgte Kollegen, wie Walter Simon und den im KZ Buchenwald inhaftierten Maspero, ein.

Die am SOS arbeitenden Chinawissenschaftler Max Pernitzsch und Walter Trittel (NSDAP- und SA-Mitglied) konzentrierten sich auf Sprachvermittlung und allgemeine Landeskunde. In welcher Weise einer von ihnen in den Entlassungsvorgang des chinesischen Lektors Zeng 1936/37 involviert war, ist aus den Quellen nicht mehr ersichtlich.[10] Der ebenfalls am SOS tätige Ferdinand Lessing, ein ausgewiesener Spezialist für Lamaismus und mongolische Volkskunde, war nach längerem US-Aufenthalt 1938 endgültig emigriert und wurde ab 1938 von Wolfgang Seuberlich (1906-1985), NSDAP-Mitglied seit 1937,[11] ersetzt.

Die Leipziger Sinologie, die sich lange Jahre als liberales Gegenstück zu der eher staatstreuen nationalkonservativen Berliner Sinologie verstanden hatte, war bereits durch Erich Haenischs Berufung nach dem Tod August Conradys (1864-1925) nahezu zweigeteilt worden. War doch mit Haenischs Berufung gerade auch der Schüler Conradys: Eduard Erkes – bekennender Atheist und Sozialdemokrat – übergangen worden. Erkes war zwar 1928 schließlich, neben seiner Museumstätigkeit, nichtplanmäßiger außerordentlicher Professor am Ostasiatischen Seminar geworden, doch für eine Berufung auf die planmäßige Professur nach dem Weggang Haenisch wurde er von den auswärtigen, so ganz im Gegensatz zu seiner politischen und wissenschaftlichen Position stehenden Gutachtern nicht ernsthaft vorgeschlagen (Leibfried 2003: 136 ff.). Nach einigem Hin und Her wurde 1934 der Japanologe André Wedemeyer (1875-1958) auf die nun als Professur für Ostasiatische Philologie denominierte Stelle berufen und mit der Leitung des Ostasiatischen Seminars betraut. Da Erkes wegen seiner SPD-Mitgliedschaft umgehend 1933 als Kustos am Museum entlassen und ihm die Lehrerlaubnis an der Universität entzogen wurde – nach späteren Aussagen wurde er von dem Kunsthistoriker und NSDAP-Mitglied Otto Kümmel (1874-1952),[12] der 1934 Generaldirektor der Staatlichen Museen in Berlin wurde, denunziert –, musste er in der Folge als Privatgelehrter sein Leben fristen. So spielte bis 1945 auch die einst attraktive Leipziger Sinologie keine Rolle mehr, zumal 1936 der Verlag der *Asia Major* liquidiert und die Zeitschrift eingestellt worden war.

Aus der Leipziger Schule stammte Gustav Haloun, der ab 1931 an der Universität Göttingen lehrte. Hier war ab 1925 versucht worden, das Fach einzurichten. Da Haloun nicht gewillt war, der NSDAP beizutreten, wurde für ihn jedoch kein ordentlicher Lehrstuhl geschaffen. Haloun bemühte sich daher um eine Anstellung in Großbritannien

---

[10] Ausführlich dazu Leutner 2001: 444 ff.

[11] Im Bericht 1942 wird Seuberlich als „in charakterlicher und politischer Hinsicht [...] nicht ganz gefestigt" bezeichnet (Bericht 1942: 8).

[12] Im Bericht 1942 fälschlicherweise als „Heinrich Kümmel" bezeichnet; hier werden sogar seine Kontakte zu „Kunstbolschewisten und Juden" problematisiert, auch wenn konstatiert wird, dass er nun zur positiven Mitarbeit bereit sei (Bericht 1942: 7). Kümmel hatte 1912 mit William Cohn die Ostasiatische Zeitschrift begründet, die noch bis 1943 erscheinen sollte.

und es gelang ihm, im Unterschied zu Erkes,[13] im Jahr 1935 eine Stelle in Cambridge zu erhalten. Im Jahr 1939 wurde in Göttingen dann eine außerplanmäßige Professur mit dem NSDAP- und SA-Mitglied Hans O. Stange (1903-1975)[14] besetzt, der sie allerdings wegen seiner Kriegsteilnahme de facto nicht wahrnehmen können sollte (Bericht 1942: 9).

Mit der Stiftungsprofessur für Richard Wilhelm (1873-1930) im Jahr 1925 hatte auch die Frankfurter Sinologie ein Sinologisches Seminar und darüber hinaus das China-Institut etabliert. Nach Wilhelms Tod im Jahr 1930 setzte der Spezialist für vergleichende Philosophie- und Religionsgeschichte Erwin Rousselle dessen Arbeit fort, wenn auch nicht als ordentlicher Professor. Als bekennender Freimaurer wurde er 1941 von seiner Funktion als Direktor des China-Instituts entbunden, sein Lehrauftrag wurde ihm entzogen und er erhielt darüber hinaus ab 1943 ausdrücklich Redeverbot an der Universität. Carl Hentze (1883-1975), der im Jahre 1942 von den Nationalsozialisten „in weltanschaulicher Hinsicht" als „einwandfrei" eingestuft wurde (Bericht 1942: 9) und eine Professur für chinesische Sprache und Kultur in Gent, Belgien, innehatte, wurde statt seiner berufen und sollte die Professur auch über die NS-Zeit hinaus innehaben.

Als vierte Universität verfügte seit 1924 die Heidelberger Universität über eine außerordentliche Professur, die mit Friedrich Ernst August Krause (1879-1942), der 1914 in Berlin bei de Groot promoviert hatte, besetzt war. Bereits 1919 hatte sich Krause mit einem Thema zur Sprache und Schrift in China und Japan habilitiert. Philip Schaeffer, der seine Promotion 1924 vollendete, Rousselle und Netty Reiling (Anna Seghers, 1900-1983) waren Krauses erste Schüler. Im Jahre 1942 ist, statt von einer Professur, jedoch nur noch von einem Lektorat im Fach Sinologie die Rede (Bericht 1942: 6). Es wurde nach dem Tod Krauses von Johannes Schubert (1896-1976) wahrgenommen, der „sich uneingeschränkt zur nationalsozialistischen Weltanschauung" bekannte (Bericht 1942: 10).[15]

Ab 1928 war auch an der Universität Bonn eine außerordentliche Professur für Sinologie eingerichtet worden, die bis 1955 Erich Schmitt (1893-1955), der sich 1927 in Berlin habilitiert hatte, innehaben sollte. Schmitt galt als „loyal" gegenüber der NS-Herrschaft. Er hielt sich Ende 1939 und wohl auch noch 1941 in Ostasien auf (Bericht 1942: 8).[16]

Mit der Errichtung des Hamburgischen Kolonialinstituts 1909, welches später umgewandelt wurde in eine Universität, entstand hier bereits früh auch eine Professur für Sinologie, die zunächst mit Otto Franke und nachdem dieser 1923 einem Ruf aus Berlin erhielt, bis 1935 mit dem Philosophiehistoriker Alfred Forke (1867-1944) besetzt sein sollte. Der auf chinesische Geschichte und Völkerkunde spezialisierte Fritz Jäger (1886-1957), Mitglied der NSDAP seit 1933, war der nächste in der Folge und prägte in den

---

[13] Erkes suchte gezielt noch einmal 1938 sowohl in den USA als auch in Großbritannien, wo sein Freund und Kollege Schindler im Exil war, nach Möglichkeiten einer Anstellung, siehe UAL (Universitätsarchiv Leipzig), PA 445 Eduard Erkes, Kasten 85 Nachlass E. Erkes Briefe A-Z 1938.

[14] Hans O. Stange, Mitglied der NSDP, 1931 bei Franke in Berlin promoviert. Seine Dissertation wurde später zugleich als Habilitationsschrift anerkannt. Er erhielt 1953 eine außerplanmäßige Professur in Göttingen, die er bis 1972 innehatte. <http://www.uni-goettingen.de/de/120795.html>, Zugriff am 23.04.2014. Siehe auch das Gutachten Fritz Jägers vom 5.12.1939 für dessen Berufung auf die Dozentur in Göttingen in Walravens 1999b.

[15] Vgl. zu Schubert: Taube 2009. In den hier veröffentlichten Briefen von und an Schubert ist ebenfalls keine kritische Sicht auf den NS-Staat zu beobachten.

[16] Einer seiner Schüler war Werner Eichhorn (1899-1990), der sich 1937 in Heidelberg habilitierte.

Jahren darauf die Hamburger Sinologie auch in politischer Hinsicht. Jäger und Forke gehörten im November 1933 zu den einzigen Sinologen, die das Bekenntnis der Professoren an den deutschen Universitäten und Hochschulen zu Adolf Hitler und dem nationalsozialistischen Staat mit unterzeichneten. Die Sinologin Ruth Krader, die auch in Hamburg studiert hatte, wurde vor ihrer erzwungenen Emigration in die USA 1939 wegen ihrer jüdischen Herkunft von den Hamburger Fachvertretern ausgegrenzt (Walravens 1996: 13; Kern 1998: 520).

Im Jahr 1922 hatte die Wiener Universität,[17] nach mehreren Jahrzehnten ohne sinologisches Lehrangebot, Arthur von Rosthorn (1862-1945), den langjährigen österreichischen Gesandten in Peking und ausgewiesenen Sinologen, auf eine Honorarprofessur berufen, die er bis 1939 wahrnehmen sollte. Der liberale und pazifistisch eingestellte Wissenschaftler hatte sich eindeutig gegen das NS-Regime positioniert und ging wohl nicht allein aus Altersgründen in den Ruhestand (Führer 2001: 101; Bericht 1942: 11).

So wurde das Fach, welches in der Weimarer Republik begonnen hatte sich breiter auszudifferenzieren und zu entfalten, ab 1933 erheblich in seiner Entwicklung eingeschränkt. Im Jahr 1942 stellte sich daher, selbst aus nationalsozialistischer Sicht, allein schon in Hinblick auf die Personalsituation, die Lage des Faches als katastrophal dar.[18] In dem bereits genannten Bericht des Chefs der Sicherheitspolizei vom Jahr 1942 heißt es, dass die Ostasienkunde an den Hochschulen nach dem Urteil fast aller Sinologen „einen besorgniserregenden Tiefstand" erreicht habe, auch wenn die Lage hinsichtlich des Nachwuchses „nicht als ganz aussichtslos" angesehen werde (Bericht 1942: 2).

Auch die chinaspezifische Kompetenz in den Museen, die sich ebenfalls erst in diesen Jahren herausgebildet hatte, war durch Entlassung und Emigration im hohen Maße betroffen. Allein acht Kunsthistoriker mit einem Schwerpunkt auf China und/oder buddhistischer Kunst wurden ins Exil gezwungen, u.a. Alfred Salmony, der Stellvertretende Direktor des Museums für Ostasiatische Kunst in Köln. Der Direktor des Museums für Völkerkunde in München, Lucian Schermann, wurde gleichfalls entlassen und ins Exil gezwungen und das Leipziger Museum für Völkerkunde verlor den Leiter der Asiatischen Abteilung, Eduard Erkes, 1933 durch Entlassung. Neben Kunsthistorikern und Ethnologen mit Schwerpunkt China hatten sich gerade jüngere Wissenschaftler spezialisiert und wiesen in ihrer Wahl der Studien- und Forschungsschwerpunkte eine große Breite auf: von den Linguisten Walter Simon, Erwin Reifler, Johannes/John Mish, über die Juristen Franz Michael und Ernst Wolff, die Spezialisten für Buddhismus bzw. Lamaismus oder Daoismus wie Walter Liebenthal, Siegfried Behrsing, Ferdinand Lessing und Erwin Rousselle, bis hin zu den Historikern und Soziologen bzw. Gesellschaftswissenschaftlern, von denen Stefan/Étienne Balázs und Karl August Wittfogel sicherlich die bedeutendsten waren, und nicht zuletzt Ethnologen wie Eberhard oder Spezialisten für klassische Literatur wie Diether von den Steinen und Joseph Kalmer oder den Geologen Peter Misch. Etliche waren interdisziplinär ausgerichtet, waren zugleich als Indologen (Liebenthal, Schermann), Altaisten (Karl Heinrich Menges) oder als Tibetologen (Rolf Stein, Philipp Schaeffer) ausgebildet oder tätig bzw. wählten entsprechende Fachkombinationen.

---

[17] Zur Wiener Sinologie siehe ausführlich Führer 2001.

[18] Ab 1938 gab es auch in München Versuche, ein Ordinariat für Sinologie einzurichten, die scheiterten. Erst 1945, mit Haenischs Wechsel von Berlin nach München, wurde die Professur realisiert.

Die Verfolgten

Insgesamt lassen sich 49 Personen[19], 43 Männer und sechs Frauen, die verfolgt wurden, identifizieren. Sie sind in der Namensliste im Anhang aufgeführt.[20] Die Mehrheit wurde wegen ihrer jüdischen Herkunft verfolgt, viele auch oder zugleich aus politischen Gründen, wie z. B. wegen aktiven Widerstandes gegen den Nationalsozialismus. Im Jahr 1933 hatten unter ihnen 38 die deutsche Staatsbürgerschaft, zehn besaßen österreichische Pässe, einzelne hatten polnische und ungarische Wurzeln, auch der Franzose Henri Maspero und der Chinese Zeng Chuiqi 曾垂祺 (selbst gewählte Umschrift: Tseng Tsui-Chi) wurden zu Opfern der nationalsozialistischen Verfolgung.

Während die in Deutschland Verfolgten bereits ab 1933 das Land verließen, emigrierten die Österreicher in der Mehrzahl erst 1938 und 1939. Die zahlenmäßig stärkste Altersgruppe unter den Verfolgten war 1933, mit 14 Mitgliedern, die der 26 bis 35 Jährigen. Die Altersgruppe zwischen 18 und 25 Jahren bestand aus zwölf Personen, die zwischen 36 und 45 Jahren aus zehn Personen. Sechs Kinder und Jugendliche emigrierten mit ihren Eltern und acht Verfolgte waren älter als 45 Jahre, nur zwei von ihnen waren über 55. Das bedeutet, dass es sich bei den China-Wissenschaftlern in erster Linie um die Nachwuchs-Generation und um Absolventen handelte, die gerade erst dabei waren, sich beruflich zu etablieren. Angesichts der geringen Zahl der Professuren im Fach Sinologie ist die Verfolgung der bereits relativ etablierten Wissenschaftler der älteren und mittleren Generation, also Eduard Erkes (Leipzig) und Erwin Rouselle (Frankfurt), sowie der Weggang von Ferdinand Lessing (SOS), Gustav Haloun (Göttingen) und Walter Simon (Berlin) besonders dramatisch für seine Entwicklung. Die Auswirkungen für das Fach werden noch deutlicher, wenn die Karrierestufen und Berufe im Einzelnen betrachtet werden: 19 Personen studierten 1933 oder in den Jahren danach (in Österreich bis 1938) noch oder hatten ihr Studium gerade abgeschlossen, 15 Personen können als Postdocs bezeichnet werden, davon arbeiteten elf Personen, meist mit kurzfristigen Verträgen, in Forschung oder Lehre an Universitäten, neun Personen hatten Professuren oder außerplanmäßige Professuren inne (nicht alle im Fach Sinologie), fünf arbeiteten im Museumsbereich, zwei als Journalisten, zwei in Bibliotheken, zwei hatten darüber hinaus andere Positionen im Staatsdienst inne und eine Person war im Kunstbereich tätig.

---

[19] Nach Fertigstellung des Aufsatzes und der quantitativen Auswertung der Daten konnten wir eine weitere Person identifizieren, die aufgrund der jüdischen Herkunft zur Emigration gezwungen war und viele Jahre in China als Wissenschaftler gearbeitet hat: Wilhelm Mann (1916-2012), der nach der Pogromnacht im November 1938 ins Exil nach China flüchtete und erst in den Jahren der Kulturrevolution nach Deutschland zurückkehrte. Siehe ausführlich dazu Unschuld 2014.

[20] Nicht mit in diese Liste aufgenommen wurden zwei österreichische China-Wissenschaftler, deren biographische Daten darauf schließen lassen, dass sie antifaschistisch und antinationalsozialistisch eingestellt waren; Arthur v. Rosthorn, der 1939 wohl nicht allein aus Altersgründen aus der Universität Wien ausschied und dessen Schüler Haloun, Reifler und Kalmer emigrieren mussten (Führer 2001: 101, 116). Der Sinologe, Geograph und Sprachwissenschaftler Josef Rock (1884-1962), der bereits 1905 in die USA emigriert war und von 1922 bis 1949 vor allem im Südwesten Chinas, außerhalb des japanisch besetzten Gebietes, lebte und u.a. über die Naxi-Minderheit und die Botanik dieses Gebiets forschte, scheint aus seiner strategisch wichtigen Position heraus – er lebte unweit der Burmastrasse – den US-Nachrichtendienst mit Informationen unterstützt zu haben, 1944 bis 1945 arbeitete er als Spezialist für den US Army Map Service in Washington (Führer 2001: 192).

Berlin als Hauptstadt mit der Berliner Universität als wichtiges universitäres Zentrum, auch für die Beschäftigung mit China, kommt hinsichtlich der Verfolgung und des Verlustes dabei eine tragende Rolle zu, wie es von Michael Wildt auch für die national-sozialistische Verfolgung allgemein festgestellt wurde.[21] Die Berliner Universität mit dem Sinologischen Seminar und dem SOS war nicht nur das Zentrum der China-Wissenschaften, sondern auch der Ort, der am meisten durch den Nationalsozialismus geschädigt wurde. 25 Personen hatten an der Berliner Universität ihren Abschluss gemacht oder dort studiert. Sieben der betroffenen Sinologen haben in den Jahren von 1919 bis 1936 bei Franke und Haenisch in Sinologie promoviert. Vier promovierten zwischen 1932 und 1934, Anneliese Bulling sogar noch 1936.

Insbesondere die Schülergruppe von Otto Franke, also der bereits 1930 promovierte Balázs, sowie Wolfram Eberhard, John Mish und Hellmut Wilhelm, sind hier zu nennen. Sieben Wissenschaftler hatten überdies zwischen 1924 und 1933 das Chinesisch-Diplom am SOS abgelegt, davon allein drei im Jahr 1933. Drei weitere Personen hatten dort Chinesisch studiert ohne einen Abschluss zu machen. Sechs der Verfolgten hatten in Berlin andere Fächer studiert oder wie Hanna Kobylinski sogar promoviert. Zwei, nämlich Walter Simon (1926) und Otto Mänchen-Helfen (1933), hatten sich überdies an der Berliner Universität im Fach Sinologie habilitiert.

Neben Berlin war die Universität Leipzig besonders betroffen; einmal durch das Berufs-verbot des Professors für Sinologie, Eduard Erkes, zum andern hatten vier der Emigranten dort ihren Abschluss in Sinologie gemacht und können als zur Leipziger Schule gehörig bezeichnet werden: Siegfried Behrsing (1927), Gustav Haloun (1923), Otto Mänchen-Helfen (1923) und Bruno Schindler (1919). Mit Schindlers Emigration nach England 1933 musste auch die von ihm finanzierte, verlegte und mit großem Engagement betriebene Zeitschrift *Asia Major* eingestellt werden, womit die deutsche Sinologie ihr prominentestes Publikationsorgan verlor (Simon 1965: 93 f). Andere Wissenschaftler hatten in Heidelberg, Wien, Frankfurt, Göttingen, München, Basel, Erlangen oder Breslau ihr Studium abgeschlossen oder dort gearbeitet, drei – Adolf Reichwein, Philipp Schaeffer, Henri Maspero – wurden wegen ihres Widerstandes gegen das national-sozialistische Regime ermordet, drei – Eduard Erkes, Erwin Rousselle, Siegfried Behrsing – wurden wegen ihrer politischen, anti-nationalsozialistischen Haltung entlassen, ver-blieben allerdings in Deutschland und konnten ihre wissenschaftliche Arbeit in den Jahren der Diktatur nur begrenzt fortsetzen. Fast 40 Personen, die Kinder nicht eingerechnet, mussten aus politischen oder „rassischen" Gründen flüchten, waren zur Emigration gezwungen oder kehrten nach 1933 von Auslandsaufenthalten nicht mehr nach Deutsch-land zurück.

Umstände der Verfolgung

Die große Mehrzahl der China-WissenschaftlerInnen wurde aus „rassischen" Gründen verfolgt, 29 von ihnen waren jüdischer Herkunft und emigrierten, darüber hinaus gingen vier China-Wissenschaftler mit ihren jüdischen Partnern oder Angehörigen ins Exil. Die

---

[21] „Beide Daten haben für Berlin eine herausgehobene Bedeutung. Als Reichshauptstadt war Berlin Schauplatz der Machtübernahme und der nachfolgenden gewaltsamen Etablierung der Diktatur. Als jüdische Metropole mit rund 160.000 jüdischen Bürgern war die Stadt zugleich von den Auswirkungen der Judenverfolgung besonders stark betroffen" (Wildt 2013b).

Tatsache, dass ein so großer Anteil der China-Wissenschaftler jüdischer Herkunft war bzw. dem jüdischen Bildungsmilieu entstammte, ist bisher kaum in der Forschung hervorgehoben worden. Möglicherweise bot gerade das noch in Entwicklung begriffene neue Fach für die nicht-traditionellen Bildungsschichten u. a. mehr Aufstiegsmöglichkeiten als schon lange etablierte Fächer wie etwa die Geschichte.

Bemerkenswert ist, dass von den 42 Emigrierten – hier sind alle Personen gerechnet – 17 bereits im Jahre 1933 ins Exil gingen oder von Forschungs- und anderen Auslandsaufenthalten nicht wieder nach Deutschland zurückkehrten.[22] Gerade auf Grund ihres außerhalb Deutschland liegenden Forschungsgegenstandes und -interesses verfügten viele von ihnen über internationale Kontakte und hatten u. a. auch enge Beziehungen nach China. In den folgenden drei Jahren gingen weitere 17 Personen ins Exil,[23] wie auch der sechsjährige Conrad Schirokauer, der erst nach dem Krieg Sinologie studieren sollte, mit seiner Familie das Land verließ. 1938 emigrierten weitere fünf[24] und 1939 schließlich noch drei Personen[25]: Willy Tonn gelang die Flucht nach Shanghai und der bereits 75-jährige Lucian Scherman, ehemals Direktor des Münchener Völkerkunde-Museums, musste mit seiner kranken Ehefrau noch vor Kriegsbeginn ins amerikanische Exil gehen (Wilhelm 2005: 700). Nach der Annexion Österreichs 1938 waren vor allem die jüdischen Österreicher geflüchtet: Der 16-jährige Ernst Schwarz und der 18-jährige Richard Frey verließen 1938 Wien, der 13-jährige Otto Schnepp konnte noch 1939 mit seinen Eltern Shanghai erreichen (Chu 1997). Alle drei begannen erst im chinesischen Exil sich mit der Sprache und dem Land zu befassen. Dies ist auch bei Hans Müller der Fall, der aus der Schweiz, in die er zunächst um ein Studium aufzunehmen emigriert war, nach Entzug seiner Aufenthaltserlaubnis Richtung China fliehen musste (Paleske 2008). Hanna Kobylinski, die bereits 1933 nach Dänemark emigriert war, sah sich dort 1943, gemeinsam mit den anderen dort lebenden Juden, von der Deportation bedroht und trat zusammen mit der überwiegenden Mehrheit von ihnen ebenfalls die Flucht nach Schweden an (Wojak 2011: 558). Ruth Schlesinger, später Krader, erhielt noch 1939 ein Einreisevisum für die USA, wenn auch ohne jede berufliche oder finanzielle Perspektive (Walravens 1996: 13; Kern 1998: 520).

Bei 17 Personen kann, wegen ihres Widerstandes gegen den Nationalsozialismus, eine Verfolgung aus primär politischen Gründen festgestellt werden.[26] Viele von ihnen waren jüdischer Herkunft. Drei waren prominent im politischen Widerstand gegen Hitler aktiv: Der Sozialdemokrat Adolf Reichwein, der 1921 mit der bahnbrechenden Arbeit über die Beziehungen Chinas und Europas im 18. Jahrhundert promoviert hatte und ein führendes

---

[22] 1933: Ecke, Fränkel, Hundhausen, Kobylinski, Krader, Löwenthal, Mänchen-Helfen, Michael, Müller, Reifler, Salmony, Schindler, Stein, von den Steinen, Wilhelm, Weiss, Wolff. Diether von den Steinen kam 1934 noch einmal als Mitglied der Theatertruppe Hundhausens zur Aufführung des Stückes „Zwei Gattinnen" nach Deutschland (Walravens/Bieg 1999: 159).

[23] 1934-37: Bachhofer, Balázs, Bulling, Alide und Wolfram Eberhard, Lessing, Liebenthal, Menges, John Mish, Peter Misch, Münsterberg, Schirokauer, Simon, Ilza Veith, Wittfogel, Zeisberger.

[24] 1938: Frey, Haloun, Kalmer, Oppenheim, Schwarz.

[25] 1939: Scherman, Schnepp, Tonn.

[26] Balázc, Behrsing, Alide und Wolfram Eberhard, Erkes, Frey, Haloun, Hundhausen, Kalmer, Mänchen-Helfen, Maspero, Menges, Reichwein, Rousselle, Schaeffer, Wittfogel. Schirokauer flüchtete mit seinem im Widerstand aktiven Vater, der zuvor im KZ inhaftiert war.

Mitglied der Widerstandsgruppe „Kreisauer Kreis" und im Falle eines erfolgreichen Umsturzes als Kultusminister vorgesehen war, wurde am 4. Juli 1944 verhaftet und am 20. Oktober hingerichtet (Kunze 2011). Philipp Schaeffer, der 1924 mit einem sinologisch-tibetologischen Thema promoviert hatte, war als KPD-Mitglied seit 1933 mehrfach festgenommen worden und 1943 als „rückfälliger Hochverräter" und Mitglied der Widerstandsgruppe „Rote Kapelle" im selben Jahr ebenfalls hingerichtet worden (Coppi 2005: 366 ff.). Der französische Sinologe Henri Maspero – seit 1918 Professor am College de France in Paris – war, ebenso wie seine Frau Hélène, aufgrund des Verdachts „terroristischer Aktivitäten" gegen das NS-Regime (Auboyer 1947: 64) und Zugehörigkeit seines Sohnes zum französischen Widerstand 1944 durch die Gestapo verhaftet und ins Konzentrationslager Buchenwald deportiert worden, wo der 62-Jährige die unmenschlichen Bedingungen im Lager nicht überleben sollte (Brooks 2004). Drei weitere China-Wissenschaftler erhielten Berufsverbot und lebten unter wirtschaftlich prekären Bedingungen in Deutschland weiter, eine Emigration war ihnen nicht möglich. Eduard Erkes, außerordentlicher Professor in Leipzig, erhielt Lehr- und Publikationsverbot, doch suchte er wissenschaftlich weiter zu arbeiten und publizierte in internationalen Zeitschriften über Themen, wie *The God of Death in Ancient China* (1939 in der holländischen *T'oung-pao*) oder *Das Schwein im alten China* (1942 in der *Monumenta Serica*, Peking). Er wurde 1943 beim Verlag Harrassowitz dienstverpflichtet, womit der inzwischen 52-Jährige der Zwangsarbeit in einer Fabrik auf Grund der Intervention seiner Frau gerade noch entgehen konnte (Lewin 1999: 449). Ebenfalls dienstverpflichtet wurde der noch junge Siegfried Behrsing, der nach seiner Entlassung Gelegenheitsarbeiten durchführte und ab 1939 beim Oberkommando der Wehrmacht als Übersetzer zum Dienst beordert wurde. Seine Frau wurde 1944 kurzzeitig durch die Gestapo verhaftet, seine Schwägerin wegen ärztlicher Hilfe für Zwangsarbeiter hingerichtet (Felber 1996: 82). Erwin Rousselle, Professor an der Universität Frankfurt, erhielt 1941, nach Rückkehr von einem zweijährigen Chinaaufenthalt, wegen seiner kritischen Haltung zum NS-Regime Berufsverbot, zwei Jahre später, wie oben gesagt, sogar Redeverbot an der Universität (Schmitt-Rousselle 2013).

Der Lektor für Chinesisch am SOS, Zeng Chuiqi wurde wegen angeblicher „jüdischer Versippung", nach 15-jähriger Lehrtätigkeit am Seminar in Berlin, entlassen. Dieser Grund war konstruiert worden, um den Lektor – aus welchen Gründen auch immer – entlassen zu können. Auf Fürsprache eines deutschen Bekannten seines Vaters, des ehemaligen Polizeipräfekten von Peking und Sohnes Zeng Guofans (1811-1872), wurde Zeng dann gestattet, selbst kündigen zu können, um sein Gesicht zu wahren (Leutner 2001: 445 ff.).

Den acht weiteren primär politisch Verfolgten gelang die Emigration. Wolfram und Alide Eberhard gingen 1937, nach zweijährigem Chinaaufenthalt, in die Türkei, wo Wolfram Eberhard eine Professur an der Universität Ankara erhielt. Gustav Haloun, der eine außerordentliche Professur in Göttingen innehatte, gelang es 1938 einen Ruf auf den Lehrstuhl für chinesische Sprache und Geschichte an der Cambridge University zu erhalten (H. Franke 1952: 2; Simon 1952: 93). Ferdinand Lessing, Dozent am SOS, konnte seine seit 1935 wahrgenommene Gastprofessur in Berkeley in eine ordentliche Professur umwandeln und kehrte nicht nach Deutschland zurück (Leutner 1987: 50). Des Weiteren verblieb Vincenz Hundhausen in Peking. Er war von seinen Funktionen am Deutschland-Institut entbunden worden, nachdem er der Aufforderung, in die Auslands-Ortsgruppe der NSDAP einzutreten, öffentlich eine klare Absage erteilt hatte (Walravens 1999a: 60). 1934 hatte er für eine Gastspielreise seines Theaters in Europa bereits Einreiseverbot für Deutschland erhalten (Jux 1999: 63; Hundhausen 1999: 60).[27] Stefan/Étienne Balász, Otto Mänchen-Helfen, Karl Menges, Josef Kalmer und Karl August Wittfogel waren anti-nationalsozialistisch eingestellt und leisteten aktiven Widerstand. Sie wurden teilweise verhaftet und waren nach ihrer Freilassung gezwungen aus Deutschland zu flüchten.

Zusammenfassend lässt sich sagen, dass insgesamt 36 Personen aktiv emigrierten, sechs weitere passiv – was bedeutet, dass sie von vor 1933 angetretenen Auslandsaufenthalten nicht wieder nach Deutschland zurückkehrten –, drei in Deutschland überlebten und drei weitere dort ermordet wurden und der Lektor des SOS als chinesischer Staatsbürger ge-zwungenermaßen 1937 nach China zurückkehrte, um dort den Tod im antijapanischen Widerstandskrieg zu finden.[28]

Exilorte

Insgesamt emigrierten also 42 der 49 Verfolgten. Die Mehrzahl der Emigranten, nämlich 20, ging zunächst nach China bzw. blieb dort. Dies war naturgemäß für Chinawissen-schaftlerInnen eine naheliegende Option, zumindest bis zum Einmarsch der japanischen Truppen im Jahr 1937 in Peking und dem Beginn des antijapanischen Widerstands-krieges.[29] Eine kleine Gruppe von China-Wissenschaftlern hatte sich bereits vor 1933 in China aufgehalten, nämlich Gustav Ecke, Vincenz Hundhausen, Diether von den Steinen und Erwin Reifler. Eine zweite Gruppe fand nach 1933 in China Berufsmöglichkeiten, wie Wolfram Eberhard, Franz Michael, Rudolf Löwenthal, Walter Liebenthal, Hellmut Wilhelm, Ernst Wolff, Ruth Weiss und Peter Misch. Einer dritten gelang es noch in den Jahren 1938 und 1939 nach China, zumeist nach Shanghai, auszuwandern, der einzig verbliebenen Zufluchtsstätte für jene, die Deutschland, Österreich oder ihre bisherigen Exilorte verlassen mussten. Zu dieser letzten Gruppe gehörten Walter Zeisberger (1936), Willy Tonn (1938), Hans Müller (1939), Richard Stein/Frey (1939), Otto Schnepp (1939) und Ernst Schwarz (1938); die vier letztgenannten hatten vor der Emigration keinen Bezug zu China. Otto Schnepp emigrierte mit seinen jüdischen Eltern und Richard Stein/Frey und Ernst Schwarz waren gerade erst 18 bzw. 17 Jahre alt. Hans Müller hatte in der Schweiz allerdings enge Kontakte zu chinesischen Studenten und Antifaschisten.[30]

---

[27] Die Theatertruppe selbst konnte 1934 einreisen und diverse Aufführungen veranstalten. Für Informatio-nen zu den Aufführungen siehe Walravens/Bieg 1999a: 158 f. Es fanden auch Aufführungen von Hund-hausens Nachdichtungen chinesischer Stücke, ohne seine Genehmigung und Nennung seines Namens, statt (Hundhausen 1999: 60).

[28] Laut persönlicher Auskunft von Wolfgang Franke im Jahr 2000. Zeng wird auch genannt im Zusammenhang mit einem *Chinesisch-deutschen Lexikon* (华德辞典), für das er eine Einleitung geschrieben hat, s. <http://www.booyee.com.cn/bbs/thread.jsp?threadid=1003735&forumid=0&get=1>, Zugriff am 05.02.2014.

[29] Auch Chinawissenschaftler ohne unmittelbaren Fluchtgrund hielten sich in diesen Jahren zu Forschungszwecken im Lande auf, so etwa Rousselle von 1938 bis 1940, also vor seiner Entlassung in Deutschland – er scheint für sich zu diesem Zeitpunkt in Deutschland keine unmittelbare Gefahr gesehen zu haben –, und der Bonner Sinologe Erich Schmitt noch zu Anfang der 1940er Jahre.

[30] Mai 2002: 216.

Als Zentren der Emigration in China sind Peking und Shanghai zu nennen. An der Peking-Universität, der Yanjing-Universität und der Furen-Universität fanden jeweils drei Migranten Arbeit, als Bibliothekare, als Deutsch-Dozenten, aber auch als Professoren für Sanskrit (Walter Liebenthal) oder Geologie (Peter Misch). Misch hatte 1936 auf Vermittlung Zhu Jiahuas eine Stelle an der Sun-Yatsen-Universität in Kanton erhalten (Han Xiao 2012: 89). Er und Liebenthal folgten den chinesischen Universitäten ins Landesinnere und waren während des antijapanischen Widerstandskrieges Mitglieder der Vereinigten Südwest-Universität (*Guoli xinan lianhe daxue* 国立西南联合大学) in Kunming, die in den von der Guomindang kontrollierten Gebieten den Lehrbetrieb fortsetzte. An der Zhejiang-Universität in Hangzhou unterrichtete Franz Michael Deutsch. In Shanghai gab es für die Emigranten Arbeitsmöglichkeiten als Deutsch- bzw. Chinesischlehrer (Erwin Reifler), als Sportlehrer (Ernst Schwarz) oder als Journalistin (Ruth Weiss). Die meisten erhielten insbesondere in den ersten Jahren in China lediglich kurzfristige Lehraufträge. Mitunter arbeiteten sie an mehreren Instituten gleichzeitig, um den Lebensunterhalt für sich und in vielen Fällen auch für die mitgeflüchteten Familienmitglieder zu verdienen. Insbesondere die relativ spät und mittellos ins Exil Gegangenen lebten in prekären Verhältnissen oder schlugen sich mit Gelegenheitsarbeiten (Willy Tonn) durch. Ernst Schwarz versteckte sich vor den japanischen Übergriffen in Shanghai ab 1941 zwei Jahre lang in einem buddhistischen Kloster (Herrmann 2008: 204), Peter Misch schickte angesichts des japanischen Vorrückens auf Kanton seine nicht-jüdische Frau und das gemeinsame Kind nach Deutschland zurück und versteckte sich, bis es ihm gelang, ins Landesinnere zu fliehen (Han Xiao 2012: 89). Hans Müller und Richard Stein/Frey gingen in die Sowjetgebiete und waren dort bis zum Ende des antijapanischen Krieges u. a. als Ärzte an der Front tätig.

Die große Mehrheit der nach China emigrierten Wissenschaftler sollte entweder noch in den Dreißiger Jahren, wie Hans Fränkel, Franz Michael und Diether von den Steinen, oder in den späten Vierziger Jahren (Rudolf Löwenthal, Erwin Reifler, Otto Schnepp, Hellmut Wilhelm, Peter Misch) weiter emigrieren. Alide und Wolfram Eberhard verschlug es 1937 zunächst in die Türkei, bevor sie 1948 in die USA gingen. Die letzten China-Emigranten mussten 1949 bzw. Anfang der 50er Jahre China verlassen oder wurden ausgewiesen, Willy Tonn ging als einziger 1949 nach Israel, Ernst Wolff 1951 nach Hongkong und dann über Japan in die USA. Gustav Ecke wurde 1949 ausgewiesen und ging in die USA, Walter Liebenthal musste 1952 China verlassen und übernahm in Indien eine Professur. Auch Vincenz Hundhausen, der in China bleiben wollte, wurde 1954 ausgewiesen und kehrte als Einziger zwangsweise nach Deutschland zurück. Ernst Schwarz konnte noch bis 1960 in China leben (Herrmann 2008: 209), während Ruth Weiss, Hans Müller, Richard Stein/Frey sowie Walter Zeisberger ihr gesamtes weiteres Leben in China verbringen sollten. Sie nahmen die chinesische Staatsbürgerschaft an, die Männer waren mit chine-sischen Frauen (bzw. Müller mit einer japanischen Frau) verheiratet und schlugen aka-demische und journalistische Laufbahnen ein. Die drei Erstgenanten waren als Mitglieder der KPCh politisch aktiv und nahmen später hohe Positionen ein.

Als weiteres wichtiges Emigrationsland – noch bevor die USA zum Haupt- und Endziel der meisten Emigranten wurde – ist Großbritannien zu nennen: neun Personen[31] flüchteten

---

[31] Bulling, Fränkel, Haloun, Alfred Oppenheim, Schindler, Simon, Wittfogel, Kalmer, Cohn

dorthin, wobei Anneliese Bulling, Hans Fränkel und Karl August Wittfogel später in die USA weiter zogen. Ähnliches kann für Frankreich festgestellt werden: vier Personen (Stefan/Étienne Balázs, Ruth Schlesinger-Krader, Alfred Salmony, Rolf Stein) wählten Paris als Exilort und davon zwei im Anschluss ebenfalls die USA. Hanna Kobylinski emigrierte zunächst nach Dänemark und 1943 weiter nach Schweden. Einzelne Wissenschaftler bzw. deren Familien gingen zunächst nach Italien, in die Schweiz, nach Polen und in die Tschechoslowakei oder suchten als Österreicher zunächst in Wien zu arbeiten. Nach dem Anschluss Österreichs an das Deutsche Reich 1938 erfolgte in der Regel die Weitermigration.

Bei der Wahl dieser europäischen Exilorte konnten die WissenschaftlerInnen meist an bestehende berufliche, universitäre oder private Kontakte anknüpfen. Als diese Exilorte auf Grund des beginnenden Krieges ab 1939 den Emigranten keinen Schutz mehr bieten konnten, traten sie die Überfahrt in die USA an. Ihre geleistete Arbeit an den Universitäten in Wien, Warschau oder in Prag war daher nicht nachhaltig. Lediglich Hanna Kobylinski kehrte aus dem schwedischen Exil nach Dänemark zurück und forschte nach dem Zweiten Weltkrieg über ostasiatische Geschichte in Kopenhagen.

Für die meisten Emigranten waren die USA allerdings zunächst nicht erreichbar, die Beschaffung von Einreisevisa, wenn überhaupt erfolgreich, stellte sich zumeist als langwieriges Unternehmen heraus. Lediglich für vier Personen – Ludwig Bachhofer, Ferdinand Lessing, Hugo Münsterberg, Lucian Scherman – sollten die USA das Erstemigrationsland sein. Als Zweitemigrationsland spielten die USA jedoch eine entscheidende Rolle und wurden so zum wichtigsten Exilort der China-WissenschaftlerInnen. Noch in den Dreißiger Jahren emigrierten 10 Personen aus China und anderen Ländern weiter in die USA.[32] Nach dem Ende des Krieges 1945 ließen sich im Zuge einer zweiten Welle weitere zehn Personen[33] in den USA nieder.

Als wichtige Zentren in den USA kristallisierten sich die University of Washington, Seattle[34] und die University of California, Berkeley,[35] heraus. Auch in San Francisco, Chicago und an der Columbia University in New York fanden Emigranten universitäre Positionen. Einige von ihnen erhielten renommierte Lehrstühle und beeinflussten die Entwicklung der Chinawissenschaften entscheidend, andere fanden sich in eher prekären Beschäftigungsverhältnissen wieder oder hatten lediglich Lehraufträge inne, teilweise an wechselnden oder mehreren Universitäten gleichzeitig. Die Vernetzung dieser Gruppen wie der EmigrantInnen im Bereich der Chinawissenschaften insgesamt bedarf noch einer genaueren Untersuchung.[36]

Eine ähnliche berufliche Situation, wie die in den USA, finden wir bei den in Großbritannien und Frankreich noch verbliebenen Emigranten. In Großbritannien hatten Walter Simon (SOAS, London) und Gustav Haloun (Cambridge University) Professuren an Universitäten inne, William Cohn konnte sich eine akademische Existenz in Oxford

[32] Fränkel, Michael, Krader, Mänchen-Helfen, Menges, Salmony, Schirokauer, Veith, von den Steinen, Wittfogel.
[33] Alide und Wolfram Eberhard, Ecke, Löwenthal, John Mish, Reifler, Wilhelm, Wolff, Schnepp, Peter Misch.
[34] Wittfogel, Wilhelm, Reifler, Krader, Wolff, Peter Misch.
[35] Wolfram und Alide Eberhard, Lessing, von den Steinen, Mänchen-Helfen.
[36] Die Verfasser sind dabei, diese Thematik weiter zu untersuchen.

aufbauen; Rolf Stein lehrte in Paris an der Ecole Nationale des Langues Orientales Vivantes und auch Stefan/Étienne Balázs gelang es, nach seinen langen Jahren in der Illegalität in Südfrankreich, in Paris an der École Pratique des Hautes Études wieder wissenschaftlich arbeiten zu können. Hanna Kobylinski, Bruno Schindler und Josef Kalmer dagegen konnten in ihren Exilländern ihre berufliche Laufbahn nur unter Einschränkungen fortsetzen.

Zusammenfassend lässt sich sagen, dass 25 der von der nationalsozialistischen Verfolgung Betroffenen nach 1945 Professuren an Universitäten und Akademien innehatten, weitere acht als Dozenten einer Lehrtätigkeit nachgingen und vier in Bibliotheken arbeiteten. Einige waren als Übersetzer, Journalisten oder als Verleger tätig, andere arbeiteten als Ärzte. Eine kleine Anzahl hatte ihren Kampf gegen den Nationalsozialismus mit dem Leben bezahlen müssen, viele hatten nur unter großen Schwierigkeiten in Deutschland und im Exil überlebt.

Viele hatten auch nicht nur in Deutschland Widerstand gegen die nationalsozialistische Diktatur geleistet, sondern ebenfalls im Exil, in ihren neuen Funktionen, ihren Widerstand gegen den Faschismus weitergeführt. Sie beteiligten sich aktiv am Kampf gegen die japanischen Invasoren (Müller, Frey), arbeiteten mit dem britischen oder amerikanischen Geheimdienst zusammen und stellten ihre China- und Deutschland-Expertise, auch zur Ausbildung von Geheimdienstoffizieren und Militär-Übersetzern, zur Verfügung. Bekannt ist, dass Walter Simon Übersetzer der britischen Armee in Vorbereitung auf ihren Einsatz in Deutschland ausbildete (Bawden 1973), John Mish ebenfalls für den britischen Geheimdienst tätig war und in Bombay als Chinaspezialist arbeitete (Stam 1984: 615), Franz Michael 1942 das U.S. Army East Asian Languages Program mit aufgebaut hat (Kern 1998: 522), Hans Fränkel als Übersetzer für die U.S.-Armee tätig war (Kern 1998: 520), Hugo Münsterberg in der U.S. Army kämpfte (Kern 1998: 522) und Rolf Stein von 1940 bis 1945 als Soldat und Übersetzer der französischen Armee in Vietnam tätig war und dort auch in japanische Gefangenschaft geriet (Kern 1998: 525).

Die Emigranten nahmen fast durchweg auch neue Staatsbürgerschaften an, einige anglisierten bzw. romanisierten ihre deutschen Namen, wie Johannes/John Mish, Stefan/Étienne Balázs und Willy/W.Y. Tonn. Einen radikalen Bruch mit seinem früheren Leben brachte Richard Stein, Kommunist und Antifaschist, durch die Wahl seines neuen Namens „Frey" zum Ausdruck. Diesen Namenswechsel nahm er direkt nach der Ankunft in den kommunistischen Gebieten und seiner Teilnahme am antijapanischen Widerstandskrieg vor.

Fast alle Migranten, die vielfach alle Arten von Gelegenheitsarbeiten und mit Glück Tätigkeiten als Lehrer oder Dozenten ausübten, lebten in prekären Lebensverhältnissen und brauchten allein zur Sicherung der nackten Existenz den größten Teil ihrer Kraft. Familien waren häufig getrennt. Hinzu kam die große Ungewissheit über das Schicksal der in Deutschland verbliebenen Angehörigen und Freunde. Es ist heute bekannt, dass kaum eine deutsche oder österreichische jüdische Familie keine Opfer des Holocaust zu beklagen hat. Insbesondere ältere nahe Familienangehörige verblieben in Deutschland und wurden ermordet oder litten im KZ.[37] Häufig wurden die Familien auseinandergerissen, da

---

[37] Walter Simons Mutter wurde im KZ ermordet, Hans Müllers Vater überlebte Theresienstadt.

es beispielsweise nicht gelang alle Kinder mit ins Exil mitzunehmen,[38] oder Geschwister und deren Familien in andere Exilländer gehen mussten.[39] Im Exil angekommen bedeutete der Aufbau einer neuen beruflichen Existenz in den meisten Fällen eine nächste Herausforderung. Nicht allein der deutsche Angriff auf die Nachbarstaaten zwang die sich dort aufhaltenden Exilanten zur erneuten Flucht oder in die Illegalität, auch die japanische Besetzung Chinas nach 1937 war für viele eine Katastrophe.

In dieser Situation des Exils war, ebenso wie für die drei in Deutschland unter Berufsverbot gestellten Sinologen, die Weiterführung der wissenschaftlichen Arbeit stark beeinträchtigt und wurde häufig, wie etwa bei Stefan/Étienne Balázs, jahrelang ganz unterbrochen. Schon im Exil, wie auch im Zuge der späteren beruflichen Konsolidierung in den Zielländern, kam es zur Verlagerung von Forschungsschwerpunkten – Walter Simon begann sich mit dem modernen Chinesisch zu befassen, Erwin Reifler wandte sich der Linguistik und später Problemen maschinellen Übersetzens zu.[40] Etliche der jungen Emigranten, die es nach China verschlug, entdeckten erst hier ihr Gastland als Studien- und Forschungsobjekt oder aber sie begannen sich mit neuen Themenbereichen zu befassen. So wurde Ernst Schwarz, der sich nach dem japanischen Angriff auf Shanghai in einem buddhistischen Kloster verstecken musste, von einem Mönch in den Buddhismus eingeführt (Herrmann 2008: 204 f.). Erwin Reifler, der bei Rosthorn über Staat und Gesellschaft im alten China promoviert hatte, wandte sich als Sprachlehrer in China linguistischen und didaktischen Fragen des Chinesischen zu (Führer 2001: 246). Auch Rudolf Löwenthal beschäftigte sich später mit der Entwicklung von Übersetzungssoftware (Pollak 1997: 415 ff.).

Der Einfluss von Verfolgung und Exil auf die wissenschaftliche Produktion, auf die Inhalte und Ausprägung der späteren Forschungsarbeiten der Betroffenen war – so kann schon jetzt gesagt werden – beträchtlich. Allein die äußeren Lebensumstände bedingten ein hohes Maß an verlorener Zeit für die wissenschaftliche Beschäftigung mit China.[41] Andererseits ist zu beobachten, dass viele Emigranten es schafften, trotz ihrer prekären Lebensverhältnisse die wissenschaftliche Arbeit weiterzuführen. Es gelang ihnen teilweise ihre Forschungsergebnisse in der ab 1934 in Peking an der katholischen Fu-Ren Universität herausgegebenen Fachzeitschrift *Monumenta Serica* zu publizieren. Wie sich im Einzelnen Verfolgung und Exil auf die Inhalte, Methoden und Theorien der wissenschaftlichen Produktion ausgewirkt haben, in welcher Weise diese Erfahrungen in der Wahl der wissenschaftlichen Themen und in den politisch-wissenschaftlichen Positionen, sowohl

---

[38] So blieb die Tochter Walther Liebenthals nach der Emigration ihres Vaters in Deutschland bei einer befreundeten Familie zurück, während der älteste Sohn Frank 1935 nach Peking folgte und dort zu studieren begann; Sohn Ludwig erhielt nach langem Bemühungen ein Visum für Argentinien. Charlotte Liebenthal konnte mit ihrem jüngsten Sohn Walter im Juli 1939 nach China emigrieren (Auskunft von Roberto Liebenthal, Buenos Aires, 6.3.2014). Peter Misch schickte 1937, angesichts der auf Kanton vorrückenden japanischen Truppen, seine Frau und sein Kind wieder nach Deutschland zurück (Molenaar 1999).

[39] Die Geschwister von den Steinen lebten in unterschiedlichen Exilorten, <http://de.wikipedia.org/wiki/Karl_von_den_Steinen>, Zugriff am 02.02.2014.

[40] In Wien hatte er 1931 bei Rosthorn über Staat und Administration im alten China promoviert (Führer 2001: 246).

[41] In besonderem Masse beklagt wird dies bezüglich Étienne Balázs, der zudem auf Grund seines frühen Todes seine wissenschaftliche Projekte und Pläne nicht realisieren konnte (W. Franke 1965: XII).

der in Deutschland Verbliebenen als auch der Emigranten, ihren Ausdruck fanden, muss Teil gesonderter Forschungen bleiben.

Nach dem Krieg

Die personell katastrophale Situation des Faches an den Universitäten, wie das Fehlen von China-Expertise insgesamt, war dominantes Kennzeichen auch der ersten Jahre nach Kriegsende. Eduard Erkes und Siegfried Behrsing, die im Osten Deutschlands überlebt hatten, wurden von den Behörden der Sowjetischen Besatzungszone und der DDR rehabilitiert und erhielten neue Berufsmöglichkeiten. Erkes wurde bereits 1945 wieder in seine Position als außerplanmäßiger Professor an der Universität Leipzig eingesetzt, ab 1947 bis zu seinem Tod 1958 hatte er dort die Professur für Ostasiatische Philologie inne. Behrsing wurde 1945 Kustos am Museum für Völkerkunde in Leipzig und nahm von 1953 bis 1969 eine Professur für Moderne Geschichte und Literatur Chinas an der Humboldt-Universität, Berlin, wahr. Im Westen Deutschlands, in der Bundesrepublik, gestaltete sich die Situation völlig anders. Erwin Rousselle erhielt seine außerplanmäßige Professur an der Frankfurter Universität nicht zurück; diese behielt der als Nachfolger Rousselles eingesetzte Hentze bei. Haenisch, der noch während des Krieges Berlin wegen der Bombardierungen verlassen hatte, baute an der Universität München die Sinologie neu auf. In Hamburg wurde Fritz Jäger als aktiver Nationalsozialist 1945 von den Besatzungsbehörden zunächst seines Amtes enthoben, 1947 allerdings wieder eingesetzt. [42] Neu berufen auf den Lehrstuhl für Sinologie wurde hier im Jahre 1950 Wolfgang Franke (1912-2007), der von 1937 bis 1945 Wissenschaftlicher Mitarbeiter am Deutschland-Institut in Peking gewesen war. An der Universität Göttingen wurde der bereits 1939 berufene Hans O. Stange wegen seiner aktiven Unterstützung der NS-Diktatur zunächst nicht wieder eingesetzt, doch 1953 erfolgte seine formelle Ernennung zum außerplanmäßigen Professor; bis 1972 leitet er das Sinologische Seminar. [43] Berufen auf zum Teil neu geschaffene Stellen wurden sukzessive auch weitere frühere NSDAP-Mitglieder, jeweils begutachtet von den in Deutschland verbliebenen wenigen Lehrstuhlvertretern. Walter Fuchs (1902-1979), der in China 1937 NSDAP Mitglied geworden war und nach seiner Rückkehr nach Deutschland 1947 als belastet interniert wurde, wurde dann nach seiner Habilitation 1956 an die neu geschaffene Professur für Sinologie an der Freien Universität, Berlin, berufen und hatte 1960 bis zu seiner Emeritierung 1970 eine Professur an der Universität Köln inne. Alfred Hoffmann (1911-1997), der wie Fuchs am Deutschland-Institut in Peking, und zwar von 1940 bis 1943 tätig gewesen war und danach bis 1945 an der Botschaft der japanischen Marionettenregierung in Nanjing gearbeitet und zugleich wichtige Funktionen im nationalsozialistischen Auslandsapparat innegehabt hatte, wurde als Nachfolger von Fuchs 1961 an die Freie Universität berufen und nahm ab 1964 eine Professur für chinesische Sprache und Literatur an der neugegründeten Ruhr-Universität in Bochum wahr (Leutner 2011: 87 ff.). An der Universität Bonn lehrte der dem NS-Regime gegenüber „loyale" Erich Schmitt (Bericht 1942:8) bis zu seinem Tode 1955 weiter. In Heidelberg wurde nach dem Tod Krauses 1942 erst im Jahre 1962 mit Wolfgang Bauer (1930-1997) die Sinologie wieder neu begründet.

---

[42] Jäger 1945 ließ sich allerdings bald pensionieren und wurde dann 1957 noch förmlich emeritiert.

[43] Vgl. <http://www.uni-goettingen.de/de/120795.html>, Zugriff am 07.02.2014.

Tatsächlich setzte keiner der Emigranten nach dem Krieg eine Berufstätigkeit in Deutschland fort, es fand keine Remigration statt. Ob dies vor allem auch den in den Nachkriegsjahren schlechten wirtschaftlichen Verhältnissen geschuldet war oder auch die, inzwischen erfolgte, neue berufliche Integration eine wesentliche Rolle für das Verbleiben in den Exilländern spielte oder inwieweit hier eine gewisse Ablehnung gegenüber den Verfolgten zu beobachten ist, muss im Einzelfall geklärt werden. Lediglich zu kürzeren Gastaufenthalten oder Besuchen kamen die Emigranten nach Deutschland bzw. Österreich zurück, vier von ihnen übernahmen Gastprofessuren[44] oder wurden durch einen Ehrendoktor (Rolf Stein in Bonn) bzw. eine Honorarprofessur (Walter Liebenthal in Tübingen) geehrt und/oder verbrachten ihre letzten Lebensjahre in Deutschland oder in Österreich. Eine Ausnahme ist der Österreicher Ernst Schwarz, der 1960, nun angesichts der politischen Entwicklungen (Großer Sprung nach vorn, Hungersnot, Anfeindungen als Ausländer) seines Exillandes China, dieses geradezu fluchtartig wieder verließ und durch Vermittlung von Anna Wang ein Einreisevisum für die sozialistische DDR inklusive dortiger Arbeitsmöglichkeit erhielt (Herrmann 2008: 209).[45]

Mehrere Emigranten wurden später, meist sehr spät, wegen ihres Kampfes gegen den Nationalsozialismus und für ihre Verdienste um ihr Land geehrt, so Richard Frey, Walter Zeisberger und Ernst Schwarz durch Österreich.[46] An Richard Frey erinnert eine Gedenktafel am Döblinger Gymnasium, das er besuchte. Zudem wurde er in China geehrt. Dem Widerstandskämpfer Philipp Schaeffer wurde durch die Umbenennung der Volksbücherei Berlin-Mitte zur Philipp-Schaeffer-Bibliothek eine Ehre zuteil. An den Widerstandskämpfer und großen Pädagogen Adolf Reichwein erinnern zahlreiche deutsche Schulen, u. a. in Berlin, die ebenso wie einige Straßen und eine Pädagogische Akademie in Celle nach ihm benannt wurden.

Rehabilitiert wurde neben Eduard Erkes und Siegfried Behrsing auch Lucian Scherman. Er erhielt noch 1945 seine Rechte als pensionierter Beamter wieder. Einige der Emigranten haben umfangreiche Nachlässe hinterlassen; Ruth Krader und Hellmut Wilhelm gaben diese nach Frankfurt an das Deutsche Exilarchiv, Anneliese Bulling an das Stadtmuseum Oldenburg. Die überwiegende Mehrheit jedoch beließ ihre Nachlässe an den Universitäten und in den Ländern, die ihre Heimat geworden waren.

Einige Emigranten stellten für das ihnen geraubte Eigentum Entschädigungsforderungen, so etwa der Sammler ostasiatischer Kunst, Alfred Oppenheim, dessen Bemühungen um Entschädigung für seine kostbare Kunstsammlung erst kurz nach seinem Tod 1953 zu einem Teilerfolg führten (Hansert 1999: 304 ff.), und Willy Tonn, der sich auch später in Israel mit prekären Beschäftigungsverhältnissen über Wasser hielt und erst 55 Jahre alt in

---

[44] Balázc Anfang der 1960er Jahre in Hamburg, Wolfram Eberhard 1979 an der FU Berlin, Ecke in Bonn, Fränkel in Hamburg, Bonn und München

[45] Schwarz erhielt mit seiner Familie nur Ausreisevisa für die DDR, nicht für sein Geburtsland Österreich, welches er wohl ab den 1980er Jahren vielfach besuchte und wohin er 1993 wieder umsiedelte.

[46] Schwarz erhielt 1992 die Ehrenmedaille der Bundeshauptstadt Wien in Gold; bereits 1981 hatte er in Berlin (DDR) den den F.-C.-Weiskopf-Preis erhalten, <http://de.wikipedia.org/wiki/Ernst_Schwarz_%28Sinologe%29>, Zugriff am 14.05.2014.

einem Schweizer Sanatorium verstarb.[47] Besonders tragisch verlief das Ende Kalmers: Er besuchte drei Mal seine Heimatstadt Wien. Jedes Mal erlitt er dort einen Herzinfarkt. Nach seinem dritten verstarb er 1959 im Alter von 61 Jahren (Führer 2001: 236).

Die Emigranten leisteten entscheidende Beiträge zur Entstehung, Entwicklung und Ausprägung der Chinawissenschaften in Großbritannien und insbesondere in den USA. Durch ihre akademische Lehre hatten sie darüber hinaus großen Einfluss auf die nächste Generation der Sinologen und Chinawissenschaftler in diesen Ländern und weltweit,[48] Deutschland inbegriffen. Auf die institutionelle Formierung des Faches in Deutschland hatten sie jedoch keinen Einfluss. Viele Namen, die deutsche Herkunft ihrer Träger und ihre Schicksale in der Emigration wurden vergessen. Beim Wiederaufbau der Sinologie und Chinawissenschaft ab den 1950er Jahren fehlte diese Generation; nur in Leipzig und an der Humboldt-Universität zu Berlin setzten zwei Sinologen – Eduard Erkes und Siegfried Behrsing –, die zuvor Berufsverbote erlitten hatten, ihre sinologische Tätigkeit fort. Das Fehlen nahezu dieser gesamten Generation wirkte sich wesentlich auf die inhaltliche Ausprägung und personelle Stärke des Faches insgesamt aus. Lediglich als sekundäre Faktoren können der Kalte Krieg und der kriegsbedingte Mangel an finanziellen Ressourcen an Hochschulen in Deutschland dafür verantwortlich gemacht werden, dass es bis in die 1980er Jahre dauerte, bis das Fach allmählich wieder an die Dimensionen der 1930er Jahre anknüpfen konnte.

Quellen- und Literaturverzeichnis

Auboyer, Jeannine (1947) „Henry Maspero (1883-1945)", in *Artibus Asiae* 10:1, S. 61-64.

Amlung, Ullrich (1999) *Adolf Reichwein: 1898–1944. Ein Lebensbild des Reform-pädagogen, Volkskundlers und Widerstandskämpfers*, Frankfurt am Main: Dipa-Verlag.

Bawden, Charles Roskelly (1973) „Walter Simon", in *Bull. School of Oriental and African Studies* 36, S. 221-223.

Bericht (1942) des Chefs der Sicherheitspolizei und des SD für die Parteikanzlei, weitergeleitet am 5. August 1942 an das Reichsministerium für Wissenschaft, Erziehung und Volksbildung über die Lage der Sinologie und Japanologie in Deutschland, 1942, in *Newsletter Frauen und China*. Berlin, Nr. 7, September 1994, S. 1-17.

Brooks, E. Bruce (2004) Sinological Profiles. Henri Maspero, in University of Massachusetts, Amherst, <http://www.umass.edu/wsp/sinology/profiles/maspero.html>, Zugriff am 25.01.2014.

Brooks, E. Bruce (2007a) Sinological Profiles. Erwin Reifler, in University of Massachusetts, Amherst, <http://www.umass.edu/wsp/sinology/profiles/reifler.html>, Zugriff am 25.01.2014.

Brooks, E. Bruce (2007b) Sinological Profiles. Hellmut Wilhelm, in University of Massachusetts, Amherst <http://www.umass.edu/wsp/sinology/profiles/wilhelmh.html>, Zugriff am 25.01.2014.

---

[47] Heute ist sein umfangreicher Nachlass als Willy Tonn Collection 1920 - 1988 1920 - 1957 (bulk) (1920) am The Leo Baeck Institute New York digital zugänglich unter: <http://www.archive.org/stream/willytonn_01_reel04#page/n224/mode/1up>, Zugriff am 15.05.2014.

[48] Der Sinologe Harry Simon, Sohn des nach London emigrierten Linguisten Walter Simon, war 1961 der Gründer der Oriental Studies, später umbenannt in East Asian Studies, an der University of Melbourne (Yeung 2010).

Chu, Henry (1997) „Shanghai's Jews Live to Tell Story at Last", in *LA Times*, 15. Juli 1997, <http://articles.latimes.com/1997/jul/15/news/mn-12725/2>, Zugriff am 28.01.2014.

Columbia University (2013) Schirokauer, Conrad <http://www.columbia.edu/cu/ealac/faculty.html>, Zugriff am 26.07.2013.

Coppi, Hans (2005) „Philipp Schaeffer, Orientalist, Bibliothekar, Widerstandskämpfer", in *IWK*, Heft 3/2005, S.366-386.

Felber, Roland (1996) „Zwischen Anpassung und Widerstand. Notizen über Schicksale von Ostasienwissenschaftlern in der NS-Zeit", in *Berliner China-Hefte* 10, S. 80-86.

Fenske, Wolfgang (2010) „Rousselle, Erwin", in *Biographisch-Bibliographisches Kirchenlexikon* (BBKL), Band 31, Nordhausen: Bautz, S. 1160-1163.

Franke, Herbert (1952) „Gustav Haloun (1898-1951) in memoriam", in *Zeitschrift der Deutschen Morgenländischen Gesellschaft* 102, 1952, S.1-9.

Franke, Herbert (1987) „Maenchen-Helfen, Otto", in *Neue Deutsche Biographie* 15, S. 636.

Franke, Wolfgang (1965) „Étienne Balázs in memoriam", in *Oriens Extremus*, 1965, S. XII.

Franke, Wolfgang (1995) *Im Banne Chinas. Autobiographie eines Sinologen 1912-1950*, Bochum: projektverlag.

Franke, Wolfgang (1999) *Im Banne Chinas. Autobiographie eines Sinologen 1950-1998*, Bochum: projektverlag.

Franke, Wolfgang 傅吾康 (2013) *Wei zhongguo zhaomi: yi wie hanxuejia de zichuan* 为中国着迷: 一位汉学家的自传 [Im Banne Chinas. Autobiographie eines Sinologen], Beijing: Shehui kexue wenchuan chubanshe. Chinesische Übersetzung von Franke 1995.

Führer, Bernhard (2001) *Vergessen und verloren. Die Geschichte der österreichischen Chinastudien*, Bochum: projektverlag.

Gransow, Bettina (1989) „[Nachruf auf] Wolfram Eberhard (1919-1989)", in Berliner Wissenschaftliche Gesellschaft e. V. (Hg.) Jahrbuch 1989, S. 69-71.

Han Xiao 韩笑 (2012) „Mi-Shi. Ba Qingshan tabian de dizhi xuejia" 米士. 把青山踏遍的地质学家 [Misch: der Geologe, der den Qingshan durchstreifte], in Beijing Daxue guoji hezuobu 北京大学国际合作部 [Center for International Cooperation der Peking-Universistät] (Hg.) *Beida yang xiansheng* 北大洋先生 [Ausländer an der Peking-Universität]，Peking: Peking University Press, S. 87-92.

Haenisch, Erich (1965) „Bruno Schindler und die alte Asia Major", in *Oriens Extremus* 12/1965.

Hansert, Andreas (1999) „Zum Schicksal der Sammlung Alfred Oppenheims während und nach der NS-Zeit", in Heuberger, Georg, Anton Merk und Moritz D. Oppenheim (Hg.) *Die Entdeckung des jüdischen Selbstbewusstseins in der Kunst*, Ausstellungskatalog Jüdisches Museum Frankfurt am Main, Köln: Wieland, S. 304-325.

Herrmann, Konrad (2008) „Über den Einfluß des Exils auf das wissenschaftlich-literarische Schaffen des österreichischen Sinologen Ernst Schwarz", in Leutner, Mechthild und Klaus Mühlhahn (Hg.) *Reisen in chinesischer Geschichte und Gegenwart, Jahrbuch der Deutschen Vereinigung für Chinastudien*, Bd. 4, Wiesbaden: Harrassowitz, S. 203-214.

Hundhausen, Vincenz (1999) „Mein Lebenslauf", in Walravens, Hartmut und Lutz Bieg (Hg.) *Vincenz Hundhausen: Leben und Werk des Dichters, Druckers, Verlegers, Professors, Regisseurs und Anwalts in Peking*, Wiesbaden: Harrassowitz, S. 59-60.

Jux, Anton (1999) „Der Enel des Montanus in China", in Walravens, Hartmut und Lutz Bieg (Hg.) *Vincenz Hundhausen: Leben und Werk des Dichters, Druckers, Verlegers, Professors, Regisseurs und Anwalts in Peking*, Wiesbaden: Harrassowitz, S. 61-64.

Kern, Martin (1998) „The Emigration of German Sinologists 1933-1945: Notes on the History and Historiography of Chinese Studies", in *Journal of the American Oriental Society* 118:4, S. 507-529.

Kern, Martin (1999) „Die Emigration der Sinologen 1933-1945. Zur ungeschriebenen Geschichte ihrer Verluste", in Martin, Helmut und Christiane Hammer (Hg.) *Chinawissenschaften – Deutschsprachige Entwicklungen. Geschichte, Personen, Perspektiven*, Hamburg: Institut für Asienkunde, S. 222-242.

Klose, Wolfgang (2014) „Dr. William Cohn. Berlin 1880 - Oxford 1961. Gelehrter Publizist und Advokat fernöstlicher Kunst", <http://www.w-ch-klose.de/html/ william_cohn.html>, Zugriff am 28.01.2014.

Kunze, Axel Bernd (2011) Adolf Reichwein (1898 - 1944) Reformpädagoge, Volks- kundler, Kulturpolitiker und Widerstandskämpfer, <http://lassalle-kreis.de/content/ adolf-reichwein>, Zugriff am 03.02.2014.

Leibfried, Christina (2003) *Sinologie an der Universität Leipzig. Entstehung und Wirken des Ostasiatischen Seminars 1878-1947*, Leipzig: Evangelische Verlagsanstalt.

Leutner, Mechthild (1987) „Sinologie in Berlin. Die Durchsetzung einer wissenschaftlichen Disziplin zur Erschließung und zum Verständnis Chinas", in Kuo Heng-yü (Hg.) *Berlin und China. Dreihundert Jahre wechselvolle Beziehungen*, Berlin: Colloquium Verlag. S. 31-55.

Leutner, Mechthild (1994) „Walter Zeisberger", in *Newsletter Frauen und China*, FU Berlin, 6/1994, S. 31-56.

Leutner, Mechthild (2001) „Vom Spracheninstitut zur NS-Auslandswissenschaftlichen Fakultät. Das Seminar für Orientalische Sprachen", in Neder, Christina, Heiner Roetz und Ines Schilling (Hg.) *China in seinen biographischen Dimensionen. Gedenkschrift für Helmut Martin*, Wiesbaden: Harrassowitz, S. 445-449.

Leutner, Mechthild (2011) „Sinologie an der Freien Universität Berlin", in Kubicki, Karol und Siegwart Lönnendonker (Hg.) *Die Kultur- und Ethno-Wissenschaften an der Freien Universität Berlin, in Beiträge zur Wissenschaftsgeschichte der Freien Universität Berlin 4. Schriften des Universitätsarchivs der Freien Universität Berlin,* , Göttingen: V&R unipress, S.81-96.

Lewin, Günter (1999) „Eduard Erkes und die Sinologie in Leipzig", in Martin, Helmut und Christiane Hammer (Hg.) *Chinawissenschaften – Deutschsprachige Entwick- lungen*, Hamburg: Institut für Asienkunde, S. 449-473.

Maas, Utz (2010a) „Menges, Karl H.", in Maas, Utz (Hg.) Verfolgung und Auswanderung deutschsprachiger Sprachforscher 1933-1945. Teil II: Katalog der 1933-1945 verfolgten und ausgewanderten Sprachforscher, <http://www.esf.uni-osnabrueck.de/ biographien-sicherung/m/254-menges-karl-h>, Zugriff am 23.04.2014.

Maas, Utz (2010b) „Steinen, Diether von den", in Maas, Utz (Hg.) Verfolgung und Aus- wanderung deutschsprachiger Sprachforscher 1933-1945. Teil II: Katalog der 1933-1945 verfolgten und ausgewanderten Sprachforscher, <http://www.esf.uni-osnabrueck.de/ biographien-sicherung/s/344-steinen-diether-von-den>, Zugriff am 23.04.2014.

Mai Huijun (2012) „Han-si Mi-le. Yi wei Deguo daifu zai Zhongguo zhanshichang" 汉斯· 米勒. 一位德国大夫在中国战事场 (Hans Müller. Ein deutscher Arzt auf Chinas Schlachtfeld) in Beijing Daxue guoji hezuobu 北京大学国际合作部 [Center for International Cooperation der Peking-Universisstät] (Hg.) *Beida yang xiansheng* 北大 洋先生 [Ausländer an der Peking-Universität], Peking: Peking University Press, S.214- 220.

Molenaar, Dee (1999) Class Acts. Peter Misch. Washington University, <http://www.washington.edu/alumni/columns/sept99/class/misch.html>, Zugriff am 06.02.2014.

Näth, Marie-Luise (1994) „Obituary. In memoriam Franz Michael (1907-92)", in *The China Quarterly* 138, S. 513-516.

Paleske, Alexander von (2008) „Rückblick: Hans Müller – Arzt im kommunistischen China", <http://oraclesyndicate.twoday.net/stories/5141920/>, Zugriff am 28.01.2014.

Pollak, Michael (1997) „Rudolf Loewenthal", in *Monumenta Serica* 45, S. 415-437.

Roy, Kshitis (1957) (Hg.) „Liebenthal-Festschrift", in *Sino-Indian Studies,* Volume V, parts 3 and 4, Santiniketan 1957.

Schmitt-Rousselle, Ardo (2013) Erwin Rousselle, <http://www.schmitt-rousselle.de/maison/erwinRousselle.asp>, Zugriff am 28.01.2014.

Simon, Walter (1952) „Gustav Haloun", in *The Journal of the Royal Asiatic Society of Great Britain and Ireland,* 1/2 (April 1952), S. 93-95.

Simon, Walter (1965) „Obituary of Dr. Bruno Schindler", in *Asia Major (New Series),* 11:2, S. 93-100.

Stam, David H. (1984) „John L. Mish (1909-1983)", in *The Journal of Asian Studies* 43:3, S. 615.

Stein, Amael Beghin (2014) Biographie Rolf Alfred Stein, <http://www.rolfastein.com/index.php?option=com_content&view=article&id=1&Itemid=2>, Zugriff am 25.01.2014.

The Social Networks and Archival Context Project (2014) Veith, Ilza, 1915- 2013. Biographical History, <http://socialarchive.iath.virginia.edu/xtf/view?docId=veith-ilza-1915--cr.xml>, Zugriff am 25.01.2014.

Taube, Manfred (2009) (Hg.) *Briefwechsel J.F. Rock – J. Schubert, 1935-1961*, Wien: Verlag der österreichischen Akademie der Wissenschaften.

Taylor, George E. (1992) „Hellmut Wilhelm. Pioneer of China Studies", in *Oriens Extremus* 35, S. 8-11.

Vanderstappen, Harrie (1983) „Ludwig Bachhofer (1894-1976)", in *Archives of Asian Art* 31:78, S. 110-112.

Walravens Hartmut (1994) „Martin Buber und Willy Tonn und ihre Beiträge zur Kenntnis der chinesischen Literatur", in *Monumenta Serica* 42/1994, S. 465-481.

Walravens, Hartmut (1996) „Ruth Krader in memoriam", in *Nachrichten der Gesellschaft für Natur- und Völkerkunde Ostasiens* 159-160, S. 13-14.

Walravens, Hartmut und Lutz Bieg (1999a) *Vincenz Hundhausen: Leben und Werk des Dichters, Druckers, Verlegers, Professors, Regisseurs und Anwalts in Peking*. Wiesbaden: Harrassowitz.

Walravens, Hartmut (1999b) „Streiflichter auf die deutsche Sinologie 1938-1943", in *NOAG* 165-166, S. 1-20, <http://www.uni-hamburg.de/oag/noag/noag1999_6.pdf>, Zugriff am 23.04.2014.

Walravens, Hartmut (2000) (Hg.) *Ferdinand Lessing (1882-1961) Sinologe, Mongolist und Kenner des Lamaismus. Material zu Leben und Werk. Mit dem Briefwechsel mit Sven Hedin*, Osnabrück: Zeller Verlag.

Walravens, Hartmut (2001) (Hg.) *Vincenz Hundhausen (1878-1955): Korrespondenzen 1934-1954, Briefe an Rudolf Pannwitz 1931-1954, Abbildungen und Dokumente zu Leben und Werk*, Wiesbaden: Harrassowitz.

Wildt, Michael (2013) „Berlin im Nationalsozialismus", <http://www.berlin.de/2013/berlin-im-nationalsozialismus/>, Zugriff am 25.1.2014.

Wildt, Michael (2013b) „Zerstörte Vielfalt", in *Das Themenjahr 2013* <http://www.berlin.de/2013/themenjahr/>, Zugriff am 28.08.2013.

Wilhelm, Friedrich (2005) „Scherman, Lucian Milius", in *Neue Deutsche Biographie* 22, S. 699-700, <http://www.deutsche-biographie.de/pnd119366304.html>, Zugriff am 28.01.2014.

Will, Pierre-Étienne und Isabelle Ang (2010) (Hg.) *Actualité d'Étienne Balazs (1905-1963): témoignages et réflexions pour un centenaire*, Paris: De Boccard.

Wissenschaftliche Gesellschaft e.V. (Hg.), Jahrbuch 1989, S. 69-71.

Wojak, Irmtrud (2011) *Fritz Bauer – Eine Biographie* , München: C.H. Beck.

Yeung, Bick-har (2010) „The Harry Simon Collection", in *East Asian Library Resources Group of Australia* Newsletter No. 56, S. 2, <http://www.ealrga.org.au/newsletter1007/1007_yeung_2.pdf>, Zugriff am 01.02.2014.

Anhang

*Übersicht der untersuchten Chinawissenschaftlerinnen und Chinawissenschaftler**

Name	Lebensdaten	Emigration	Akademische Forschung
Bachhofer, Ludwig 路德维希·巴赫霍夫	1894-1976	1935	Kunsthistoriker, Spezialgebiet asiatische Kunst
Balázs, Étienne (Stefan) 白乐日	1905-1963	1935	Sinologe, Wirtschafts- und Sozialgeschichte Chinas
Behrsing, Siegfried 贝尔森	1903-1994	/	Sinologe, Schwerpunkt Buddhismus
Bulling, Anneliese 卜爱玲	1900-2004	1936	Kunsthistorikerin und Sinologin
Cohn, William	1880-1961	1938	Kunsthistoriker, Spezialgebiet asiatische Kunst
Eberhard, Wolfram 艾伯华	1909-1989	1937	Sinologe und Ethnologe
Eberhard-Römer, Alide 阿莉德·艾伯哈特-罗美尔	1911-1994	1937	Sinologin
Ecke, Gustav 艾克，艾锷风	1896-1971	(1923)	Kunsthistoriker
Erkes, Eduard 何可思	1891-1958	/	Sinologe, Historiker
Fränkel, Hans Hermann 傅汉斯	1916-2003	(1933)	Sinologe, Altphilologe, Literatur Chinas
Haloun, Gustav 霍古达	1898-1951	1938	Sinologe, Historiker, Ethnologe

* In Klammern ist bei einigen Wissenschaftlern das Jahr angegeben, in dem sie ins Ausland, meist nach China, gegangen sind; nach 1933 war eine Rückkehr nach Deutschland nicht möglich. Daher sprechen wir von „passiver Emigration".

Hundhausen, Vincenz 洪涛生	1878-1955	(1924)	Literaturwissenschaftler, Dichter, Übersetzer
Kalmer, Joseph 约瑟夫·卡尔梅尔	1898-1959	1938	Sinologe, Ethnologe
Kobylinski, Hanna	1907-1999	1933/34	Historikerin, Geschichte Chinas
Krader-Schlesinger, Ruth 史蕾仙	1911-1996	1933	Sinologin, Ethnologin
Lessing, Ferdinand 佛狄南·烈辛	1882-1961	1935	Sinologe, Mongolist, Spezialgebiet Lamaismus
Liebenthal, Walter 李华德	1886-1982	1934	Indologe, Sinologe, Spezialgebiet Buddhismus
Löwenthal, Rudolf 罗文达	1904-1996	1933	Zeitungs- und Bibliothekswissenschaftler, Schwerpunkt China
Mänchen-Helfen, Otto 门琴-黑尔芬	1894-1969	1933	Sinologe, Ethnologe, Schwerpunkt euro-asiatische Kontakte
Maspero, Henri 昂利·马伯乐	1883-1945	/	Sinologe, Althistoriker
Menges, Karl Heinrich	1908-1999	1936	Altaist, Sprach- und Kulturkontake im zentralasiatischen Raum
Michael, Franz 梅谷	1907-1992	1933	Sinologe, Politikwissenschaftler
Misch, Peter 米士	1909-1987	1936	Geologe, Schwerpunkte u.a. Himalaya, Guangdong, Yunnan
Mish, John 约翰内斯·米仕	1909-1983	1934	Sinologe, Mandschurist
Müller, Hans 汉斯·米勒	1915-1994	1933/1939	Mediziner, Arzt
Münsterberg, Hugo	1916-1995	1935	Kunsthistoriker, Spezialgebiet asiatische u. chinesische Kunst
Oppenheim, Alfred	1873-1953	1938	Maler und Sammler ostasiatischer Kunst
Reichwein, Adolf 利奇温	1898-1944	/	Pädagoge, chinesisch-europäische Beziehungen im 18. Jh.
Reifler, Erwin 罗逸民	1903-1965	(1932)	Sinologe, Linguist, Sprachdidaktiker
Rousselle, Erwin 鲁雅文	1890-1949	/	Sinologe, Religionswissenschaftler
Salmony, Alfred 萨尔莫尼	1890-1958	1933	Kunsthistoriker, Spezialgebiet asiatische Kunst
Schaeffer, Philipp 菲利普·谢费尔	1894-1943	/	Sinologe, Bibliothekar

Scherman, Lucian	1864-1946	1939	Indologe, Spezialgebiet buddhistische Kunst Chinas
Schindler, Bruno	1882-1964	1933	Sinologe, Herausgeber der Zeitschrift *Asia Major*
Schirokauer, Conrad 希诺瓦考	1929-	1935	Sinologe, Historiker
Schnepp, Otto	1926-	1939	Chemiker, Wissenschaft und Technik in China
Schwarz, Ernst	1916-2003	1938	Sinologe, Übersetzer
Simon, Walter 西门华德	1893-1981	1936	Sinologe, Linguist
Stein, Rolf Alfred 石泰安	1911-1999	1933	Sinologe, Tibetologe, Mongolist
Stein/Frey, Richard 理查德·傅莱	1920-2004	1938	Arzt, Medizintechniker
Steinen, Diether v.d. 石坦安	1903-1954	(1927)	Ethnologe, Sinologe
Tonn, Willy (W. Y. Tonn)	1902-1957	1939	Sinologe
Tseng, Tsui-Chi 曾垂祺	1900-?	1937	Lektor für Chinesisch am Seminar f. Orientalische Sprachen, Berlin
Veith, Ilza 伊尔扎·威斯	1915-2013	1934	Medizinhistorikerin, u.a. Geschichte chinesische Medizin
Weiss, Ruth 魏璐诗	1908-2006	1933	Journalistin, Übersetzerin
Wilhelm, Hellmut 卫德明	1905-1990	1933	Sinologe
Wittfogel, Karl August 魏特夫	1896-1988	1934	Soziologe, Sinologe, Historiker
Wolff, Ernst 恩斯特·沃尔夫	1910-?	1933	Sinologe, chinesische Literatur
Zeissberger, Walter 蔡思克	1914-1993	1936	Ethnologe, Linguist, Sinologe

Emmelie Korell

Constructing Identity in Tourism: The Transformation of Zhongdian County into Shangri-La

The idea of Shangri-La, since its first appearance in James Hilton's 1933 novel *Lost Horizon*, has evolved into a myth of popular culture, inspired movies and explorers, and has become an iconic name for tourism marketers and tourists alike. Restaurants, hotels and towns utilize the name to attract visitors, and in 2002, Zhongdian County in northwestern Yunnan Province, China, renamed itself 香格里拉 Xianggelila (Shangri-La) County (*Xianggelila xian* 香格里拉县)[1] after a team of experts had – arguably – proven that this region displays the landscapes that had inspired the scenery described in Hilton's novel and can also be linked to the name itself. A decade later tourism has arrived in Xianggelila County and has not only introduced change to the region's industry and economy, but also to the County's identity.

Local identities function as brands in tourism marketing and even the development plan for Xianggelila County states: "[…] in order to create further opportunities and impulses for developing the tourism industry, the County's Chinese Communist Party (CCP) Committee and government immediately designed a strategy to develop […] Shangri-La as a brand" (Wang 2008c). Drawing from the myths and paradisiacal concepts related to the name of Shangri-La, the development plan aimed to capitalize on Xianggelila County's local identity.

This paper will analyze the impacts of tourism on Xianggelila by examining the ways in which tourism constructs Xianggelila County's local identity. Similarly, Åshild Kolås (2004, 2007) has extensively studied the impacts of tourism on representation practices of Tibetan identity in Xianggelila County. Huang Jiyuan (2001) and Cai Weiyan (2005) discussed the relationship between tourism and cultural changes in Diqing Tibetan Autonomous Prefecture (TAP), while Xiong and Yang's 2007 essay sketches the shifts that occurred in the County when it was transformed from Zhongdian into Xianggelila. Chen, Liu and Li (2009) provide an analysis of the suggestions for the development of Xianggelila County which can be gleaned from Hilton's novel. Other works have focused on the economic benefits of tourism (Li and Zhou 2006; Long 2008) and tourism's impacts on the environment (Qi 2001). In contrast to the works focused on representation practices (Kolås 2007) and transformation processes (Xiong and Yang 2007), this paper will discuss Xianggelila's local identity as it has been redefined by being renamed and reshaped as a tourist destination. For this purpose, the paper examines the construction of the local *Other* and three central scenic spots in Xianggelila County: Ganden Sumtseling Monastery (*Gadan songzanlin si* 噶丹松赞林寺)[2], Dakar Dzong[3] and Tiger Leaping

---

[1] The majority of localities in China use the Pinyin transcriptions of their names, but Xianggelila County employs Hilton's spelling instead. In this paper, Xianggelila is used to refer to the County and Shangri-La is used to refer to the place named in *Lost Horizon*.

[2] This paper primarily employs the names used in English materials and uses English transcriptions of Tibetan names.

[3] In January 2014, most of Dakar Dzong was destroyed in a fire (Nanfang Zhoumo, 13.01.14). This paper examines Dakar Dzong prior to the fire. Official sources usually transliterate Dakar Dzong from its

Gorge[4]. In the same way as Xianggelila County, their local identities have been redefined by their designation as tourism destinations; and by employing the concepts of simulacra (Baudrillard 1981) and hyperreality (Eco 1986), this paper traces their contemporary identities as scenic spots in Xianggelila County.

After a short introduction to tourism theories, the concepts of simulacra and hyperreality and tourism in China, this paper will focus on Xianggelila County and the myths that feed its identity. By analyzing three sites and the conception of the local *Other* – all serving as symbols for Xianggelila County as a tourism destination – a general outline will be formulated to show how tourism constructs have romanticized the identities of places and how tourist sites function.

Tourism in China

The World Tourism Organization defines tourism as

> [...] a social, cultural and economic phenomenon which entails the movement of people to countries or places outside their usual environment for personal or business/professional purposes. These people are called visitors (which may be either tourists or excursionists; residents or non-residents) and tourism has to do with their activities, some of which imply tourism expenditure.

Other definitions put forward in academic literature reflect diverse aspects and approaches to the subject. John Urry (1990) views tourism as an act of consumption of "[...] goods and services which are in some sense unnecessary. They are consumed because they supposedly generate pleasurable experiences which are different from everyday life" (quoted in Burns 1999: 31). In contrast, Neil Leiper (1995) defines tourism as the behavioral manifestations of ideas and opinions that cause people to travel and further inform their ideas on where to go and how to relate to a specific location.

Dean MacCannell (1976) suggests that the search for authenticity is a basic motivation for tourists. However, the moment the tourist arrives at his destination, a cultural *Heisenberg effect* (cf. van den Berghe and Keyes 1984) occurs: "the search of the exotic [becomes] self-defeating because of the overwhelming influence of the observer on the observed" (Mac Cannell 1976: 345). Tourists searching for an authentic location will not find it because of their own presence. Any authenticity at a tourist site then must be staged, and MacCannell anticipates that tourists will abandon such a destination (ibid 2001: 388).

This predicted scenario has not yet occurred, and indeed it seems that rather the opposite is taking place. Staged shows surrounding ethnic or local cultural practices are extraordinarily popular with Chinese tourists (Xu 2001: 167-172; Oakes 2005), and theme parks flourish across the globe. Dennison Nash (1996) points out that "there are, indeed, other types of tourists (and, one might add, hosts) for whom the issue of authenticity does not come up" (Nash 1996: 82). Perhaps then, tourists do not, as MacCannell assumed, seek authenticity – perhaps what they seek is difference or *Otherness*[5].

---

original Tibetan as *dukezong gucheng* 獨克宗古城 – the old town of Dukezong – in Chinese. Sometimes, it is also referred to as the old town in Jiantang, or (Shangri-La) Old Town (*Lonely Planet* 2011: 675).

[4] Among western travelers, Tiger Leaping Gorge is well-known by its English name. In Chinese sources, *hutiao xia* 虎跳峡 is used.

[5] *Otherness* constitutes a concept used among postmodernist and postcolonial scholars that denotes a relationship informed by power asymmetries, perceived differences and deviations from (constructed)

In this paper, therefore tourism is considered in terms of an individual's conscious immersion in a perceived or constructed *Otherness*, affecting the economy, ecology and culture of the tourist and the host simultaneously. The nature of this immersion may be superficial, visual, spatial, ritualistic or adopt any other shape imaginable; once the individual assumes the identity of the tourist, geographical distances lose their significance[6]. *Otherness* constitutes the attribute that appeals to tourists: a destination needs to be different in order to be attractive. While difference may be inherently negative when associated with social change or migration (Davies 2009: 38) and tourism tends to produce orientalist images (Said 2003 [1978]: 202), tourism also romanticizes difference.

Analogous to the previously mentioned *Heisenberg effect,* difference in the context of tourist destinations results from their designation as tourist destinations. However, places such as Xianggelila County and its sites are not only tourist destinations but also sites of historic or religious significance. Obviously constructed sites, such as Disneyland, have been called hyperreal by Jean Baudrillard (1994). The concept of hyperreality commonly refers to spaces where differentiating between "reality" and "simulated reality" is either impossible or pointless; Umberto Eco has called this "the absolute [authentic] fake" (Eco 1986: 8) and Baudrillard "a real without origin or reality" (Baudrillard 1994: 2). Tourists engage with these hyperreal spaces that are designed to meet their imagined desires. Baudrillard points out that the superimposed identity "engenders the territory and if we were to revive the fable today, it would be the territory whose shreds are slowly rotting across the map": the identity constructed at tourist destinations becomes the local identity. In this reading, Disneyland is Disneyland; it is a theme park of itself. Xianggelila, as a tourist destination, also functions as a hyperreal space, and can be understood as a simulacrum, since it represents an idea of itself. It is not any kind of reality – and indeed, Baudrillard has suggested that the real is "a fantasy generated by doubling the signs of an unlocatable reality" (Baudrillard 1994: 81), that is represented through performances and symbols. Symbols of Xianggelila narrate the fictions and myths that construct Xianggelila's identity.

While contemporary mass tourism appears as a new phenomenon in the People's Republic of China, literati in imperial China engaged in leisure travel centuries ago. Wu (2005: 68) points out that the terms used in today's tourism terminology, such as *fengjing* 风景 (scenery) and *mingsheng* 名胜 (short for *mingshan shengdi* 名山胜地: famous mountains and unexcelled places), date back to the Qin dynasty (221-206 b.c.e.). Leisure travel constituted an established practice for the gentry by the 16th century, and a canon of "scenic spots" had been developed. The canon included vistas and locations described in the writings of famous poets and scholars (Teng 2001), and travel to these places functioned as a part of Confucian self-cultivation (Strassberg 1994: 20)[7].

---

norms. The *Other* in relation to tourism can be the destination or the local; tourism itself requires them to be the *Other* opposite the tourist. The usage of *Other, Otherness* or *Othering* in italics and capitalized indicates a reference to said concept.

[6] This definition allows for a local to turn into a tourist or a tourist to turn into a local; both processes are common and crucial for domestic tourism, since the individual here seeks out difference in his or her own country or region.

[7] Strassberg discusses the relationship between travel and Confucianism in detail, naming both the negative and positive connotations.

Views formed a central component of literati leisure travel. Local gazettes regularly printed local canonical views and, from time to time, they added new views or scenic spots to their canon (ibid; Brook 1998). Nyíri (2003: 9) observes that this practice came to a halt during the 1930s, and was only revived after the end of the Cultural Revolution (1966-1976). After the victory of the Communist Party in 1949, tourism became taboo: as a bourgeoisie hobby it was out of place in the young communist country (Zhang 2003: 15). However, pilgrimages during the Cultural Revolution that saw large numbers of Red Guards traveling to revolutionary sites posed one exception. Analogous to scenic spots the revolutionary sites had been state-approved and (in a somewhat ironic reference to literati traditions) canonized (Wagner 1992: 380-386).

After Mao's death in 1976 and the beginning of the "Reform-and Opening Era" (1978 – present), tourism took off in China. During the first decade, the Chinese state almost exclusively encouraged inbound tourism in an attempt to gain foreign currency. Although a domestic travel department was set up as early as 1985 (Wei et al. 1999: 145), it was only in 1997 that developing domestic tourism became a priority. The importance of internal tourism became apparent when it was employed as a strategy to counter lagging economic growth rates. Subsequently, in 1999, the number of official holidays was raised, creating the "Golden Weeks" around May 1st and National Day on October 1st (Qian 2003: 148).

Today, dramatically increased numbers of domestic tourists traveling during the Golden Weeks question the Golden Weeks' continued existence. On October 3rd, 2012, as many as 182.000 tourists visited the Forbidden City in Beijing, and 215.000 were counted at the Sun Yat-sen Mausoleum in Nanjing. Overcrowding led to potentially dangerous situations in Huashan, dead camels in Dunhuang and monstrous traffic jams on China's busy roads (Li 2012). For this reason, there have been calls to replace the fixed-date holidays with variable ones; the number of domestic tourists is expected to continue rising (Liang and Li 2012).

At the heart of tourism in China lies the scenic spot: seeing it, engaging it by taking part in certain ritualistic gestures, such as taking pictures, purchasing tickets or eating local specialties, and consuming it are tourism's standard practices[8]. While many scenic spots possess historical roots and were among the catalogued views collected prior to the 20th century, recently established sites have joined the canon. The process of adding a new site – such as Xianggelila – to the canon sees the extensive use of symbols, references to already known scenic spots or even (re-)constructions of historical traditions. For example, in the process of developing a Guizhou village for tourism, Nyíri observed the addition of a clock tower that had never existed in the village. This particular type of clock tower, however, could be found in all surrounding villages and constituted part of the areas' canonical vistas (Nyíri 2003: 13). Therefore, the addition of the clock tower did not cause the site to become inauthentic, but rather shaped the village to match its canonical identity. These linkages between site and canon figure prominently in Xianggelila County as well; the canon provides the narrative for presenting and developing the site. At Xianggelila County, the canon draws from the myths surrounding its name as well as the historical and fictional ties to Tibetan culture. Establishing scenic

---

[8] Due to its ritualistic nature, MacCannell (1976) and Graburn (2001) have described tourism as a religion-replacement of the 20th century.

spots in border regions as a firm part of China's scenic spot canon (ibid) also constructs a narrative on that intimately links these sites to the Chinese nation. The narrative bracket affirms those localities as parts of the People's Republic of China regardless of their ethnic or cultural *Otherness* (Anagost 1997: 161-165).

Shangri-La: the Myths and the Place

James Hilton's *Lost Horizon* rapidly became an international best-seller after its publication in 1933. Subsequent translations into other languages spread the idea, and frequent references in popular culture turned Hilton's invention into a myth (Eco 2013). Xianggelila County now looks to invoke the myth and reconstruct itself in the tradition of Shangri-La.

In the novel, a group of four expatriates is evacuating from fictional Baskul[9] in the 1920s when their aircraft is hijacked. Eventually, they crash in a barren, "this looks like the end of the world" (47)[10] area, after which they are rescued and taken to Shangri-La by a group of monks. The novel's protagonist, Conaway, meets the high lama, who, it is revealed, was originally a missionary from Luxembourg. During his century-long stay at Shangri-La, the missionary converted to the local variety of Buddhism. Meanwhile, the group's third member falls in love with a local Chinese princess and, together with Conaway, the two escape from Shangri-La. For the couple in love, the attempt to escape is fatal, while at the end of the novel, the surviving Conaway sets his sights on finding a way to return to Shangri-La.

Landscape and cultural identity expressed in architecture and practices configure Hilton's Shangri-La. Hostile but beautiful mountains enclose the arable Blue Moon Valley of Shangri-La. Its visual splendor including "[…] the loveliest mountain on earth" (51) posits a leitmotif throughout the novel and the landscape descriptions that mirror those found in today's travel literature. The idea of Shangri-La still includes those towering, snow-capped peaks and fertile valleys – and routine association with Tibet. Xianggelila County uses both, by invoking the scenery of Tiger Leaping Gorge and the mountains of Deqin, as well as capitalizing on its Tibetan heritage. In the novel, two clues point toward Tibet: the vague location of Shangri-La itself, somewhere north of the Indus valley, and the Tibetan lamasery situated above Blue Moon Valley. In the novel, the lamasery functions as a governing institution, although Hilton's characters point out that it is the principle of moderation that governs life in the valley where religions peacefully coexist. Nowadays, Shangri-La is imagined as a version of the Garden of Eden, as an "oriental version of Paradise" (Kolås 2007: 5), or as a "concept of an earthly paradise after Western cultural and moral viewpoints" (Wang 2008b). In 2009, Chen, Li und Liu presented a paper using *Lost Horizon* in order to develop suggestions for Xianggelila County[11], and

---

[9] Based on a line within the novel – "Fact is, an Afghan or an Afridi or somebody ran off with one of our buses" (Hilton, 2004: 2). Mitra believes Baskul to be located in modern-day Afghanistan, perhaps even to be identical with Kabul (cf. Mitra 2006).

[10] All page numbers provided here refer to the 2004 edition of *Lost Horizon* as named in the bibliography below.

[11] It may be of interest to note that Hilton's Shangri-La is constructed as a western vision of paradise; studies have looked at orientalist and colonial markings (Masuzawa 1999). The inclusion of visions of

Origins of Shangri-La continues to state that "*Lost Horizon* became the *Peach Blossom Spring* of the West".

Tao Yuanming's (372–417) poem *Peach Blossom Spring*[12] tells the tale of a fisherman, who upon following a stream reaches a remote community. The locals warmly welcome him and he is deeply impressed by the tranquility and peace that he finds there. However, the locals in Peach Blossom Spring caution him not to tell anybody in the outside world of their existence – their ancestors relocated to this hidden place after a war, and they have not involved themselves in worldly affairs since. After the fisherman returns to his home, nobody else is able to find the place again.

Peach Blossom Spring resembles Hilton's Shangri-La in its fundamental identity of a remote idyll. Differences reveal themselves in the details: conflict in Peach Blossom Spring is relegated to the outside world, and avoided through strict moderation in Shangri-La. Being self-sufficient, society in Peach Blossom Spring has eschewed contact with the outside world, whereas Shangri-La depends on the outside world for trade and modern amenities. However, the parallels of peace and prosperity between these two fictional places influence the perception of Xianggelila. The concept of Shambhala (also known as Shambala, Shambahla, or Shamballa) possesses the same characteristics and is linked to Xianggelila, not only by these parallels, but also by its association with Tibetan Buddhism and the resemblance to its Chinese name – Xiangbala. When Zhongdian was looking to transform itself into a tourist destination, Xiangbala had been considered an option (Kolås 2004).

Shambhala is a loanword from Sanskrit that migrated into Tibet with the *Kalachakra Tantra* in the 11th century (Frost 2007). In the context of Tibetan Buddhism, it is sometimes used as a synonym for the *Pure Land*, but more commonly, it is used to refer to a remote, hidden kingdom located somewhere in central Asia[13] that is characterized by peace and social harmony; inhabitants of Shambhala have presumably attained enlightenment[14]. For Xianggelila, the association with the Shambhala myth works to affirm an identity constructed around paradisiacal concepts. It also tightens its links to Tibetan Buddhism, and the development plan views religion and spirituality as a resource to be developed (Wang 2008c). Shangri-La, Peach Blossom Spring and Shambhala primarily function as different versions of paradise that are by name or location linked to Xianggelila. However, Xianggelila's connection to these myths goes beyond loose associations and paronyms; in 1996, a group of experts arguably proved that Hilton's Shangri-La is located in Diqing TAP.

---

paradise originating in the east, such as Peach Blossom Spring and Shambhala, indicate the intention to efface potential cultural discrepancies.

[12] The Chinese title is *taohuayuan ji* 桃花源记 and translates into "records of the source of the peach blossom river"– *Peach Blossom Spring* is the commonly used translation, and will consequently be used in this paper. Further, this paper will differentiate between the location and the poem by setting the poem in italics.

[13] The vision presented in the *Kalachakra* texts appears to have been appropriated from an older Hindu myth, which itself can arguably be read as the mythologization of an actual culture in another part of Asia, with Tibet being a distinct possibility (Newman 1985: 54).

[14] Shambhala may be understood as a synonym for the Pure Land.

Hilton's detailed descriptions indicate that he based his narration on travelogues and accounts from travelers, although his exact sources remain uncertain. An interview Hilton gave to the New York Times in 1936 hints that he used "Tibetan Material" from the British museum (Crisler 1936), which may have included the 1928 translation of a travelogue[15] by two French missionaries who travelled from Beijing to Lhasa in 1844 on a route 250km north of Yunnan (McRae 2002). Another possible source consists of articles by the botanist and explorer, Joseph Rock, who lived in Yunnan during the 1920s and travelled the region extensively. Travel guidebooks (*Lonely Planet* 2011; Goodman 2009) claim that the older inhabitants of Xianggelila County still remember him. At the time when Hilton was writing his novel, the *National Geographic* magazine covered Rock's excursions, including photographs and illustrations. While there is no evidence to prove that Hilton used these, the descriptive markers utilized within *Lost Horizon* indicate that Hilton had visual sources. However, Rock's accounts and photographs cover Yunnan, Sichuan, Tibetan and Qinghai, and the French missionaries did not pass through Yunnan or Xianggelila County. If these constituted Hilton's sources, his inspirations may not have originated from the landscapes of today's Xianggelila County.

The 1996 expert group sent into the field by Yunnan officials consisted of more than 40 Chinese academics from various fields and provinces. They examined Hilton's descriptions of Shangri-La's landscapes to determine whether Xianggelila is Shangri-La. They suggested that *Lost Horizon's* Mount Karakal is identical with Kawa Karpo in Xianggelila County's neighboring Deqin County, and three rivers that are mentioned as crisscrossing the area in the novel could also be identified: the Nujiang, the Mekong (Langcan) and the Jinsha (Kolås 2007: 6).

In the *Shangri-La book series*, experts on the Tibetan language and history suggested that the Tibetan name of the Old Town at Jiantang, Dakar Dzong, can be translated as "Blue Moon Township". In *Lost Horizon*, Hilton locates Shangri-La in Blue Moon Valley. In *Tibetans at Diqing's Shangri-La*[16], Huang Zhongcai declares that the renaming is not really a renaming: Shangri-La had been the region's name all along. He claims that "Shangri-La", as a Tibetan term, translates as "the sun and the moon are in our minds" (5)[17]and the ancient names of two towns located at the site of today's Jiantang "尼玛寨 Nimazhai" and "独肯寨 Dukenzhai" (also: Yang 2002:2) refer respectively to sunlight and moonlight. From this, Huang concludes that the region encompassing them includes both the sun and

---

[15] The material in question is presumably the translation of the travelogue by Evariste Regis Huc and Joseph Gabet that was published in 1928.

[16] Full title: *Vistas of China's minorities: Tibetans of Diqing's Shangri-La*. The book forms part of a series introducing China's *minzu* – covering history, customs, food, dress and holidays on about fifty pages.

[17] The original Chinese is: 心中的日月 *Xinzhong de riyue*, and the English translation is provided on the same page. Qi (1999) suggests that the pronunciation of this term in the local Tibetan dialect is phonetically similar to Xianggelila. He demonstrates this as follows: 香 *Xiang* replaces 心 *xin*, 格 *ge* in local dialect functions like 的 *de*, 里 *li* represents 日 *ri* and is also pronounced similar to 尼 *ni*, and finally 拉 *la* stands for 月 *yue* (Qi 1999: 9 f.).

the moon, since the term "Shangri-La" includes them both when translated as "the sun and the moon are in our minds"[18].

While *History of Shangri-La* and *Tibetans at Diqing's Shangri-La* [19] interlink Xianggelila's history with Shangri-La by using linguistic markers, historical sources mainly utilize two names – Zhongdian (Chinese) [20] and Gyalthang (Tibetan) – to refer to the area. Zhongdian translates as "middle pasture": conquerors from Lijiang's Mu kingdom chose Zhongdian and a Naxi alternative[21] for the region in the 15th century (Kolås 2004: 28). "Gyalthang" can be traced back to different origins. One account sees it as deriving from the name "Jie" of an ethnic group "Jie Qiang" which settled in the Jinsha area in the third century AD (Duan 1997: 46). Another version suggests that the name means "victory plain", combining the Tibetan words for victory (rgyal) and plain (thang), and commemorating battles fought here between Tibet and Lijiang in the 7th century AD (Kolås 2007: 4). Gyalthang is also historically cited together with Lithang and Bathang as the "land of the three brothers", with reference to a legend that these three were fiefdoms awarded to the three sons of one Tibetan king (Wang 2008a).

Historical sources present a variety of other names, most of them variations on Jiantang. The variations on Jiantang, similar in pronunciation or writing, appear from the Tang dynasty onwards (Yang 2002: 25), corresponding roughly with the founding of Dakar Dzong. While Jiantang was used until the County's renaming (and is still used on maps), the name, Dakar Dzong, posits one more link to the new name of Xianggelila. The ruling Tubo Kingdom erected a fortification (ca. 676–679) on the site of modern-day Jiantang and named it Dakar Dzong (Wang 2008a)[22]. In the following centuries, Zhongdian remained a sphere of struggles, and was invaded by the Mu of Lijiang in 1499 (Yang 2002: 25). According to *History of Shangri-La,* the Mu misunderstood Dakar Dzong's name. Since another settlement was founded nearby, their names soon merged in the spoken language, resulting in the name of "Xianggenima" (ibid), which means as much as "city of sun and moon" (*riyuecheng* 日月城). This not only parallels the above-mentioned authors' translation of Shangri-La as "the sun and the moon are in our minds", but also appears phonetically similar to the Chinese transcription of Shangri-La: *Xianggelila.*

Regardless of the explanation chosen, the linkage of Xianggelila's new name with past names or a novel constitutes what Eric Hobsbawm considers an *invented tradition*. It constructs a narrative that converts or establishes historical elements into a teleological order that must legitimize the renaming and the identification of Shangri-La with Xianggelila County. The identity construct of Xianggelila County as Shangri-La, in return, provides

---

[18] An alternative, etymological tracking of "Shangri-La" may lead to the conclusion that it translates to "Shang Mountain Pass" (cf. Das et al. 2005). Furthermore, Shang refers to a region in western Tibet, thus rather distant from Yunnan.

[19] Both titles have been named semi-academic by Kolås (2007). As their publication coincides with the renaming of the County, it is not unlikely that their purpose is to reinforce the notion that Xianggelila County is Shangri-La.

[20] 忠甸 *Zhongdian* was an abbreviation for 忠于明王朝 *Zhong yu Ming wangchao*. By the time of the Qing (1644–1911) it had become 中甸 *Zhongdian* (Yang 2002: 26).

[21] The Naxi name can be transcribed as "Zhushu" and means "here the ruler of the west resides" (Xiong and Yang 2007: 64).

[22] The capital of the Tubo Kingdom (648–877) was in Lhasa; it can be understood as a Tibetan kingdom.

the basis for the region's practice of referencing Hilton's novel in its tourism advertisement campaigns. And in turn, the campaigns transformed Xianggelila County from a hinterland county dependent on forestry into a popular tourist destination.

The symbols: Ganden Sumtseling Monastery, Dakar Dzong, Tiger Leaping Gorge and the local *Other*

Ganden Sumtseling Monastery, Dakar Dzong and Tiger Leaping Gorge constitute Xianggelila's three main scenic spots. They all function as symbols for Xianggelila County and construct its identity. And at the same time, they represent their identity and the County's identity to tourists; this identity is being transformed by tourism.

In 1674, the fifth Dalai Lama, with the help of the Koshut Mongols and troops from the Mu Kingdom, brought Zhongdian into the Tibetan kingdom, replacing the local Kagyu School and converting their temples to the Gelug school of Buddhism. After hearing the report on local conditions, the fifth Dalai Lama himself, in 1679, selected the location on which the first Gelug Monastery of the region was to be built. After the completion of the initial building – with the capacity to house 530 monks – the fifth Dalai Lama chose the name, Ganden, with reference to the Gelug School's founder, Tsongkhapa (1357-1419), and Sumtseling, meaning the thirty-three heavens (Jiedang 1995: 105). Ganden Sumtseling Monastery continued to grow and by the dawn of the 19th century, constituted the most important Gelug Monastery in Yunnan. Jiedang (1995: 114) writes that relations between the Monastery and the Chinese state remained friendly; the Monastery supported passing troops in 1936, and in 1950, in accordance with CCP instructions, took up agricultural production to sustain itself. During the Cultural Revolution, the Monastery was severely damaged and many treasures were lost. Local Buddhist practitioners initiated reconstruction in 1982, while the state joined the project in 1984 and has, since then, invested in the Monastery's restoration and maintenance. New constructions established by 2012 include a visitor center housing a ticket office, a restaurant, a hotel and a souvenir shop. In the grounds of Ganden Sumtseling Monastery, signposts direct tourists and provide them with information for their visit. The information provided on these signposts comprises the names of individual buildings, the dates of their construction, and, at times, additional information related to the context of their construction or religious usage. This sparse information policy leaves some buildings unmarked and unexplained, and further only presents a very abbreviated and superficial narrative of the place. The tourist may construct their own narrative from the visual signage. Or they may elect to take a guided tour in order to hear a longer narrative of Ganden Sumtseling's identity. The published development plan (Wang 2008c) for Xianggelila County emphasizes the instruction and training of travel guides. Their narratives introduce and affirm Ganden Sumtseling's identity to tourists and are capable of subverting or reaffirming official narratives as these are presented on television or in guide books. The conformity of narratives is at the heart of the training and representation of the guides. The on-site signs support the state-sanctioned narrative. The splendidly restored buildings symbolize former glory and a state engaged in the upkeep of its cultural heritage (Shepherd 2006:249). Tibetan architecture and writing invoke Tibetan culture, while mandalas and thangka underscore the site's religious significance. But in their function as signs and symbols for an obscure notion of Tibetan culture or Lama Buddhism, they have become hyperreal, and possibly empty;

Ganden Sumtseling Monastery, then, can be seen as a simulacrum to tourists: a symbol of itself.

Another site on the tourism map of Xianggelila County is the "old town" of Dakar Dzong in Jiantang. It is on the map because of its visual values and its historic significance, having once been a trading site on the Tea-Horse-Road. Founded as a walled fort by the Tubo Kingdom between 676 and 679, it became a major trading hub between Tibet and the Qing Empire, and with the rise of the mining industry, merchants flocked to the area. After the heydays of trade and mining, Dakar Dzong was rediscovered as a potential tourist destination in the late 1990s. Mirroring Ganden Sumtseling Monastery, the narrative of Dakar Dzong is constructed in travel guides and through visual signage: architecture, dress and consumable local specialties, such as Yak meat, Tibetan knifes and related souvenir paraphernalia. In fact, at Dakar Dzong not one store unrelated to tourism can be found. This resembles what Nyíri (2003) observed at Songpan, where tourism developers rebuilt the old town by tearing down new houses, and moving out residents in order to create an enclosed area only for tourists (2003: 48).

To tourists on their (imagined) quest for authenticity and unspoiled landscapes[23], the obvious intervention of tourism planners must then be understood as a repellant (MacCannell 2001; Llamas and Belk 2011: 2). But Nyíri (2003) has pointed out that "tourism does not invalidate authenticity", and it is within the symbol-based construction of Dakar Dzong after its imagined identity that Dakar Dzong is able to meet tourist expectations and match the narrative proposed in tourism guidebooks. Like Ganden Sumtseling Monastery, Dakar Dzong functions as a symbol unto itself and as a hyperreal space.

The use of ancient signs and symbols, however, heralds their rise back into the public consciousness. They may be appropriated to visually construct an identity – regardless of their former meanings or context – but in their new function, they gain meaning as symbols of identity. As such, the utilization of symbols of Tibetan culture to attract tourists paradoxically causes both: a commoditized, constructed narrative of a fictional local identity built on myths and tourist expectations as well as growing awareness and critical discussion of local identity and local culture.

While Dakar Dzong emphasizes its cultural heritage and Ganden Sumtseling Monastery capitalizes on its religious significance – in both cases through symbols and simulation – Tiger Leaping Gorge's main attraction is its landscape. *Lonely Planet China* hails it as one of China's "30 Top Experiences" (2011: 6), and then goes on to make skeptical observations about recent construction efforts on the site. As of September 2012, easily accessible walkways have been constructed at the bottom of the gorge and these have changed Tiger Leaping Gorge from an exclusive hiking destination to a popular day excursion site. Mass tourism, with all its implications and impacts, has discovered the gorge.

Close to the gorge, a village consisting of hotels, restaurants and shops is being constructed (Wang 2008c). The construction of the settlement in Tibetan style may be understood as an attempt to widen the gorge's range of attractions. Currently, tourists visit the gorge mainly for its scenery; a nearby village may inspire tourists to spend more time

---

[23] Urry (1990) developed the concept of the *tourist gaze*, according to which the object is reduced to its visual components. With reference to this concept, *romantic gaze* suggests an inclination on the viewer's side to perceive the object of his gaze as special, and, basically, different.

and money in the area. Simultaneously, the leitmotif of the Tibetan heritage of the entirety of Xianggelila County is introduced to the site.

A small memorial building expands on Tiger Leaping Gorge's historical significance. During the Long March (1934-1935), part of the Red Army passed through the gorge and through some areas of Xianggelila County[24]. Entrepreneurs at the gorge offer to rent uniforms to tourists who then have their photographs taken. This behavior mirrors the stalls outside and near the entrance of the gorge, where colorful minority dress can be rented for the same purpose. These clothes, like the uniforms, are rarely historically accurate (Mackerras 2003: 73). Instead, they appeal to fashions and images with which the tourists will already be familiar through propaganda and media[25]. The dress is a simulacrum, imitating an idea rather than attempting to recreate the past, and relying heavily on visual symbolism in the process.

Tiger Leaping Gorge's spatial identity, however, is not shaped by local dress and culture, but rather by its vistas. The symbols of the locality – the gorge, the mountains and the river – do not function as simulacra: Tiger Leaping Gorge is not quite a symbol of itself. The signs that include Tiger Leaping Gorge in the construct of Xianggelila – the hotels in Tibetan style, the dresses rented on site – simulate an imagined identity of the place. If Tiger Leaping Gorge is understood not as a tourist site, but as a place of wilderness and adventure (as *Lonely Planet* suggests), then its landscapes must be seen as simulacra.

To tourists, these three sites constitute Xianggelila's three main scenic spots. And yet these symbols are simulations of their own identity: Ganden Sumtseling Monastery as a tourist site is a symbol of the County's religious significance, the site of Dakar Dzong represents its cultural heritage and Tiger Leaping Gorge symbolizes dramatic landscapes. As simulacra, the sites are neither inauthentic nor truly real – they can be tourist sites and place of worship, culture and nature simultaneously. Xianggelila County, too, functions as a simulacrum of Shangri-La, Peach Blossom Spring and Shambhala: places invented through myth and fiction. And within the simulacra at Xianggelila County, tourists may encounter the difference they seek.

Difference in general may assume various forms; tourists require difference from their everyday lives. As tourism development seeks to capitalize on imagined different places, destinations and sites become touristified. Llamas and Belk (2011) criticized Xianggelila County, saying that it had been turned into a theme park, and tourism has constructed these simulacra according to its own desires. But aside from history and local culture, myths and fiction inspire the symbols utilized to signify Xianggelila County. And these fictional identities are what tourists encounter and locals negotiate with on site.

For example, the anthropomorphic representation of difference at Xianggelila County is the local inhabitant. Local residents at Xianggelila include individuals from different parts of China and the world. Some families may have lived in Xianggelila for generations, others may have moved there for economic reasons (Kolås 2007: 89). Furthermore,

---

[24] Yang (2002: 124-129) mentions the fact that a unit crossed through Zhongdian between April 25th, and May 12th, 1936. While this differs from the dates commonly associated with the Long March – 1934-35 – a number of units took different routes, or ended their trek on differing dates.

[25] For example, both *A Complete Guide to Yunnan Province* (157) and Huang's 2004 *Tibetans at Shangri-La* provide pictures of locals in traditional dress.

guidebooks advertising Xianggelila usually represent the locals as Tibetan[26], while in fact less than 50% of the local population is actually ethnically Tibetan (Diqing Nianjian Bianjibu 2003: 44). Tourism advertisements created the image of an *Other* that is Tibetan. On site performers – including tour guides, sales personnel and actors – meet that image by donning Tibetan dress regardless of their actual ethnicity (Kolås 2007: 90). It is the dress that demarcates Tibetan identity at Xianggelila and the individual functions as a simulacrum suggesting a Tibetan identity of place and people regardless of the individual's actual background. The Tibetan *Other* at Xianggelila simulates a fiction of Tibetan-ness, constructed from myths and escapist fantasies. Symbolism signifies Tibetan-ness, and Gladney (2002), Oakes (1998 2000), Diamond (1988), and Thierry (1989) observe that there is a stringent pattern to the representation of minorities in China. Women are generally depicted as "highly feminine and sexualized" (Nyíri 2008: 39), whereas men may appear strong, strange, extraordinary and generally exotic[27]. While this underscores the difference constructed in these fictional visions of *Otherness*, the political agenda still seeks to portray all *Others* as "patriotic Chinese citizens" (ibid). Yet the Tibetan *Other* portrayed posits a simulacrum and a generic Tibetan *Other*.

As simulacra for tourists, the Tibetan *Other* and the scenic spots symbolize fictions. They draw inspiration from circulated images, myths and history, but in their construction they become artificial. The difference tourists encounter when engaging with these simulacra then posits a fictional, simulated difference.

Conclusion: Romanticized Simulacra

In tourism, names invoke their own kind of brand magic by summoning particular images fueled by advertisements, fiction and fantasy. New York is as much a place as it is an idea to tourists, the same as Bora Bora or Macchu Picchu. Indeed, some place-images have become so current in the popular vernacular that they are applied to descriptions of other locations, such as descriptions of Suzhou as the "Venice of the East" (Lonely Planet China 2011: 219) and of Frankfurt am Main as "Mainhattan". Ideally, the tourist is attracted by these names and their familiar fictions. The transformation of Zhongdian to Xianggelila invokes the same "magic". The myths behind the name provide ideas for tourists who are unfamiliar with the actual place[28].

Xianggelila County invokes the myths that originated in *Lost Horizon*, *Peach Blossom Spring* and the *Kalachakra Tantra* to design the identity it portrays to tourists. By establishing connections to the myths through landscape descriptions, etymological markers and history, the County constructs a narrative as Xianggelila County. This new narrative replaces the other narrative Zhongdian, but does not overwrite it. History is not being rewritten so much as it is being re-imagined.

Simultaneously the County's designated scenic spots become simulacra. Ganden Sumtseling Monastery to tourists is a symbol of a fictional, generic Tibetan Lamaist Monastery. Mandala and thangka inform tourists of this; the general condition of the

---

[26] This occurs in both, *Lonely Planet* and *A Complete Guide to Yunnan Province*.

[27] Gladney (2002: 241 f.) remarks that the portrayal of minorities in a way that is useful to the state is not particularly new, but can be traced back to imperial times.

[28] The only other contemporary example is the temporary re-naming of New Zealand to Middle Earth in response to the popularity of the cinematic adaptions of Tolkien's novels

Monastery furthermore proposes a state concerned with its upkeep. And the monks living in the Monastery signify the place's continued religious significance. Tourism does not invalidate Ganden Sumtseling Monastery as a place of worship: tourists engage with a fiction, while monks and pilgrims interact with the site in its spiritual function. At Dakar Dzong, symbols, too, proclaim the place's Tibetan heritage and historic age to the visitor, simulating itself. And at Tiger Leaping Gorge, tourists encounter a domesticated form of nature that stands in for wilderness and unspoiled landscapes. Tourists encounter fictions of spaces, simulacra constructed after their own wishes.

The *Other* that tourists meet at Xianggelila County is a fiction, too. Performers adapt this identity by donning ethnic dress or simply by functioning as the *Other* in an encounter. The identity of the *Other* is a role that may be assumed by anyone – and yet the generic Tibetan *Other* together with the scenic spots represent the touristified brand identity of Xianggelila County. Any difference that tourists encounter in the County uses a simulacrum for comparison. In this, difference itself becomes semi-fictional; it exists as a difference between the tourist and a simulacrum constructed after their imagination. The tourist experiences this difference as difference – and even 21st century awareness of the constructivist nature of tourism sites among travelers does not invalidate the difference experienced.

In conclusion, as a constructed simulacrum, Xianggelila County is capable of meeting tourist expectations. Tourists seeking difference do encounter it, even if they are engaging a fiction realized through symbolism on site. While this brand identity does not keep the sites from maintaining other functions or does not aim to erase other narratives of place, it becomes prevalent and representative since tourism constitutes the County's main source of income and designs the terms of engagement with the world. The image constructed includes generic, orientalist and backward images of Tibet, religion and rural areas – tourism capitalizes on exotic ideas in order to create a sense of *Otherness*. But tourism also tends to display sympathy for its subjects: it romanticizes their lives, the past and their cultural practices by emphasizing unique qualities and special accomplishments. And for Xianggelila County, tourism has constructed a romanticized, fictional simulacrum as a representative brand identity.

References

Anagost, Ann (1997) *National Past-times. Narrative, Representation, and Power in Modern China*, Durham: Duke University Press.

Baudrillard, Jean (1994 [1981]) *Simulacra and Simulation*, Ann Arbor: University of Michigan Press.

Breidenbach, Joanna and Pál Nyíri (eds.) (2005) *China Inside Out, Contemporary Chinese Nationalism and Transnationalism,* Budapest: Budapest Central European University Press, pp. 237-291.

Brook, Timothy (1998) *The Confusions of Pleasure: Commerce and Culture in Ming China*, Berkeley, Los Angeles and London: University of California Press.

Burns, Peter (1999) *An Introduction to Tourism & Anthropology*, New York: Routledge.

Cai Weiyan 蔡维琰 (2005) *"Xianggelila lüyou wenhua yunhan de lishi he shenmei"* 香格里拉旅游文化蕴涵的历史和审美意识 [The historical and aesthetic consciousness embodied in the tourism culture at Shangri-La], in *Yunnan Minzu Daxue Xuebao* 云南民族大学学报 [Journal of Yunnan Nationalities University] 5, pp. 84-88.

Chen Yizhi 陈一智, Liu Li 刘丽 und Li Qiang 李强 (2009) " 'Xiaoshi di dipingxian' dui goujian hexie lüyou de ji dian qishi" "消失的地平线"对构建和谐旅游的几点启示 [Some inspirations from Lost Horizon to establish harmonious tourism], in *Bianjiang jingji yu wenhua* 邊疆經濟與文化 [The Border Economy and Culture] 3, pp. 10-13.

Crisler, B. (1936) "Film gossip of the week", in *The New York Times*, 16.7.1936, p. 3, section 9.

Das, Sarat Chandra, Graham Sandberg and August William Heyde (2005[1902]) *A Tibetan-English Dictionary with Sanskrit synonyms*, Delhi: Motilal Banarsidass.

Davies, Gloria (2009) *Worrying about China: The Language of Chinese Critical Inquiry*, Cambridge: Havard University Press.

Diamond, Norma (1988) "The Miao and Poison: Interactions on China's Southwest Frontier", in *Ethnology* 27:1, pp. 1–25.

Diqing Nianjian Bianjibu 迪庆年鉴编辑部 (2003) *Diqing nianjian* 迪庆年鉴 [Yearbook of Diqing Prefecture], Kunming: Yunnan daxue chubanshe.

Duan, Z. (ed.) (1997) *Zhongdian xianshi* 忠甸现史 [Zhongdian County History], Kunming: Yunnan renmin chubanshe.

Eco, Umberto (1986) *Travels In Hyperreality*, New York: Harcourt Brace Jovanovich.

Eco, Umberto (2013) *The book of legendary lands*, New York: Rizzoli Ex Libris.

Frost, Carrie Fredrick (2007) Text Analysis of the Kalachakra Tantra, <https://collab.itc.virginia.edu/wiki/renaissanceold/Text%20Analysis%20of%20the%20OK%C4%81lachakra%20Tantra.html>, accessed 4 November 2012.

Gladney, Dru (2005) "Alterity motives", in Breidenbach, Joanna and Pál Nyíri (eds.) *China Inside Out, Contemporary Chinese Nationalism and Transnationalism*, Budapest: Budapest Central European University Press, pp. 237-291.

Goodman, Jim (2009) *Yunnan: China South of the Clouds*, Hong Kong: Odyssey Books & Guides.

Graburn, Nelson (2001) "Secular ritual: A general theory of tourism", in Smith, Valene and Maryanne Brent (eds.) (2001) *Hosts and Guests Revisited: Tourism Issues of the 21st Century*, New York: Cognizant Communication Corp., pp. 23-34.

Han Huiqin 韩慧琴 and Liu Zhongbo 刘忠波 (2012) *Yunnan lüyou: wanquan zhinan* 云南旅游:完全指南 [A Complete Guide to Yunnan Province], Beijing: Zhongguo jinggongye chubanshe.

Harper, Damien, Shawn Low and Daniel McCrohan (2011) *Lonely Planet China*, 12th edition, London: Lonely Planet Publications.

Hilton, James (2004[1933]) *Lost Horizon*, New York et al.: Harper Collins.

Hobsbawm, Eric and Terence Ranger (eds.) (1983) *The Invention of Tradition*, Cambridge: Cambridge University Press.

Huang Zhongcai 黄忠彩 (ed.) (2004) *"Zhongguo minzu mingpian" diqing xiangelila zangzu* "中国民族名片"迪庆香格里拉藏族 [Vistas of China's Minorities: Tibetans of Diqing's Shangri-La], Beijing: Minzu chubanshe.

Huc, Evariste Regis and Joseph Gabet (transl. by William Hazlitt) (1928) *Travels in Tartary, Tibet and China, 1844-46*, London: Routledge.

Jiedang Xiraojiacuo 杰当·西绕嘉措 (1995) "Songzanlin si shilüe" 松赞林寺史略 [Records of Songzanlin Si] in *Zhongguo zangxue* 中国藏学 [*China Tibet Studies*] 1, pp. 104-115.

Kolås, Åshild (2004) *Ethnic Tourism in Shangrila: Representations of Place and Tibetan Identity*, Oslo: University Press.

Kolås, Åshild (2007) *Tourism and Tibetan Culture in Transition: a Place Called Shangrila*, New York: Routledge.

Leiper, Neil (1995) *Tourism Management*, Collingwood: TAFE Publications.

Lew, Alan et al. (eds.) (2003) *Tourism in China*, New York: The Haworth Press.

Li, Zoe (2012) "34 million visitors and other China Golden Week records", <http://travel.cnn.com/explorations/life/182000-visitors-and-other-china-golden-week-records-419951>, *CNN*, 8.10.2012, accessed 16 October 2012

Liang Jun 梁军 and Li Zhenyu 厉振羽 (eds.) (6.10.2012) "Scenic Spots' gridlock triggers criticism", <http://english.peopledaily.com.cn/90882/7968137.html>, accessed 14 October 2012.

Liu Zhiyun 刘之耘 (ed.) (13.1.2014) "Xianggelila gucheng dahuo: 'yuericheng' banbijiangshan bei shaohui" 香格里拉古城大火: "月光城"半壁江山被烧毁 [Great Fire at Shangri-La Old Town: half of the scenery of "Moonlight Town" burnt down], in *Nanfang zhoumo* 南方周末 [Southern Weekly], <http://www.infzm.com/content/97493>, accessed 20 January 2014.

Llamas, Rosa und Belk, Russell (2011) "Shangri-La: messing with a myth", in *Journal of Macromarketing*, pp. 1-19.

Long Yanqing 龙彦青 (2008) "Kuaisu fazhan zhong de xianggelila xian lüyou ye cunzai wenti yanjiu" 快速发展中的香格里拉县旅游业存在问题研究 [Study on the existing problems in the rapidly developing tourism of Shangri-La County (sic.)], in *Anhui nongye kexue* 安徽农业科学 [Journal of Anhui Agricultural Science] 36, pp. 14690-14692.

MacCannell, Dean (1999 [1976]) *The Tourist: a New Theory of Leisure Class*, Berkely and Los Angeles: University of California Press.

MacCannell, Dean (2001) "Remarks on the commodification of cultures", in Smith, Valene and Maryanne Brent (eds.) *Hosts and Guests Revisted: Tourism Issues of the 21st Century*, New York: Cognizant Communication Corp., pp. 380-390.

Mackerras, Colin (2003) *China's Ethnic Minorities and Globalisation*, London: Routledge.

Masuzawa, Tomoko (1999) "From empire to utopia: the effacement of colonial markings in Lost Horizon", in *Positions* 7:2, pp. 541-572.

McRae, Michael (2002) *The Siege of Shangri-La: The Quest for Tibet's Sacred Hidden Paradise*, New York: Broadway Books.

Mitra, Amitabh (19.2.2006) James Hilton's Lost Horizon, <http://www.amitabhmitra.com/index.php?option=com_content&task=view&id=24>, accessed 10 November 2012.

Newman, John (1985) "A Brief History of the Kalachakra", in Sopa, Geshe Lhundub, Roger Jackson and John Newman (eds.) *Wheel of Time: The Kalachakra in Context*, Ithaca: Snow Lion Publications, pp. 51-90.

Newman, John (1996) "Itineraries to Shambhala", in Cabezón, José and Roger Jackson (eds.) *Studies in Indo-Tibetan Buddhism*, Ithaca: Snow Lion Publications, pp. 485-499.

Naquin, Susan and Yü, Chün-Fang (eds.) (1992) *Pilgrims and Sacred Sites in China*, Berkeley et al.: University of California Press.

Nash, Dennison (1996) *Anthropology of Tourism*, Oxford and New York: Pergamon Press.

Nyíri, Pál (2003) *Scenic Spots: Chinese Tourism, the State, and Cultural Authority*, London: University of Washington Press.

Oakes, Tim (1998) *Tourism and Modernity in China*, London: Routledge, 1998.

Oakes, Tim (2000) "China's provincial identities: reviving regionalism and reinventing 'Chineseness'", in *The Journal of Asian Studies* 59:3, pp. 667-692.

Oakes, Tim (2005) "Land of living fossils: scaling cultural prestige in China's periphery", in Wang, Jing (ed.) *Locating China. Space, Place and Popular Culture*, Abingdon: Routledge, pp. 31-51.

Qi Zhala 齐扎拉 and Leianwangdui 勒安旺堆[29] (1999) *Yunnan diqing – xianggelila jiemi* 云南迪庆 – 香格里拉揭秘 [Yunnan Diqing: Uncovering the Secret of Shangri-La], Kunming: Yunnan renmin chubanshe.

Qi Zhala 齐扎拉 (2001) "'Xianggelila' baohu yu fazhan de tansuo ji xingdong" "香格里拉"保护与发展的探索及行动 [The conservation and development of "Shangri-la"]", in *Sixiang zhan xian* 思想战线 [The Ideological Front] 1, pp. 70-72.

Qian, Wei (2003) "Travel agencies in China at the turn of the millenium", in Lew, Alan A. et al (eds.) *Tourism in China*, New York: Haworth Hospitality Press, pp. 143-64.

Rock, Joseph (1924) "Land of the Yellow Lama: National Geographic Society Explorer Visits the Strange Kingdom of Muli, Beyond the Likiang Snow Range of Yunnan, China", in National Geographic Society: *National Geographic* 47, pp. 447-491.

Rock, Joseph (1930) "Glories of the Minya Konka: Magnificent Snow Peaks of the China-Tibetan Border are Photographed at Close Range by a National Geographic Society Expedition", in National Geographic Society: *National Geographic* 58, pp. 385-437.

Rock, Joseph (1930) "Seeking the Mountains of Mystery: An Expedition on the China-Tibet Frontier to the Unexplored Amnyi Machen range, One of Whole Peaks Rivals Everest", in National Geographic Society: *National Geographic* 57, pp. 131-185.

Said, Edward (2003 [1978]) *Orientalism*, London: Penguin Books.

Shepherd, Robert (2006) "UNESCO and the Politics of Cultural Heritage in Tibet", in *Journal of Contemporary Asia* 36:2, pp. 243 – 257.

Smith, Valene and Maryanne Brent (eds.) (2001) *Hosts and guests revisted: tourism issues of the 21st century*, New York: Cognizant Communication Corp.

Sopa, Geshe Lhundub, Roger Jackson and John Newman (eds.) (1985) *Wheel of Time: The Kalachakra in Context*, Ithaca: Snow Lion Publications.

Strassberg, Richard (1994) *Inscribed Landscapes: Travel Writing from Imperial China*, Berkeley, Los Angeles and London: University of California Press.

Teng, Xincai (2001) "On tourist culture in the Mid- and Late Ming Dynasty", in *Tourism Tribune* 6, pp. 64-69.

Thierry, Francois (1989) "Empire and minority in China", in Chaliand, Gerad (ed.) *Minority Peoples in the Age of Nation-States*, London: Pluto Press, pp. 76-99.

Urry, John (1990) *The Tourist Gaze – Leisure and Travel in Contemporary Societies*, London: Sage publications.

Van den Berghe, Pierre and Charles Keyes (1984) "Introduction: tourism and re-created ethnicity", in *Annals of Tourism Research* 11, pp. 343–352.

Wei Xiaoan 魏小安, Liu Zhaopin 刘赵平 and Zhang Shumin 张树 (1999) *Zhongguo lüyouye xin shiji fazhan da qushi* 中国旅游业新世纪发展大趋势 [The Big Trends in the Development of China's Tourism Industry in the New Century], Guangzhou: Guangdong lüyou chubanshe.

Wagner, Rudolf (1992) "Reading the Chairman Mao Memorial Hall in Beijing: the tribulations of the implied pilgrim", in Naquin, Susan and Chün-Fang Yü (eds.)

---

[29] This seems to be a foreign name (probably Tibetan?) transliterated into Chinese. As no English spelling was suggested, the name was transliterated from Chinese.

Pilgrims and Sacred Sites in China, Berkeleyet al.: University of California Press, pp. 378-423.

Wang Zheng 王政 (2008a) Xianggelila gaikuang 香格里拉县概况 [Summary on Shangri-La*], <www.shangri-la.gov.cn>, accessed 21.09.2011).

Wang Zheng 王政 (2008b) Xianggelila de youlai 香格里拉的由来 [Origins of Shangri-La*], <www.shangri-la.gov.cn>, accessed 11 September 2011.

Wang Zheng 王政 (2008c) Xianggelila xian lüyou gongzuo qingkuang jianjie 香格里拉县旅游工作情况简介 [Introducing the current situation of Shangri-La's tourism enterprise], <www.shangri-la.gov.cn>, accessed 14 July 2012.

World Travel & Tourism Council (2012) Global Travel & Tourism industry defies economic uncertainty by outperforming the global economy in 2012 – and predicted to do it again in 2013, <http://www.wttc.org/news-media/news-archive/2013/global-travel-tourism-industry-defies-economic-uncertainty-outpe/>, accessed 21 January 2013.

Wu, Peiyi (1992) "An Ambivalent Pilgrim to T'ai Shan in the Seventeenth Century", in Naquin, Susan and Chün-Fang Yü (eds.) *Pilgrims and Sacred Sites in China*, Berkeley et al: University of California Press, pp. 65-88.

Xiong Yan 熊燕 und Yang Zhuhui 杨筑慧 (2007) "Cong 'zhongdian' gengming wei 'xianggelila' kan difang wenhua de chongjian" 从"中甸"更名为"香格里拉"看地方文化的重建 [Reconstruction of local culture: from the change of "Zhongdian" to "Shangri-La"], in *Zhongyang minzu daxue xuebao: zhexue shehui kexue ban* 中央民族大学学报：哲学社会科学版 [Journal of the Central University for Nationalities: Philosophy and Social Sciences Edition] 5, pp. 63-68.

Yang Shiguang 杨世光 (2002) *Xianggelila shihua* 香格里拉史话 [History of Shangri-La], Kunming: Yunnan renmin chubanshe.

Zhang, Guangrui (2003) "China's tourism since 1978: policies, experiences, and lessons learned", in Lew, Alan et al. (eds) *Tourism in China*, New York: The Haworth Press, pp. 13-33.

International Conference: "China in Latin America – Who are the actors?", Freie Universität Berlin, 24.-25. October 2014

This international conference was organized by Katja Levy, Freie Universität Berlin/Universität Würzburg and Enrique Dussel Peters, Universidad Nacional Autónoma de México, Ciudad de México in cooperation with the Friedrich-Ebert Foundation, Peking University, the Institute for Latin American Studies and the Confucius Institute at Freie Universität Berlin.

In her keynote speech, Levy sketched the three main points that informed the concept of the conference. Firstly, she explained that the actor-centered approach, as conceptualized by Renate Mayntz and Fritz Scharpf, would be employed to analyze Sino-Latin-American relations, since this enables scholars to draw a clearly differentiated picture and allows them to recognize the actors' characters and motivations. Secondly, Levy emphasized the importance of moving beyond merely tackling economic questions, by incorporating political factors and analyzing them against the backdrop of international power shifts. Lastly, she pointed to the valuable contribution that is being made to contemporary China Studies by locating the conference in a current paradigm shift that involves conducting research on contemporary China using methods and theories drawn from other disciplines as well as embracing a complementary approach to area studies in order to reveal the similarities and differences between countries. Levy emphasized the fact that this sort of research required the participation of multidisciplinary and multinational teams.

The first panel chaired by Svenja Blanke (Friedrich-Ebert-Foundation) adopted a broad perspective to discuss the actors in Sino-Latin-American relations. Bettina Gransow (Freie Universität Berlin) analyzed the strategies, actors and risks of Chinese infrastructure projects in Latin America, asking whether China, in this case, was applying a specific development strategy characterized by heavy investment in infrastructure sectors, such as, transport, energy, telecommunications and water provision. Such a strategy had been applied within China since the 1990s and had proved successful for China's own development path, but it had also led to environmental and social problems and grievances. Undertaking a preliminary analysis of the impacts on Latin American society, Gransow identified the main governmental and private stakeholders: Chinese financial institutions and companies, Latin American governments, implementing agencies, international and local NGOs as well as the international and local public. She argued that similarities to China's national policy were visible and that extensive infrastructure investment might contribute to social polarization and environmental degradation unless the actors developed counter-measures based on social and environmental assessments in their project evaluations.

Dussel Peters investigated the role of China's "public sector", including the institutions of central, provincial and municipal governments and state-owned enterprises. He found that while the public sector in most Latin American countries had decreased rapidly, the Chinese public sector with its ability to conceptualize, design, finance and implement "general guidelines" remains very important for both the Chinese national economy and economic relations between China and Latin American countries. He argued that this difference had not been sufficiently understood in Latin American countries and that this had resulted in multiple tensions. In conclusion, he pointed out that it is crucial for negotiators from Latin-American countries to be aware of the role played by their Chinese counterparts in the Chinese politico-economic system, in order to be able to grasp decision-making powers and to adjust their negotiation strategies.

The prominent role played by state actors in economic relations between China and Latin American countries was also one of the findings of Barbara Hogenboom's (University of Amsterdam) study on China's transnationalizing oil industry in Latin America. After identifying the Chinese government, state-owned enterprises, banks and companies under state guidance as the main actors within the infrastructure sector, Hogenboom showed, by drawing on Brazil, Venezuela and Ecuador, that the oil industry was of key importance for the countries' complementary economic interests, that is, the exchange of natural resource reserves and capital reserves as well as diversification and security. The large-scale investments by Chinese state-owned oil companies in Latin America, which played a key role in these transnational oil-backed interactions, are supported through new arrangements by Chinese government agencies and state-owned banks, such as oil-backed loans and joint funding arrangements. While these new actors and interactions have generally been receiving a positive response, Hogenboom, in accordance with Gransow's findings, pointed to concerns regarding their impact on the Latin American development path, because "Chinese attitudes" to environment and local stakeholders revealed that improving companies' accountability and the implementation of host state regulations was necessary.

The panel's last speaker, Dong Jingsheng (Peking University) shed light on the historical and current relations between China and the Caribbean, focusing on the economic aspects. In his view, the region has not been given sufficient attention because the depth of relations appears limited when compared with the relations between China and South America. The main actors identified by Dong were private and state-owned enterprises, mostly in the mining and manufacturing sector, banks, governments acting as coordinators and promoters, and various other agents such as, research institutions and associations. While growing trade relations and investments held out mutual opportunities, he also saw two main challenges. Since China's engagement with Caribbean countries was predominantly organized at the bilateral level, competition for Chinese assistance among the Caribbean states might ensue. Dong further stressed the fact that the significant and constantly increasing trade deficit between the Caribbean countries and China might eventually have a detrimental impact.

The second panel, chaired by Katja Levy, shifted the focus towards environmental aspects within Sino-Latin American relations. Eva Sternfeld (Freie Universität Berlin) opened the panel with a discussion on the political aims and achievements of the so-called BASIC group, a climate policy alliance between Brazil, South Africa, India and China that convenes regularly at ministerial level and is influential in international climate change negotiations. Employing Brazil and China as case studies, she showed that while the BASIC-group was highly influential, it was not homogenous since its members pursued different interests and set themselves different goals. This shows in vague definitions of their adherence to the principle of equity in the distribution of the remaining global carbon budget and dissent over binding agreements among the members of the BASIC group. Although Brazil and South Africa had already signaled their readiness to undertake binding agreements in 2011, China has delayed considering this option until after 2020 and India has firmly resisted making any such promises.

Ruben Gonzáles-Vicente (City University of Hong Kong) argued that early literature on Sino-Latin American relations usually homogenized or overlooked the variety of Chinese actors engaged in the region. In his analysis of Chinese investments in the mining and oil sectors, he looked closely at the institutions, companies and individuals involved. Exploring the complex industrial organization of extractive sectors, he found that Chinese companies relied heavily on local and international partners and that a significant number of the actors involved were, in fact, non-Chinese. Using Chinese investment in Peru as a case study, Gonzáles-Vicente showed the wide range of actors involved at different levels, from the internationalized processes of project acquisition to local legislation and complexities pushing companies to hire local staff, as well as the relations between Chinese and Peruvian workers. He finally argued that researchers needed to understand the complexities of the specific sectors and the variety of actors involved in order to grasp the rationale and impacts of Chinese investments.

The third panel, chaired by Eva Sternfeld, focused on social issues. Adrian Hearn (University of Melbourne) underlined the importance of citizens as actors: given China's growing demand for food, large-scale imports have become commonplace, but after looking at the case of Chinese soybean-imports from Brazil and analyzing ethnographic data related to the Brazilian states, Matto Grosso and the Cerrado Savanna, Hearn called into question the long-term sustainability of the current Brazilian agribusiness. His investigation revealed infrastructure bottle-necks, such as the poor roads, the growing distrust of Chinese state-owned enterprises among the local population and the demands of Chinese buyers for unprocessed soybeans, which are all leading to losses. These dim prospects for the current agribusiness practices had led Hearn to seek alternatives based on a local approach and, as a result, he was able to present the initiative of the "Cidades sem Fome" (Cities without Hunger), an urban gardening project in Sao Paolo that comprises 700 gardeners and over 4,000 community residents.

Ariel Carlos Armony (University of Miami) focused in his paper, written together with Nicolás Velasquez, on the public sphere, with an investigation into the negative perceptions of China that are found in Latin America. According to Armony, data retrieved from online communities revealed a diverse, unrestricted and spontaneous discourse as well as a combination of contradictory perspectives and socially dominant narratives. Analyzing user comments obtained from the official Facebook profiles found in nine major newspapers in Argentina, Chile, Colombia Mexico and Peru, he found that China's rise had triggered anxiety mainly as a result of issues linked with the environment, outward migration and the demand for natural resources. Specific engagement with China's presence centered on criticism of the quality of Chinese products while information beyond the business realm was fragmented and superficial. He further discerned strong negative attitudes towards Chinese culture. Lastly, the analysis revealed that relations with China gave rise to questions about Latin America's domestic conditions and development path.

Yang Zhimin (Chinese Academy of Social Sciences) examined the role played by semi-state organizations and provided a detailed description of the evolution and activities of the CCPIT (China Council for the Promotion of International Trade). Identifying the CCPIT as the most influential semi-state organization in Sino-Latin-American relations, he described its core function as providing a platform for dialogue. Yang emphasized the fact that the organization had started to influence China's economic policy towards Latin America after the China-LAC business summit organized by the CCPIT, when a government White Paper (published in 2008) described the CCPIT as a key mechanism. However, Yang also drew attention to the limitations of the influence of the organization, pointing out that some large companies did not rely on the CCPIT.

The last panel at the conference, chaired by Dussel Peters, considered the actors from the perspective of International Relations. José Luis Léon-Manríquez (Universidad Autónoma Metropolitana, Xochimilco) compared the expectations and the realities of China with those of Latin American left-wing governments against the backdrop of the international system. Drawing on government speeches and news conferences, he dissected convergences and differences between "hard" left-wing and "soft" left-wing Latin American governments, social movements and trade unions. This did not reveal a unified discourse or any common expectations from China. For Léon-Manríquez, the most surprising findings were the low levels of open anti-US imperialism found on the Chinese side and the lack of interest shown by leftist Latin American countries with regard to adapting the so-called 'China Model'.

Eduardo Daniel Oviedo (Universidad Nacional de Rosario) zoomed in on the relations between China and Argentina, with a particular focus on actors in the soybean trade and in migration flows, since these are the most important components of this bilateral relationship. His presentation contradicted the commonly held opinion that migration and economic actors eroded the state's monopoly. In contrast, he found that the state remained the key actor in international relations. Although, in his case, interactions were often presented as non-governmental or private linkages, he found that the states guided the soybean business and controlled migratory flows.

Niu Haibin (Shanghai Institute for International Studies) looked into the implications of the presence of new actors such as small businesses, Confucius Institutes, media, tourists and migrants. He was further interested in how these actors could become a source of soft power. Moving away from a focus on economic relations alone, he attempted to provide a more comprehensive picture of the diverse actors. The new actors, in his view, demonstrated stronger social and cultural ties as well as the strengthening of China's presence in the region. They nevertheless pursued self-serving interests, which could challenge China's engagement with the region. As a way of increasing China's soft power, he suggested promoting the teaching of Corporate Social Responsibility and adherence to the local business culture.

Sun Hongbo (Chinese Academy of Social Sciences), in his analysis of China-Venezuelan collaboration in the oil sector, presented a cooperation model of the oil sector, infrastructure, high-tech, agriculture and other industries and identified the oil sector as the main cooperation axis. The core mechanism that Sun identified - as a special case in China's energy collaboration with Latin America - was that China finances investment and loans and expects Venezuela to repay these with oil exports. According to Sun, the model's sustainability depends on the congruence of the motivations and expectations of actors at different levels, but he admitted that it was difficult to obtain full explanation of the political and economic interactions in the policy-making process between the governments and national oil companies.

Finally, Julie Klinger (University of California, Berkeley) explained the changing scales within China-Brazil mining relations. Drawing on stakeholder interviews undertaken in Brazil and China during the last two years, she described and analyzed the ways in which practices have changed in China's overseas activities. Since these are no longer character-ized by state-directed and state-supported investments, looking at the scale of the state or the firm is no longer sufficient for comprehensive analyses. The case of Minas Gerais showed that municipal governments had independently initiated outreach efforts to attract Chinese investment, while Chinese buyers had opted to direct their investments toward purchasing minority stakes in established local mining operations. Klinger also found that this diverged greatly from China's overseas mineral acquisitions in other countries, where the strategy focused on Chinese-owned and -managed mining operations.

In her concluding remarks, Levy emphasized several key issues. First, referring to a con-troversial discussion on the role of semi-state organizations, she observed that the use of specific terms was sufficient to draw the implications of actors' characteristics. As a meth-odological issue underlying many contributions, she identified the multiple connections between the local and the global and the resulting need to discuss these on a case-to-case basis. Overall, one common outcome was that a differentiated picture that did not conceptualize countries as monolithic actors had proved useful. Along these lines, Levy suggested that such a focus should not only look into different policy fields but should also incorporate the analyses of mutual perceptions. She further highlighted some different areas that would be well worth investigating in the future, including environmental aspects, such as, urban gardening and the relationship between growth and pollution, as well as the field of legal studies and the question of the ways in which the differences between China's and the Latin American legal systems impacted on Sino-Latin-American relations. The conference covered a very broad range of topics associated with China-Latin American relations, which might be a sign for the topic area still being under-researched. However, on each of the two conference days, the lively and thought-provoking discussions among the numerous participants showed that the topic area is gaining increasing attention. Selected papers are currently being prepared for publication in a special issue of a leading journal.

(Sabine Mokry and Sören Vogler)

Governance, Adaptability and System Stability under Contemporary One-party Rule. Comparative Perspectives, Nanchang, VR China, 27.-29. März 2014

Diese international hochkarätig besetzte Konferenz bildete den Schlusspunkt für die erste Projektphase des Kompetenznetzwerks „Regieren in China", das 2010 von sozialwissen-schaftlich ausgerichteten Chinawissenschaftlern der Universitäten Duisburg-Essen, Trier, Tübingen und Würzburg sowie dem German Institut for Global and Area Studies (GIGA) gegründet wurde und vom Bundesministerium für Bildung und Forschung finanziert wird. Sie wurde gemeinsam mit dem China Center for Global Governance and Development (CCGGD), der Nanchang Universität sowie der Zhejiang Universität ausgerichtet. Konfe-renzort war die Stadt Nanchang, die Hauptstadt der Provinz Jiangxi, die als Ort des kommunistischen Nanchang-Aufstands vom 1.8.1927 einen wichtigen Platz in der Partei-geschichte der Kommunistischen Partei Chinas (KP China) einnimmt.

Die Netzwerkmitglieder präsentierten während der drei Konferenztage auf insgesamt sechs Panels Forschungsergebnisse der ersten vier Jahre des Kompetenznetzwerks; internationale Wissenschaftler waren dazu eingeladen, diese Beiträge zu kommentieren.

Das erste Panel, das von Thomas Heberer organisiert und moderiert wurde, bildete insofern eine Ausnahme, als dass hier Nicht-Netzwerkmitglieder ihre Sicht auf „Regieren in China" schilderten. Adam Przeworski vertrat die These, dass die KP China anders als andere Ein-Parteien-Systeme durch ihre wirtschaftliche Entwicklung und die partielle politische Öffnung einen Weg gefunden hat, die für solche Systeme typischen Friktionen zwischen Staat und Partei produktiv in eine Anpassungsstrategie umzulenken. Chu Yun-han stellte die Ergebnisse des Asian Barometer Survey hinsichtlich der Frage vor, inwiefern die KP China heute Legitimität genießt. Das erstaunliche Ergebnis dieser großangelegten Befragung ist, dass die Regimelegitimität keineswegs von der ökonomischen Leistung des Systems, sondern vielmehr durch traditionelle Konzepte politischer Legitimität sowie die von den Befragten wahrgenommenen Eigenschaften des politischen Systems abhänge. John Keane nahm anschließend die Rolle eines modernen Alexis de Tocqueville ein, der in China nach Spuren von Demokratie sucht. Er stieß bei seinen Untersuchungen auf die, wie er sie nannte, „Phantom-Demokratie", die auf der einmaligen Konstellation von ökonomischen und politischen Reformen in der VR China basiert. Yu Keping stellte seine Forschungsergebnisse zur chinesischen Kaderausbildung und ihre Auswirkungen auf die Verbesserung chinesischer Governance vor.

Heike Holbig organisierte und moderierte das zweite Panel über die Rolle von Ideologie in der Regierung und Parteilegitimation in China. Zuerst referierte He Zengke über den aktuellen politischen Strategiewandel in der VR China von „social management" (*shehui guanli* 社会管理) hin zu „social governance" (*shehui zhili* 社会治理), also von dem Bestreben nach Kooptation gesellschaftlicher Akteure in die staatliche Politik hin zur Kooperation des Staates mit gesellschaftlichen Akteuren zur Erreichung bestimmter staatlicher Ziele. Holbigs Beitrag analysierte die Parteiideologie seit dem 18. Parteitag der KP China 2013 und kommt zu dem Ergebnis, dass sich unter der neuen Führung Xi Jinpings und Li Keqiangs ein Wandel in der Parteiideologie abzeichnet, der einerseits eine Betonung auf die praktische Lösung von Problemen legt und durch die Formulierung des „Chinesischen Traums" den Erwartungsdruck auf die Parteitheorie abschwächen soll. Dai Changzhengs Vortrag über „Ideological Discourse Formation" beschäftigte sich mit chinesischer Politik an der Basis. Frank Pieke stellte seine Untersuchungsergebnisse zur Parteihochschulausbildung der Provinz Yunnan vor.

Der zweite Konferenztag wurde durch das dritte Panel mit dem Titel „Policy-making and adaptive governance" eröffnet. Scott Kennedy untersuchte zunächst, wie die politische Förderung von indigener Innovation in China funktioniert. Anschließend stellte Chen Ling Ihre gemeinsam mit Barry Naughton durchgeführte Untersuchung über die die kleinen Führungsgruppen der KP China (*lingdao xiaozu* 领导小组) vor. Zhu Xufeng beschäftigte sich dann mit dem neuen Verwaltungsgenehmigungssystem der VR China, das er in 283 Städten mit Hilfe einer Ereignisanalyse untersucht hat.

Björn Alpermann organisierte und moderierte ein Panel zu sozialer Schichtung und politischer Partizipation in China. Er selbst präsentierte die qualitative Untersuchung, die er zusammen mit Katja Yang und Baris Selcuk zu politischen Werten von urbaner Bevölkerung durchgeführt hat. Ein wichtiges vorläufiges Ergebnis ihrer Forschung ist, dass die bisherige sozialwissenschaftliche Praxis der Untersuchung von politischen Werten in Kategorien sozialer Schichten sich in China als wenig hilfreich erweist, weil sich die Individuen, die den sozialen Schichten zugeordnet werden sich aufgrund ihrer unterschiedlichen Lebenswege und Erfahrungen zu sehr von einander unterscheiden, als dass verallgemeinernde Aussagen über ihre politischen Werte aussagekräftig sein könnten. Marc Blecher und Daniel Zipp leisteten mit ihrem Vortrag einen Beitrag zur Forschung über das Klassenbewusstsein von Migrantenarbeitern. Gang Shuge sprach schließlich über die politische Partizipation chinesischer Privatunternehmer.

Der dritte Tag wurde mit einem Panel eingeleitet, das Gunter Schubert zusammen mit Thomas Heberer leitete und das sich mit der Rolle des lokalen Staates für die Entwicklung Chinas befasste. Die beiden Mitglieder des Kompetenznetzwerkes stellten zunächst ihr Forschungsprojekt vor, das die Interaktion von Privatunternehmern und den lokalen Regierungen mit Hilfe des theoretischen Konzepts der strategischen Gruppen theoretisch zu fassen sucht. Elena Mayer-Clement wandte dieses Konzept anschließend auf die Urbanisierung des chinesischen ländlichen Raumes an. René Trappel stellte seine Untersuchung über die Rolle der Verwaltung auf Gemeinde- und Kreisebene in der Reform der Landwirtschaft vor, und Yang Xuedong betrachtete in seinem Beitrag den Einfluss der Globalisierung auf die Leistungsfähigkeit und Legitimität der lokalen chinesischen Regierungen.

Das letzte Panel der Tagung wurde von Yu Keping organisiert und moderiert und konzentrierte sich auf soziale Organisationen und die Reform der Partei Governance. Chu Songyan zeigte anschaulich, dass die Massenorganisationen der KP China in der letzten Zeit einen erheblichen Legitimationsverlust erlitten haben und nun vor der Entscheidung stehen, wie darauf zu reagieren ist. Yu Jianxing zeigte in seinem anschließenden Vortrag, dass sich gerade ein Wandel der Beziehung zwischen Staat und Gesellschaft vollzieht, bei dem Kontrolle an Bedeutung verliert, während stärkeres Gewicht auf Governance gelegt wird. Jude Howell stellte die Ergebnisse ihrer Untersuchung über die aktuelle Praxis der chinesischen Regierung, soziale Dienstleistungen von Arbeiter-NGOs zu kaufen, vor. Das Panel wurde mit Zeng Mings Vortrag über Stabilitätswahrung am Beispiel der Kohleförderungsindustrie abgeschlossen.

Diese Konferenz brachte fast 40 China- und Politikwissenschaftler aus Europa, den USA, der VR China und Taiwan an einem geschichtsträchtigen Ort in China zusammen. Die Beiträge bildeten einen beeindruckenden Überblick über die aktuelle Erforschung der chinesischen Politik und zeigten dabei auch die Vielfalt der Entwicklungen in Chinas politischem System. Die spannenden Diskussionen zwischen den TeilnehmerInnen dürften zur weiteren Erforschung der chinesischen Politik angeregt haben. Es ist erfreulich, dass das Kompetenznetzwerk nun für zwei weitere Jahre verlängert wurde und noch einige ähnlich erkenntnisreiche Konferenzen stattfinden werden. Eine davon fand bereits im November 2014 an der FU Berlin statt; die Abschlusstagung wird im November 2015 in Würzburg folgen.

(Katja Levy)

Kennosuke Ezawa und Annemete von Vogel (Hg.) 2013: *Georg von der Gabelentz. Ein biographisches Lesebuch.* **Tübingen: Narr, 341 S. (ISBN 978-3-8233-6778-9)**

Kennosuke Ezawa, Franz Hundsnurscher und Annemete von Vogel (Hg.) 2010: *Beiträge zur Gabelentz-Forschung.* **Tübingen: Narr, 301 S. (ISBN 978-3-8233-6861-8)**

Im Kontext und in Folge der Internationalen Konferenz zu Georg von der Gabelentz im Jahr 2010 an der Humboldt-Universität zu Berlin, die auch von einer Ausstellung begleitet wurde, haben die Veranstalter nun zwei Bände vorgelegt. Zum einen ein biographisches Lesebuch dieses Pioniers der chinesischen Sprachwissenschaft deutschsprachigen Raum. Gabelentz, lange in seiner wissenschaftlichen Bedeutung viel zu wenig rezipiert, eignet sich mit seinen bahnbrechenden Arbeiten und nicht zuletzt angesichts des umfangreichen Nachlasses vorzüglich, um die Anfänge des Faches in wissenschaftstheoretischer Hinsicht aufzuarbeiten. Dieser hervorragend zusammengestellte Band, zahlreich bebildert, zeigt zunächst die grundsätzliche Bedeutung des Sprachforschers Gabelentz auf. Er ist darüber hinaus eine Dokumentation seines und seiner Familie Lebens und Wirkens. Die Herausgeber haben unveröffentlichte biographische Materialien seiner Schwester Clementine aus dem Jahre 1913 und frühe Biographien über Hans Conon und Georg von der Gabelentz (1938) sorgfältig zur Veröffentlichung ausgewählt. Sie dokumentieren anlässlich der Berliner Ausstellung gehaltene Würdigungen und machen spätere wissenschaftliche Beiträge zu Einzelaspekten des Gabelentz'schen Werkes erneut einer breiteren Öffentlichkeit zugänglich. Den LeserInnen wird ein breiter Einblick in die sozialen und familiären Prägungen und die Netzwerke des gebildeten Adels im 19. Jahrhundert geboten, die genau die Grundlage für eine fruchtbare wissenschaftliche Tätigkeit – neben oder nach der politisch-administrativen Tätigkeit – boten. Der Band bietet einen informativen und kurzweiligen Einblick in eine die Sinologie prägende Wissenschaftlerpersönlichkeit und regt an zur weiteren wissenschaftlichen Beschäftigung mit Georg von der Gabelentz – reiches, bisher nicht aufgearbeitetes Material liegt im Familienarchiv der von der Gabelentz im Thüringischen Staatsarchiv Altenburg.

Zum anderen wird in Folge der Tagung ein Sammelband vorgelegt, der die bahnbrechende fachliche Leistung des großen Sprachforschers würdigt. Im Vordergrund stehen seine wegweisenden Thesen zur allgemeinen Sprachwissenschaft, seine Innovation im Bereich der Grammatik, insbesondere der chinesischen Grammatik und seine Rolle als Begründer der Sprachtypologie. Im ersten Teil dieses Bandes werden acht Forschungsbeiträge zu Gabelentz' Stellung in der Wissenschaftsgeschichte und zur neueren Rezeption und zum Einfluss seiner Thesen in der Linguistik nachgedruckt. Weitere, auf der o.g. Konferenz vorgetragene Beiträge von Christian Lehmann (Zur wissenschaftsgeschichtlichen Bedeutung von Gabalentz), Karl H. Rensch (Wilhelm von Humboldt, Hans Conon und Georg von der Gabelentz) und Hans Frede Nielsen (Otto Jespersen's Progress-in-Language Theory and Georg von der Gabalentz) beleuchten das Werk Gabelentz' aus aktueller sprachwissenschaftlicher Perspektive. Im zweiten Teil geht es um Analysen von Roland Harweg, Sven Staffeldt und Wilfried Kürschner der Beiträge Gabelentz' zur allgemeinen Sprachwissenschaft und speziell zur Chinesischen Grammatik. Barbara Meisterernst (Chinesische Grammatikstudien seit Georg von der Gabelentz), Martin Gimm (Hans Conon von der Gabelentz, sein Sohn Georg und die Rolle des Manjurischen für das Chinesischstudium im 19. Jahrhundert) und Feng Xiaohu

(Zur Rezeption der „Chinesischen Grammatik" (1881) von Georg von der Gabelentz in China) präsentieren durchweg anregende und informative Studien, die auch für Nicht-Linguisten spannend sind. Die große wissenschaftshistorische Bedeutung von Georg von der Gabelentz und seine bahnbrechenden, bis heute wirkenden Erkenntnisse bezüglich der Sprachwissenschaft im Allgemeinen und bezüglich der chinesischen Sprache im Besonderen wird in diesem sorgfältig edierten Band noch einmal deutlich gemacht.

(Mechthild Leutner)

Mechthild Leutner, Andreas Steen, Xu Kai, Xu Jian, Jürgen Kloosterhuis, Hu Wanglin und Hu Zhongliang (Hg.) 2014: *Preußen, Deutschland und China. Entwicklungslinien und Akteure (1842-1911)* (Berliner China-Studien 53). Berlin, LIT-Verlag, 368 Seiten. (ISBN: 978-3-643-12487-6)

Nach dem Abschluß des Vertrages von Nanjing (1842) gingen westliche Mächte dazu über, in China ein koloniales System zu errichten. Dieses System bildete auch den Rahmen für die jeweiligen bilateralen Beziehungen. Im Falle Preußen/Deutschland und China handelte es sich dabei zunächst um punktuelle Kontakte durch deutsche bzw. deutschsprachige Missionare und Geschäftsleute. Nach der Unterzeichnung des deutsch-chinesischen Freundschaftsvertrages (1861) traten noch die Akteursgruppen der Diplomaten, der Berater bzw. Experten und der Studenten hinzu. Gleichzeitig nahmen politische und wirtschaftliche Interaktionen zu (u.a. in den Bereichen Rüstung und Bildung). Eine Verräumlichung, Verdichtung und Internationalisierung erfuhren die deutsch-chinesischen Beziehungen durch die Inbesitznahme der deutschen Kolonie Qingdao (1897), aber auch durch den Boxerkrieg 1900/01.

Kontakte jeglicher Art zwischen den Akteuren zweier Länder haben beidseitige Veränderungen zur Folge. Das Andere läßt sich nicht in einer rigiden Entgegensetzung einer rationalen gegen einen irrationale Gesellschaft bestimmen, sondern immer nur als relationale Positionierung. Gegenüber Begriffen wie „Einfluss", „Rezeption", „Wirkung" oder „Kulturkontakt" wird mit dem Begriff des Kulturtransfers versucht, interkulturelle Vermittlungs- und Durchdringungsvorgänge zu erfassen. Der von WissenschaftlerInnen der Freien Universität Berlin und der Universität Peking im Rahmen eines Forschungsprojektes zu den deutsch-chinesischen Beziehungen 1842-1911 vorgelegte Sammelband hat es sich zum Ziel gesetzt, diesen Anspruch einzulösen. Dies dokumentiert sich allein darin, dass der vorgelegte Band auch auf Chinesisch in China veröffentlicht wurde. Zudem bilden die Quellengrundlage aller Beiträge sowohl Akten aus dem Geheimen Staatsarchiv Preußischer Kulturbesitz in Berlin als auch aus dem Ersten Historischen Archiv in Peking.

Die Aufsätze des Sammelbandes lassen sich verschiedenen Themenkomplexen zuordnen: Zunächst geht es um die (1) frühe Phase der deutsch-chinesischen Beziehungen, in der noch keine zwischenstaatlichen Vereinbarungen existierten. Auch wenn das Interesse der chinesischen politischen Elite in der ersten Hälfte des 19. Jahrhunderts unübersehbar auf England, Frankreich, Russland und Amerika gerichtet war, holte es auch Informationen über Preußen/Deutschland ein. Han Yongfu zeigt in seinem Beitrag, daß die Chinesen bereits in den 1840er Jahren und damit lange vor den bekannten Deutschland-Beschreibungen Kang Youweis auf Schilderungen deutscher Länder zurückgreifen konnten. Allerdings beschränkte sich der Zugang zu diesem Wissen auf einen sehr geringen Teil einer ohnehin kleinen Elite, da die konfuzianischen Gelehrten und Beamten westlich geprägte Systematisierungen des Auslandes ablehnten. Während es in diesem Beitrag um Texte und Dokumente als Zeugen und Instrumente einer Dokumentation kulturellen Wissens geht, widmet sich Cord Eberspächer dem Bereich der Politk. Mit Blick auf das Chinawissen politisch Handelnder in Deutschland analyisert er die Entstehung deutscher Konsulate in China 1842-1859. Dabei macht er eine extrem kleine Chinalobby aus: Nur in (nord)deutschen Handelskreisen konnte von einer spürbaren Begeisterung für die Öffnung des chinesischen Marktes überhaupt die Rede sein. Hingegen war das Interesse der politischen Entscheidungsträger an China gering. Eine koloniale Begeisterung kann allenfalls rudimentär in Kreisen des Bildungsbürgertums festgestellt werden.

Der zweite Themenkomplex (2) befaßt sich mit den deutsch-chinesischen Beziehungen während und nach dem Abschluß des deutsch-chinesischen Vertrages 1861, wobei der Akzent deutlich auf dem Wissen und den Erfahrungen der Diplomaten liegt. Im Mittelpunkt des Beitrags von Andreas Steen stehen die rund sechs Monate dauernden Verhandlungen zwischen deutschen und chinesischen Diplomaten, die zum Abschluß des Vertrages führten. Erstmals werden in diesem Aufsatz die Motivationen und Beweggründe der chinesischen Verhandlungspartner genau dargelegt und nicht nur vage auf den Taiping-Krieg (1851-1864) und den so genannten Zweiten Opiumkrieg (1858-60) verwiesen. Dagegen wendet sich Hu Zhongliang dem ersten chinesischen Gesandten in Deutschland, Liu Xihong, zu, der 1877/78 in Berlin weilte. Hierbei lotet er dessen Arbeitsbedingungen und Handlungsspielräume aus. Liu Xihongs diplomatisches Agieren war geprägt von strengen Direktiven des Zongli Yamen, aber auch von Machtkämpfen mit chinesischen Gesandten in anderen europäischen Städten, wobei Fragen der Anpassung an westliche Gewohnheiten (u.a. Kleidung, Musik) und der Wissensaneignung für China im Mittelpunkt standen.

Mit einem vielschichtigen Detailaspekt in der Gestaltung der deutsch-chinesischen Diplomatiegeschichte befaßt sich der Aufsatz von Xu Kai - der Vergabe von chinesischen Orden an Ausländer, speziell an Deutsche. Orden, verstanden als staatliche Abzeichen für geleistete Dienste, waren insofern neu für die chinesischen Politiker, als Beamtenhüte die traditionelle Auszeichnungsform gewesen waren. Mit der Verleihung von Orden wollte sich die chinesische Regierung den internationalen Gepflogenheiten anpaßen, gleichzeitig aber auch „wahre Freundschaft" (S. 302) schließen. Es zeigte sich, daß zwar beide Seiten Orden ausgaben, dabei aber äußerst unterschiedliche Bedeutungen mit diesen verbanden. Stand für die deutsche Seite eher die Inszenierung von Freundschaft im Vordergrund, so gingen die chinesischen Akteure davon aus, sich mit der Verteilung von Orden die Loyalität und Freundschaft der ausgezeichneten Personen zu sichern.

Ein dritter Schwerpunkt (3) des Sammelbandes befaßt sich in einer Zeit der intensivierten deutsch-chinesischen Beziehungen mit Strategien, das Wissen über die jeweils anderen zu vertiefen und zu systematisieren. Mechthild Leutner stellt eine Texte und Dokumente produzierende Person in den Mittelpunkt ihrer Überlegungen. Anhand des Konsuls und Sinologen Carl Arendt (1838-1902) zeigt sie unterschiedliche Motive und Möglichkeiten der Wissensaneignung und –verwertung über China auf. Es handelte sich um Wissen, das einerseits den Rahmen eines fachwissenschaftlichen Kenntnisstandes schuf und andererseits – entgegen dem Humboldtschen Ideal – dem Zweck der Ausübung kolonialer

Herrschaft diente. Wissen über den jeweils anderen wurde freilich nicht nur von einzelnen Personen, sondern auch von Gruppen transferiert. Mit der Entsendung von chinesischen Studenten nach Deutschland in der späten Qing-Zeit 1876-1911 beschäftigt sich deshalb Xu Jian. Da Anhänger der Verwestlichungsbewegung Deutschlands Rüstungsgüter sowie seine Militärausbildung schätzten, wurden zunächst chinesische Militärstudenten nach Deutschland geschickt; später folgten Studenten der Sprachenschule Tongwenguan. Ab 1901 nahm die Zahl der nach Deutschland entsendeten Studenten stark zu. Es stellt sich die Frage, wo, wie und in welchem Ausmaß sie nach ihrer Rückkehr in China wirkten. Drei Bereiche können bisher ausgemacht werden: Militär, Konstitutionalistische Bewegung und Bildung.

Konflikte und Konfliktlösungen innerhalb der deutsch-chinesischen Beziehungen (4) stellen einen weiteren Themenkomplex des Sammelbandes dar. Bei den von Qu Chunhai analysierten deutsch-chinesischen Verhandlungen zum Markenschutz in der Qing-Zeit - Marken sind Warenzeichen und Symbole der Industrie- und Handelsunternehmen, die die Qualität, Normen und Merkmale bestimmter Waren definieren – handelt es sich nur auf den ersten Blick um ein strikt ökonomisches Thema. Deutsche Vertreter verhandelten mit chinesischen Ministerien, um ihre Industrie- und Handelswaren zu schützen. Auseinandersetzungen gab es jedoch nicht nur wegen der hohen Gebühren für die Registrierung der Markennamen, sondern auch wegen der Ausübung der Konsulargerichtsbarkeit. Waren deutsche Geschäftsleute in Streitfälle involviert, sollten keine chinesischen Behörden eingeschaltet werden. Das Problem der Markenanmeldung war damit zu einem Problem der Souveränität Chinas geworden. In dieser Frage konnte letztlich erst 1921, als sich die Bedingungen der gegenseitigen Beziehungen vollkommen verändert hatten, eine Einigung erzielt werden. Auch Andreas Steen beschäftigt sich in seinem zweiten Beitrag mit einer Konfliktsituation in den deutsch-chinesischen Beziehungen, die jedoch deutlich globale Züge trägt. Es handelt sich um den Transfer, die Anwerbung und den Widerstand von Kulis 1850-1914. Da die Dampfschiffahrt zumindest teilweise in deutschen Händen lag, war auch Deutschland am Kulihandel beteiligt. Ein Problem entstand daraus, als chinesische Arbeiter für deutsche Kolonien angeworben wurden, so vor allem für Deutsch-Samoa. Die Verhandlungen hinsichtlich der Behandlung dieser Arbeitskräfte wurden über drei Kontinente geführt und endeten mit einem Erfolg für die chinesische Seite. 1911 wurde die Prügelstrafe für Chinesen in Deutsch-Samoa abgeschafft.

In dem neuen Sammelband zu den deutsch-chinesischen Beziehungen werden die bilateralen Beziehungen konsequent als Transferprozesse zwischen Akteuren beider Länder dargestellt. Es werden nicht nur Akteursgruppen betrachtet, die sich von Deutschland nach China, sondern auch solche, die sich von China nach Deutschland bewegten. Chinesische Akteure stehen nicht nur als Schatten im Hintergrund, sondern erhalten Gesicht, Namen und agency; ihre Handlungsmotivationen werden aufgedeckt. Dies wiederum verdeutlicht, daß nicht nur die deutsche Seite rational agierte, sondern auch die chinesische. So gelingt es, die deutsch-chinesischen Beziehungen auch im Zeitalter des Imperialismus und der ungleichen Verträge vom „Einfluß-Paradigma" zu lösen und symmetrisch darzustellen.

Explizit oder implizit klingt in allen Beiträgen an, daß sich die deutsch-chinesischen Beziehungen in einem internationalen Umfeld abspielten und kaum von diesem isoliert werden können. Vielmehr waren sie Teil eines Umfeldes, das sich entweder als koloniales System in China präsentierte – sozusagen als übernationaler bzw. koordinierter Imperialismus – oder aber als globales System, wie etwa im Falle des Migrationstransfers. Letzteres führte zu einer Deterritorialisierung der deutsch-chinesischen Beziehungen, da sie sich diese nicht mehr ausschließlich auf chinesischem oder deutschem Territorium abspielten. Der vorliegende Sammelpunkt gibt damit in mehrfacher Hinsicht die Richtung für nachfolgende Studien zu den deutsch-chinesischen Beziehungen vor.

(Susanne Kuss)

Ulrike Unschuld 2014: *You banfa – Es findet sich immer ein Weg. Wilhelm Manns Erinnerungen an China, 1938-1966* **(Reihe Jüdische Memoiren, Bd. 22). Berlin: Hentrich & Hentrich, 240 S. (ISBN 978-3-95565-040-7)**

Spannend zu lesen sind diese Erinnerungen Wilhelm Manns. Und verdienstvoll ist ihre politische und wissenschaftshistorische Kontextualisierung und Präsentation durch Ulrike Unschuld. Sie hat viele Gespräche mit Wilhelm Mann geführt und seine Erinnerungen aufgenommen. Zahlreiche Passagen sind im Text wörtlich wiedergegeben; anderes ist aus Briefen an und von Wilhelm Mann zitiert worden oder hat indirekt Eingang in die Gesamtdarstellung gefunden. Es ist eine sehr geglückte Collage, die die Chinajahre des Emigranten Mann sehr bildhaft beim Leser aufscheinen lassen – und die zugleich das historische Geschehen dieser Jahre auf die Mikroebene des Schicksals und der Erfahrungen und Erlebnisse einer Person, einer Persönlichkeit herunterbricht. Für die Chinahistorikerin bieten die *Erinnerungen* zudem neue Ansätze für weitergehende Fragestellungen, etwa zu den „chinesischen industriellen Kooperativen" (INDUSCO) oder zu den naturwissenschaftlichen Forschungsschwerpunkten im China der 1950er Jahre. Nicht zuletzt handelt es sich um eine eindrucksvolle Darstellung von Emigration und Exil, von der Annäherung an China und dem Versuch, sich dort zu integrieren.

Wilhelm Mann, geboren 1916, einer gebildeten und assimilierten jüdischen Familie aus Mannheim entstammend, hatte angesichts der Härte der nationalsozialistischen Verfolgung (fast) noch Glück: Seine Geschwister konnten rechtzeitig ins Exil in die USA und nach Großbritannien gehen, seine Eltern sollten im französischen Internierungslager Gurs überleben und er selbst konnte nach einer geradezu unbeschwerten Jugend noch bis 1936 an der Heidelberger Universität, zwar nicht das gewünschte Fach Medizin, aber immerhin Chemie studieren. Im Oktober 1938 allerdings wurde er als letzter jüdischer Student der Universität Heidelberg exmatrikuliert, nach der Reichskristallnacht gelang es ihm noch rechtzeitig im Dezember 1938 eine Schiffspassage nach Shanghai zu beschaffen. Hier hätte nun das bereits mehrfach beschriebene Shanghaier Exil der „kleinen Leute", die auf Weitermigration warteten und suchten, sich irgendwie durchzuschlagen, beginnen können. Doch Wilhelm Mann kam in Kontakt mit Erich Landauer, einem seit mehreren Jahren in China lebenden Arzt, der ihn einlud, mit ihm gemeinsam nach Guiyang, also in das von der Guomindang noch kontrollierte Innere Chinas, zu gehen. Dort sollte er im Hauptquartier des Medizinischen Hilfskorps des Roten Kreuzes arbeiten, zunächst verantwortlich für die Lagerbestände, ab 1942 dann beim Sanitätsdienst der nationalchinesischen Armee und bei der Army Medical Field Service School, wo er zuständig wurde für die gesamte Laborarbeit. In der Lagerabteilung des Medizinischen Hilfskorps stieß er erstmals auf die große Korruption, die Bereicherung von höheren Militärs und Beamten, die ihm nach 1945 auch in Shanghai begegnen sollte und die ihm die große Akzeptanz der Kommunisten durch die Bevölkerung, darunter viele Ärzte und Wissenschaftler, plausibel machten. Bis 1945 arbeitete er hier, gemeinsam auch mit ausländischen Ärzten, die vorher in Spanien auf Seiten der Franco-Gegner gekämpft hatten. Später, nach Beginn des Pazifischen Krieges, wurde hier auch amerikanisches Militär stationiert – deutliche Einblicke gibt Wilhelm Mann in die mühsamen Versuche des für den Aufbau des chinesischen Militärs in Indien zuständigen US-Generals Stilwell, Guomindang-chinesische Truppenteile, teils noch aus dem Burmafeldzug, wieder für den Krieg gegen Japan auszurüsten. Eine wichtige Episode war Wilhelm Manns Versuch, in Zhejiang für die INDUSCO zu arbeiten. Als die Finanzierung des Projektes ausblieb, machte sich Mann zu einer mehrere Monate dauernden Tour quer durch China und hinter den Frontlinien auf, um die Gründe dafür zu klären. 1945 hatte Wilhelm Mann den sehnlichen Wunsch, nach Hause, nach Deutschland zurückzukehren. Jedoch wird er aus verschiedenen Gründen davon abgehalten – die Nachrichten aus Deutschland sind nicht viel versprechend und ihm bot sich in Shanghai, wo er immer noch im Dienste Guomindang-chinesischer Forschungsinstitute stand, die Möglichkeit zu studieren. Mann belegte Chemie am St. John's College in Shanghai, arbeitete zugleich als Hilfsassistent, erhielt 1949 sein Diplom und feierte mit Kollegen die Befreiung 1949. Sein früherer Arbeitgeber, das Guomindang-Verteidigungsministerium, war nach Taiwan gegangen, er selbst blieb in Shanghai, erhielt eine Stelle am Medizinischen Forschungsinstitut, das später zur Akademie der Wissenschaften umbenannt wurde. Er arbeitete hier bis zum Beginn der Kulturrevolution mit renommierten Forschern zusammen, etliche waren aus dem Ausland nach China zurückgekehrt. Die Liste seiner Veröffentlichungen zeugen von den Ergebnissen und Erfolgen seiner wissenschaftlichen Forschung in diesen Jahren: Es gelang dem Forscherteam des Instituts, auf eigenen Wegen eine Insulin-Synthese herzustellen. Diesen Erfolgen entgegen standen allerdings die wiederkehrenden Kampagnen, die Wilhelm Mann in ihrer Bedeutung eher zurückhaltend wertete. Erst als die Kulturrevolution begann und die Labore geschlossen wurden, wurde ihm sein „Ausländer-Sein", sein – durchaus auch Vorzüge besitzendes Außenvorbleiben – so deutlich, dass er, der sich seit Mitte der 1950er Jahre erfolgreich um eine Anerkennung als DDR-Bürger bemüht hatte, China verließ. Er nutzte eine Dienstreise nach Berlin/DDR, um mit Hilfe eines früheren Kollegen aus seinen China-Jahren, dort zu bleiben. Er promovierte noch und arbeitete weiter wissenschaftlich am Institut für Mikrobiologie. Ab Ende der 1980er Jahre stand er auch wieder im engen Kontakt mit seinen Shanghaier Kollegen.

Wilhelm Mann starb 2012 in Berlin.

(Mechthild Leutner)

Gary Bettinson (Hg.) 2012: *Directory of World Cinema: China*. Bristol, Chicago: Intellect, 232 S. (ISBN 978-1-8415-0558-9)

Seit etwa der Jahrtausendwende sind zahlreiche Publikationen erschienen, die den chinesischen Film im Großen zu definieren versuchen, entlang spezifischer Schwerpunkte (Chris Berry/Mary Farquhar 2006, *China on Screen: Cinema and Nation*; Olivia Khoo/Sean Metzger 2009, *Futures of Chinese Cinema: Technologies and Temporalities in Chinese Screen Cultures*), entlang sprachlicher Definitionen (Sheldon H. Lu/Emilie Yueh-yu Yeh

2004: *Chinese-Language Film: Historiography, Poetics, Politics*) oder im Sinne der Film-geschichte einer ,Greater China'-Region, die die Filmtraditionen der Volksrepublik, Taiwans und Hongkongs umfasst (Yingjin Zhang 2004: *Chinese National Cinema*).
Der 2010 von Gary Bettinson herausgegebene und bei Intellect in der Reihe „Directory of World Cinema" erschienene Band „China" folgt letzterem Ansatz, versteht sich dabei aber eher als ein allgemein verständliches Überblickswerk denn als wissenschaftliche Arbeit. Mit der Tatsache, dass auf 232 Seiten kaum eine umfassende Enzyklopädie der drei be-troffenen Filmindustrien zu leisten wäre, geht der Band offensiv um und entscheidet sich für einen sehr selektiven Ansatz, der nicht auf Vollständigkeit bedacht ist.
Den Anfang machen drei Überblicksartikel zu den Themen „Chinese Opera and Cinema", „Taiwanese Documentary" und „Hong Kong Action Cinema", die sich also mit spezifi-schen intermedialen Beziehungen, Produktionsmodi und Genres beschäftigen. Es schließen sich unter den Rubriken „Three Action Heroes", „Three Female Stars" und „Hong Kong New Wave" biographische Artikel an, gefolgt von drei ebenfalls biographischen Sektionen zu repräsentativen Regisseuren der Volksrepublik, Taiwans und Hongkongs, wobei nur solche Filmemacher ausgewählt wurden, die auch heute noch aktiv und einflussreich sind. Den Rest des Buches machen Kritiken wichtiger Filme aus, sortiert nach den Kategorien „Drama: Mainland China", „Drama: Taiwan", „Kung Fu and *Wuxia Pian* (Swordplay Film): Hong Kong and Taiwan", „Action Cinema and Heroic Bloodshed: Hong Kong", „Independent and Art Cinema: Hong Kong", „Comedy/Musical: Taiwan and Hongkong" sowie „Documentary: Mainland China and Hongkong". Die einzelnen Kritiken sind jeweils in eine kurze Zusammenfassung des Filminhalts und eine kompakte Analyse seiner Bedeutung unterteilt.
Der Schwachpunkt von „Directory of World Cinema: China" liegt auf der Hand: Ein solch schmales Buch kann unmöglich die Breite des chinesischen Filmschaffens aller drei Filmindustrien und –traditionen abdecken, so dass die Auswahl der Themensektionen, der repräsentativen Persönlichkeiten (drei pro Kapitel) sowie der Filme (drei bis siebzehn pro Kapitel) zwangsläufig einer gewissen Willkürlichkeit unterliegt. Von den drei chinesischen Filmindustrien steht Hongkong klar im Vordergrund, Action- und Martial-Arts-Filme sind gegenüber anderen Genres sehr prominent vertreten, was auch mit den thematischen Vorlieben des Herausgebers zusammenhängen mag.
Auf der anderen Seite fällt zum einen die hochkarätige Autorenriege auf, die renommierte Filmwissenschaftler/-innen wie Esther M.K. Cheung (Hong Kong University), Mette Hjort (Lingnan University) und Tony Williams (Southern Illinois University) umfasst; zum anderen beleuchten viele der Porträts der Filmschaffenden ihren Gegenstand von einer neuen Seite, indem sie das Augenmerk auf jeweils einen spezifischen Aspekt von deren Schaffen richten – um nur ein Beispiel zu nennen: Bruce Bennett sucht in seinem Artikel zu dem festlandchinesischen Regisseur Lu Chuan, in dessen ausgesprochen diversem Schaffen sich inhaltlich kaum ein roter Faden erkennen lässt, nach übergreifenden Themen und Motiven und konstatiert, Lus Filme beschäftigten sich stets auch mit Maskulinität und männlicher Gewalt, verwendeten fremde Landschaften nicht als realistischen Hintergrund, sondern als symbolträchtigen Bestandteil der Inszenierung, und zeichneten sich durch eine fatalistische Grundhaltung sowie transnationale Verständlichkeit aus. Auf ähnliche Weise charakterisieren die meisten der biographischen Artikel das künstlerische Schaffen von Regisseurinnen und Regisseuren,

Schauspielerinnen und Schauspielern anhand eines prägnanten Leitgedankens oder einer Leitfrage und bilden so aufschlussreiche Porträts der jeweiligen Persönlichkeiten. So zeichnet *Directory of World Cinema: China* zwar kein vollständiges und auch kein ganz ausgewogenes Bild des chinesischen Kinos, aber doch eines, das dessen Vielseitigkeit und Breite erkennbar werden lässt und mit manch neuer Perspektive aufwartet. Zudem ist derzeit ein zweiter Band im Erscheinen, der dieses Bild womöglich zu ergänzen und zu erweitern vermag.

(Clemens von Haselberg)

Kimiko Suda 2013: *Chinese Lala Organizing. Identität und Repräsentation lesbischer Frauen in Beijing* **(Berliner China-Studien 50). Berlin: LIT-Verlag, 128 S. (ISBN 978-3-643-11975-9)**

With Kimiko Suda's study on forms of lesbian identity and organization in Beijing German China studies have not only gained an important facet on their course to further diversification and interdisciplinarity. Suda's study, published as the 50th edition of the Berliner China-Studien, sheds a vital and long overdue light on an often marginalized and neglected topic.

Suda's study examines the formation of lesbian identity during China's political transition from a socialist towards a neoliberal society. It was originally submitted as her master's thesis in 2008, and has since been consecutively revised to include the latest in relevant literature in the field, as well as updates on the professional and private lives of Suda's in-group interview partners. In employing the Beijing-based lesbian non-governmental organization (hereafter, NGO) *Tongyu* as her main focal point Suda analyzes new spatial, organizational and identity-constituting processes among Beijing's urban lesbian community, and beyond. In opposition to the usage of lesbian identity and lesbian women as support for "essentialist and narrow views of biological and social bodies" Suda instead employs these terms within the context of strategic essentialism in order "to create a position to speak from." This 'audibility', or own voice, manifests itself within the context of a new terminology, and new sets of implications that arise thereof: China's lesbian circles have since replaced derogatory, limiting, and locally demarcated medical terms with the term *lala* (拉拉), which according to Suda can be considered "the most popular transnational Chinese-language term for lesbian/s". *Lala*, as Suda notes, is the affirmed "positive self-identification" of lesbian women in China, and is generated through participating in social and virtual interaction. The growing theoretical and social vociferousness of *lala* is in turn complemented and further carried into Chinese urban public re-presentation and discourse by the visibility of organizational structures, such as Suda's empirical example of *Tongyu*. This 'space of their own' has in recent years advanced to an important spatial entity for the maintenance of lesbian identity and community in a Beijing urban context.

In her introduction Suda prepares the ground for her ensuing discussion on the interconnectivity between lesbian identity and organization. She presents new female agents in Chinese discourse on gender, sexuality, and social representation, and locates her discursive starting point in the United Nation's (hereafter, UN) world women's conference in 1995 as a hotbed for the emergence of transnational networks for young Chinese women's NGOs. It is here that Suda positions her main argument that women's

NGOs in their role as female players (*Akteurinnen*) inscribe marginalized gender identities on public discourse both within the context of the ideological and social specifics of Chinese women's state and non-governmental organizations, as well as within the framework of a transnational Chinese women's public sphere. In this contextualization or positioning Suda heavily draws from Mayfair Mei-hui Yang's extended, Habermasian (civil public, *bürgerliche Öffentlichkeit*) notion of the development of a women's public sphere in the context of transformation processes and the increasing impact of globalization on the People's Republic of China. Yang's sphere is as much 'local' as it is transnational, and blends well with Suda's use of theoretical work, in particular that of Maria Jaschok, Cecilia Milwertz and Ping-chun Hsiung (2001), which affirms the development of a new "women's public sphere" in China since the mid-1990s, as well as the active use of this, as Suda terms it, "scope of action" (*Handlungsspielraum*) by Chinese women in urban intellectual settings. According to Suda, the main difference between state-coordinated efforts at organization, such as the All-China Women's Federation, and recent women NGOs lies in the area of representation. Whereas the All-China Women's Federation represents women's interests vis-à-vis the state, new Chinese women's NGOs mainly develop through a common interest among certain groups of women to represent their issues not only towards the state, but towards and as part of the general Chinese public. Suda argues that this active self-representation of the new organizations is changing women's role from "passively represented objects" to protagonists of their own social destiny.

Not only does Suda place her own theoretical contributions within the research genealogy of gender and queer studies in China since the 1920s, she also rightly emphasizes that the roots of non-governmental women's organizations in China as well as issues of women's representation should be traced back to the late Qing and to the Republican era. In chapter 2, Suda elaborates the latter point and provides a short overview over the genealogy of women's representation in China within the political and social transition during this particular historical period. The characteristics of this period, its structures of representation, and the public and legal establishment of new gender categories to replace traditional and/or limited concepts, e.g. from *funü* to *nüxing*, re-embed Suda's discussion of post-reform lesbian subject identity formation and structures of social organization within overall modern Chinese social history and gender. According to Suda, the historical developments of the transition from the Qing dynasty to the Republican era continue to exert a strong influence on discourses of gender, sexuality, and urban public representation, and thus continue to serve an important function within the social 'localization' (*Verortung*) of lesbian identity in contemporary Chinese society. Moreover, by illustrating the historical continuities of certain categories, structures and processes, Suda further strengthens her argument regarding the substantial impact, which the 1995 Fourth World Conference on Women and its aftermath have since had on Chinese women's social organization.

In chapter 3 Suda further elaborates on specific examples of forms of social organization and lesbian identity formation in China since the 1990s. She discusses examples and issues of Chinese urban lesbian identity coordinates, such as voice/visibility, vocabularies, and categories, as well as virtual (cyberspace, internet) and physical spaces (lesbian bars). These examples all play together to support Suda's argument that the social situation of lesbian women in Beijing has experienced a definite improvement since the late 1990s. According to Suda, lesbian identity has become more visible as part of urban public life, and has thus provided young women with options, role models and social contacts, which are particularly vital in the early phases of lesbian identity formation. As part of this public representation, the internet, and particularly numerous lesbian websites, have greatly contributed to the exchange and communication between lesbian women on issues ranging from finding friends and dating all the way to discussions of everyday relevance and gender theory. Apart from these virtual spaces lesbian bars have also come to act as a main mode of bridging the increasing anonymity, which goes hand in hand with Beijing's permanent urban and social expansion. Perhaps most importantly, the formation of a 'cosmopolitan lesbian subject' (with, if we wish, Chinese characteristics) and the increasing collective awareness, as well as the outside awareness of the Chinese public, of constituting a social group (*shehui qunti*) is increasingly motivating lesbian women to move beyond the virtual and often mostly symbolic confines of lesbian representation and organization into spaces, which allow for a real-time participation and self-presentation as part of urban public life.

As an example for the new organization efforts chapter 4 features a portrait and discussion of the lesbian NGO *Tongyu*. Based on a description of *Tongyu*'s definition, organization structures, social and theoretical aims, and projects as well as interviews with some of its protagonists and supporters Suda effectively illustrates how *Tongyu* has advanced from a support structure for lesbians in and around the greater Beijing area to a key constituent within an infrastructure for a type or social space, which in turn complements lesbian cyberspace community, and also manages in a sense to move beyond it. In Suda's words, by offering "innovative practices of organizing" *Tongyu* "open[s] up collective spaces and new modes of representation" beyond *lala* cyberspace and the growing importance, which the internet and social platforms have gained in social networking and group formation in China since the late 1990s. According to Suda lesbian communities were in dire need of a space and infrastructure beyond 'offline', which would in turn act as a precondition for lesbian individuals to provide support in identity affirmation, urban public representation, and future representation of political interests (for instance regarding legalization of same-sex marriages) for the lesbian social group (*shehui qunti*). In its role of co-constituent of such a new infrastructure, *Tongyu* has so far proven to be especially crucial in teaming lesbian women with varying social and educational backgrounds to form, among other networks, transnational lines of communication and project cooperation between different localities in the People's Republic, Taiwan, Hong Kong, and beyond. Suda vividly sketches how, via structures such as *Tongyu*, lesbian communitas in China is increasingly interconnected with international and transnational discourse and interests regarding social and political representation. Here, comparison of social and identity issues first happens virtually, e.g. by means of the Chinese-speaking internet, and is then strengthened via communication and exchange with NGOs, female researchers and cultural producers (*Kulturproduzentinnen*). Last but not least, perhaps one of the most remarkable features of *Tongyu* and this new type of lesbian organization in general is that these physical, social and discursive spaces are created without any form of (local Chinese) institutional support.

Certainly one of the most striking results of Suda's study is her observation that Chinese lesbian women living and working in urban contexts now acknowledge or define themselves according to a separate identity category of gender. Back in 2002, when I was engaging in a study of ethnicity and gender among women belonging to the Yi ethnic minority, who were then living and working in Beijing, the category of 'gender', which I had carefully selected to complement questions regarding the adaptation from a culturally and socially 'other' locality and context to a complex, urban and politically invested Beijing, raised only questions marks and empty looks. My interview partners simply understood themselves as women, and did not consider this 'fact' to be in any substantial way relevant for the self-positioning within their own ethnic cultural background, or within their urban career and family environment. Another path-breaking aspect of Suda's study is the process of terminological emancipation, which has been accompanying lesbian identity in its move from the shadows of homosexual identity in China to the clarity and colors of an own stance and social and subject identity. However, in talking about categories and/or 'markers' of identity it remains to be seen how the spaces and heterophony created by organizations such as *Tongyu* can and/or will continue to influence and support lesbian community in China and beyond, and vice versa: As Suda notes in her concluding remarks and outlook, lesbian identity in China is increasingly determined by a type of identity reciprocity. This reciprocity manifests itself in the formation of a 'transnational Chinese lesbian sisterhood', which is currently expanding across several continents, and which is based on the same forms of personal dedication and 'organization' as a set of innovative and creative working techniques, which also make possible the existence of NGOs such as *Tongyu*.

This book is a must-read for scholars of gender, sociology, and social organization in contemporary China. It provides clear-cut, in-depth and insightful information on alternative structures and processes of social organization and formation, and enriches both the discussion on social identity, society-state relations, gender issues, and homosexuality in China today.

(Olivia Kraef)

Notes on Contributors

Chen Hsien-wu is Professor at the Graduate Institute for National Development, National Taiwan University, Taipei. His main research interests include legal theory, constitutional law, law and politics, and law of the PR China.

Gao Quanxi is Dean of the Institute for Advanced Studies in Humanities and Social Sciences at Beihang University and law professor at Beihang University Law School. He is a leading scholar of political constitutionalism in contemporary China. His research interests include political philosophy and constitutional law.

Clemens von Haselberg has studied Chinese studies, psychoanalysis and American studies in Frankfurt/Main. He has specialized in Chinese film and written his master thesis on the combination of documentary and fictional film techniques in the work of director Jia Zhangke. He is currently working as a research associate at the University of Cologne and is writing his PhD-thesis on constructions of cultural identity in the Chinese wuxia film genre.

Huang Hui is Associate Professor, Executive Director of the German Legal Study Centre, and Vice Director of the Research Centre of Constitutional and Administrative Law at Beihang University Law School in Beijing. Her main research interests include consititutional law, state liability law, juristic methodology, and guiding case systems in civil law countries. Professor Huang received her doctoral degree of law at Humboldt University and was Humboldt Scholar in 2009.

Emmelie Korell is a Research Associate and Lecturer at the Institute of Chinese Studies, Freie Universität Berlin. Her main research interests include tourism in China, its impact on culture and society and perceptions of the Chinese periphery.

Olivia Kraef is a research associate and Ph.D. candidate with the Institute of Chinese Studies at Freie Universität Berlin. She began conducting research on the Nuosu-Yi of Liangshan, Sichuan province, in early 2002 as part of her master's thesis on gender and intellectual migration. Her doctoral dissertation focuses on Nuosu-Yi music, cultural policy, and change in Liangshan.

Susanne Kuss is Privatdozent in Modern History at the University of Bern (Switzerland). Following her study of history and philosophy in Berlin and Freiburg, she obtained her PhD in history from the University of Freiburg. One focus of her research lies on the German colonial wars in Africa and China.

Martin Leutner is currently obtaining his master's degree at the School of International Studies, Peking University. His research interests include Sino-German relations, post-Cold War international relations and the introduction and use of English loan words in Chinese.

Mechthild Leutner is Professor of Chinese History and Culture at Freie Universität Berlin. Her main research interests lie in Chinese social and political history, German-Chinese relations and Chinese women's history.

Katja Levy is Assistant Professor at the Institute of Chinese Studies, Freie Universität Berlin. Currently she is on leave to act as Chair for Contemporary Chinese Studies at the University Würzburg. Her main research interests include legal sociological questions in the PRC, politics in the PRC and foreign policy of the PRC.

Benjamin L. Liebman is the Robert L. Lieff Professor of Law and Director of the Center for Chinese Legal Studies at Columbia Law School. His current research focuses on Chinese tort law, on Chinese criminal procedure, on the impact of popular opinion and populism on the Chinese legal system, and on the evolution of China's courts and legal profession.

Lin Po-Wen is Doctorate Researcher of the Graduate Institute of National Development of the National Taiwan University, majoring in Constitutional Law. He holds bachelor degrees in both economics and law and earned a Masters in law from the University of California. His research focuses on Constitutional law and the comparison of cross strait law.

Sabine Mokry recently graduated from the master's program International Relations and currently writes her master's thesis in Chinese Studies at Freie Universität Berlin. Her main research interests include the Chinese International Relations community as well as China's foreign policy and relations between state and society.

Sören Vogler currently writes his master's thesis in Chinese Studies at Freie Universität Berlin. His research interests include dynamics of political contention, social inequality, and social change in contemporary China.

Zhu Yi is a Research Associate at the Mercator Institute for China Studies (MERICS) in Berlin. Her main research focus are Chinas society, contemporary media development (especially social media), and the changing rights awareness in Chinese society. Prior to taking on this position, Zhu Yi was Head of Programs at the Heinrich Böll Foundation's Beijing office. She is also a PhD candidate at the Institute for Media and Communication Studies, Freie Universität Berlin.